Queer Vietnam

QUEER VIETNAM

*A History of
Gender Transgression,
1920–1945*

Richard Quang-Anh Tran

Stanford University Press
Stanford, California

Stanford University Press
Stanford, California

Library of Congress Cataloging-in-Publication Data
Names: Tran, Richard Quang-Anh, author.
Title: Queer Vietnam : a history of gender transgression, 1920-1945 /Richard
    Quang-Anh Tran.
Other titles: History of gender transgression, 1920-1945
Description: Stanford, California : Stanford University Press, [2025] |Includes
    bibliographical references and index.
Identifiers: LCCN 2024041850 (print) | LCCN 2024041851 (ebook)
    | ISBN 9781503615380 (cloth) | ISBN 9781503642744 (paperback) |
    ISBN 9781503642751 (ebook)
Subjects: LCSH: Gender nonconformity—Vietnam—History—20th century.
    |Gender identity—Vietnam—History—20th century.
Classification: LCC HQ77.95.V5 T73 2025 (print) | LCC HQ77.95.V5 (ebook) |
    DDC 306.76/80959709041—dc23/eng/20240922
LC record available at https://lccn.loc.gov/2024041850
LC ebook record available at https://lccn.loc.gov/2024041851

Cover design: Daniel Benneworth-Gray
Cover art: Dinh Thi Tham Poong, *Seeing Myself,* 2007, paper & watercolor, Judith
Hughes Day Vietnamese Contemporary Fine Art, New York.

CONTENTS

ACKNOWLEDGMENTS

One of the great joys of researching and writing this book was the opportunity to engage with a lively community of learned and generous scholars worldwide. I have incurred more debts than I can acknowledge here.

I remain grateful to Peter Zinoman and the community of historians who welcomed me to their discipline and taught me the intricacies of their craft. The book, in part, reflects this profound influence. I would also like to thank my colleagues, scholars of premodern East and Southeast Asia, who helped clarify the often subtle historical, linguistic, or conceptual issues in the course of the research and writing. I am especially grateful to C. Michele Thompson and Catherine Churchman for reading relevant portions of the manuscript and providing their incisive feedback.

I would also like to thank George E. Dutton for reading my work and for his support during my time as a visiting scholar at the University of California, Los Angeles. Tamara Loos took the time out of her very busy schedule to provide valuable feedback on a much earlier version of this manuscript, thereby helping to make the current one stronger. Brett de Bary at Cornell has been a steady and encouraging ally.

Numerous other colleagues and friends have provided support and sustenance along the way. In no particular order they include Howard Chiang, Nguyễn Tân Hoàng, Marguerite Nguyễn, Gail Hershatter, Trịnh T. Minh-hà, Claire Liên-Thị Trần, Christina Firpo, Liam Kelly, John Phan, Frank Proschan, Oona Paredes, Ivan Small, Christina Schwenkel, Alexander M. Cannon, Nguyễn Nguyệt Cầm, Tường Vũ, Nguyễn Võ Thu Hương, Martina Nguyễn, Alec Holcombe, Jason Picard, Mariam B. Lam, Eileen Võ, Eric Huỳnh, Nicole Nguyễn, Shawn Ratcliff, Caroline Martinez.

Thanks to Việt Lê for introducing me to the wide array of beautiful paintings by contemporary Vietnamese artists. In surveying the works available, I was immediately struck by Đinh Thị Thắm Poong's art, one of which graces the book's cover.

At the Ca' Foscari University of Venice, Italy, I would like to thank Laura de Giorgi and Nicoletta Pesaro. During my time in Venice, I was most inspired by Nicoletta's organizing of the annual literary readings on migration titled "L'autro sono io" (The other is I). Thanks also to Giulia Baccini for our conversations about premodern Chinese literature and to Attilio Adreini for his ongoing encouragement in learning classical Chinese.

I would also like to acknowledge the memory of the late Marco Ceresa, to whom I would very much have liked to have shown the completed book.

Many archivists and librarians at numerous institutions worldwide helped track down references or answered my many queries. Although regrettably I do not have a list of all their names, the research for the book certainly would not have been possible without their assistance. They hail from the University of California, at Berkeley, Los Angeles, and Irvine, Cornell, the Bibliothèque Nationale de France, Archives Nationales d'Outre Mer, École Française d'Extrême-Orient, Leiden University Libraries, Vietnam National Archives, the National Library of Vietnam, and the General Sciences Library in Ho Chi Minh City.

At Stanford University Press, I wish to thank Marcela Maxfield and Dylan K. White for their kind assistance throughout the process, as well as the team at the press, including Caroline McKusick, David Zielonka, Tiffany Mok, Katherine Faydash, and many others, who helped bring the manuscript into the world. Heartfelt thanks go to the anonymous readers whose generous, meticulous, and constructive readings helped strengthen the manuscript.

At UC Berkeley, a warm thanks goes to Poulomi Saha and the Program in Critical Theory for sponsoring me as a scholar-in-residence during the 2023–2024 academic year. I am also most grateful to the Association for Asian Studies for the support through its book subvention.

The debt, intellectual and otherwise, to Judith Butler is enormous. I remain forever grateful for Judith's mentorship—a model of scholarly generosity, analytical acumen, ethical clarity, and profound humanity.

The book is dedicated to my family and fierce sisters who imagine otherwise.

INTRODUCTION

AT THE LONG GIÁNG Buddhist temple, located in a remote rural region of Vietnam, Ngọc, a young man dressed in modern urban clothing, observes from afar a young monk in traditional garb. The two had exchanged introductory greetings upon Ngọc's arrival at the temple. "How strange," Ngọc thinks to himself as he considers the monk's delicate features. "How is it possible that in the countryside there is someone so handsome with such fair skin and a sweet, pure voice, just like that of a young woman."[1] Ngọc becomes engrossed by his increasing suspicion that the other person may, in fact, be a woman and embarks on a mission to force disclosure. When he discovers that the monk is indeed a woman named Lan, resolutely devoted to the religious faith, the hero realizes that his growing feelings toward Lan can never be consummated. The story concludes with Ngọc vowing forever to love Lan platonically.[2]

This story is from Khái Hưng's novella *Butterfly Soul Dreaming of an Immortal* (*Hồn Bướm Mơ Tiên*). Serialized in ten parts from 1932 to 1933, the novella was first published in *Mores* (*Phong Hóa*), the periodical of the Self-Reliant Literary Group, which sought to modernize Vietnamese culture.[3] The novella's stylistic innovations certainly departed from classical literary conventions, but classical antecedents persisted in the story's mise-en-scène, which parallels the renowned premodern tale of the Bodhisattva of Mercy (Quan Âm Thị Kính, or Kuan-yin or Avalokiteśvara).[4] In that tale, the heroine Thị Kính, dressed as a man, seeks refuge at a temple and becomes a monk. On a visit to the pagoda,

Thị Mầu, the daughter of a wealthy family, immediately falls in love with Thị Kính and attempts to seduce him. When Thị Mầu later becomes impregnated by another man, she blames her condition on Thị Kính. The latter's innocence is revealed only after she dies and her body is discovered to be female.[5] This well-known Buddhist tale was inscribed into verse by at least the nineteenth century and translated into the modern Vietnamese vernacular in the early twentieth century, at about the same time Hưng's novella was published.[6] Both the no-vella and premodern tale share a concern with cross-dressing.[7] Insofar as dress is considered a symbolic marker of gender and sexual difference,[8] revealing the cultural conceptions of masculinity and femininity, the topos of cross-dressing raises questions about gender—its constitution, its limits, its instabilities, and its potential transgressions in a given culture.

The modernist version of this story, for example, could be read as an affirma-tion of the binary conception of gender and sexuality, for the hero Ngọc believes that the cross-dressing monk he pursues is a woman in disguise. Alternatively, the story could be read as an invitation to explore other modalities of sexual erotics. In this view, even though the hero ultimately declares his love for the woman, the story nevertheless intimates the possibility of same-sex desire: the demarcation between the hero's desire for the monk versus the actual woman could be rather ambiguous and difficult to disentangle. Finally, the story could also be read as an allegory of gendered embodiment. In this reading, the focus would be on the heroine's act of gendered transformation. In each case, the question of gender is central to how readers understand the story.

The two stories mentioned here were by no means exceptional cases in Viet-namese culture of the interwar period. Gender crossing—as well as other sexual variant subjects—was conspicuous in Vietnam's public sphere during this time. In short stories, novellas, poetry, reform theater, urban reportage, and jour-nalistic accounts of tales both local and foreign, hundreds of such narratives involving gender- and sexual-variant subjects were circulating, which reveals a Vietnamese society in which the fixity of gender and sexual norms was less rigid than scholars have previously assumed.

Queer Vietnam: A History of Gender Transgression, 1920–1945 explores the meanings of variant genders and sexualities in late French colonial Vietnam to glean something of the overall cultural norms of the time. The book focuses on the interwar period, from about 1920 to 1945. With the arrival of the French in the nineteenth century in the region that we today call Vietnam and the eventual dissolution of Asian dynastic systems by the middle of the twentieth century, the period was one of cultural disorientation, transition, change, and modernization. The period witnessed, to varying degrees, many of the conditions of European modernity: the rise of capitalism, the formation of the bourgeois world, the establishment of state systems, and the foundation of modern science.[9] Scholarship on queer Asia and the transnational histories of sexuality in Asia has shown that these conditions, together with Western imperialism, generally led to a reorganization of sexual norms, typically a narrowing and delegitimization of what had been a wide range of acceptable practices.[10] In the case of late French colonial Vietnam, however, my research on popular culture and literature suggests a slightly different picture. While the period certainly witnessed the modern reorganization of Vietnamese society, the efflorescence of gender and sexual variance in the Vietnamese cultural archive suggests that certain fundamental questions concerning the periodization and conceptualization of sexual modernity need to be rethought.

Queer Vietnam argues that a far more capacious vision of gendered personhood existed in this period than has been supposed. Vietnamese popular culture and literature embraced the dynamic plasticity of the human body: stories both fictional and biographical involving "queer" subjects abounded. This period of gender and sexual dynamism can be explained, I suggest, in large part because Sino-Vietnamese and Southeast Asian traditions that tolerated greater gender and sexual variance persisted far into the early decades of the twentieth century. While certain modern strands of French and European discourses on the plasticity of sex and gender entered Vietnamese culture, sexology's pathologizing rhetoric was not yet the dominant signifying frame in and through which the period understood queer subjects.

While the term "queer" is increasingly used in today's general discourse, often to refer to LGBT identities, its meaning is nevertheless worth clarifying here. In this book, the historical subjects we can understand as "queer" depart from the ideological fiction that naturalizes one's sex, gender, desire, morphology, and psyche into neatly aligned and mutually complementary binary oppositions: male-female, heterosexuality-homosexuality, normal-abnormal, and so forth. Queer studies scholars are particularly interested in the dislocations of the prior elements in revealing how such alignments are arbitrary, though no less powerful, normative constructs. One aim of critical historiography is to reconstruct the ways and means by which some identities and practices in certain times and places are rendered normative while others are not.[11]

The term "transgression" in the book's subtitle follows from the prior definition of "queer" in referring to the crossing of a normative limit. The transgression need not be indefinite. Nor does it need to entail a subversion or overthrowing of the status quo. Rather, by "transgression," the study implies acts or performances that Bataille once called "limited" transgressions that interrupt the world of the profane, a world characterized by interdictions and prohibitions.[12] Bataille points to historical examples such as potlatches, festivals, rituals, and unbridled sexual activity that exceed the limits of utilitarian models or restricted economies based on the principle of scarcity.[13] Likewise, I focus on historical cases in Vietnam that transgress the limits of the heteronormative model. Because the Vietnamese sources are primarily preoccupied with gender embodiment, and less so on biological "sex" or sexual desire, the book's subtitle reflects the historical and thematic centrality of both the cultural interpretations of masculinity and femininity and of the body, here understood as irreducible to anatomy.[14]

From an emic perspective, however, the empirical cases of gender transgression that this book examines, while certainly context bound and governed by internal rules, were not necessarily nonnormative to the actors or the social world from which they came. So using less judgmental language, the "transgressions" that the study identifies are akin to gender "crossings" that lead to a remaking or rearrangement of elements that, at times, might also lead to individual subjective transformation. But these latter terms, "crossings," "remakings," and "rearrangements," do not quite capture the powerful normative constraints on gender and sexuality both in the past and today: a history of gender "remaking" seems to evoke a world in which one could alter at will the normative organization of sex, gender, or desire. Vietnam's interwar period, relative to today's heteronormative regime, saw greater tolerance for gender plasticity in popular culture and literature. But that does not mean there were no limits. Therefore, the term "transgression" more accurately captures the central narrative arc that this book seeks to reconstruct and the historical and contemporaneous disjuncture that it brings into relief. Like the word "queer," then, "gender transgression" does not serve historical verisimilitude but offers a useful analytical category for understanding cases of gender ambiguity or androgyny.[15]

By "Vietnam," this study generally refers to the geographic region that we today associate with the corresponding nation-state. Before the twentieth century, this nation-state had not yet been formed politically. For most of the nineteenth century, the area that we call Vietnam was ruled by the Nguyễn dynasty. Founded in 1802, the Nguyễn dynasty emerged in the aftermath of a brutal civil war between the Lê dynasty in the north and the Nguyễn dynasty in the central and southern regions.[16] Gia Long, the founding Nguyễn emperor, united the kingdom and relocated the capital from Hà Nội in the north to Huế in the central region. Under his reign, the kingdom stretched from the north to the south, assuming for the first time the country's geographical S shape noticeable in today's political maps.[17] This territorial expansion southward had already begun in the fifteenth century, leading the Vietnamese ethnic majority, the Kinh, to come into contact with indigenous populations such as the Cham and Khmer who resided in the central and southern regions.[18] In founding the new kingdom, Gia Long and his heirs sought to emulate China and its imperial gravitas, turning Vietnam, its symbols, its customs, and its rituals into the image of the great northern neighbor.[19]

When the French arrived in 1858, they fragmented the country once again. They first seized the southern region of Cochinchina and gradually moved northward, claiming the middle and northern regions of Annam and Tonkin, respectively. Eventually, the French also seized what today are considered the countries of Laos and Cambodia. The territories of the three mainland countries of Southeast Asia—Vietnam, Laos, Cambodia—would form what was then called French Indochina. The southern region of Vietnam was formally deemed a French colony. The central and northern regions of Vietnam were French protectorates, indirectly governed by France in consultation with the Nguyễn Court in Huế.[20] So in the early twentieth century, Vietnam as a nation-state had not yet been formed. Nevertheless, I retain the usage of the term "Vietnam" in this study on the basis of the study's focus on Vietnamese perspectives drawn from Vietnamese-language sources, as opposed to the state-centric French perspective of Indochina, and on the basis of its utility: "Vietnam" is presumably more familiar to the contemporary reader and thus usefully serves as a concise descriptor of the region of this study.

The book focuses on the years 1920–1945 for several reasons. First, this was the first time in the modern period when Vietnam evinced a flourishing public sphere.[21] It was largely ushered in at the turn of the twentieth century by the advent of modern print technology and the adoption of the romanized alphabet as the national script (*quốc ngữ*). This alphabet marked a departure from the previous predominant use of classical Chinese and *nôm*—the Vietnamese demotic script that employed Chinese ideographs to transcribe the Vietnamese language. Due in part to its ease of learning and rapid dissemination, the adoption of the modern vernacular helped create an available Vietnamese readership and explosion in print publications. According to French colonial state records, the northern region of Tonkin had four newspapers in 1918. By 1937, the number had ballooned to sixty-three. In the same year, the southern region boasted thirty-seven periodicals. Between 1919 and 1939, in the southern region alone, 163 Vietnamese-language periodicals were reportedly in circulation. Between 1922 and 1940, 13,381 different books and tracts were published in Vietnamese.[22] These numbers all point to an increasingly robust forum in which literate Vietnamese from a wide variety of walks of life could participate.[23] In so doing, this public sphere provides unusual access to Vietnamese perspectives on matters pertaining to gender and sexuality.

While the French colonial state did impose press censorship, it did so only selectively, according to region and subject matter. Regionally, metropolitan laws guaranteeing press freedoms were mostly applied only to the southern region of Cochinchina, a direct French colony. In the absence of such legal guarantees, censorship in the protectorates of the central and northern regions was more stringent. This uneven distribution of press freedom partly explains why the south was historically renowned for its flourishing journalistic culture.[24] The French colonial state's censorship was also selective in terms of subject matter. Concerned primarily with security issues that could subvert its continued existence, the colonial state was relatively indifferent to almost all other matters, including writings on sex, gender, and desire.[25]

Second, the years from 1920 to 1945 are widely considered the period of Vietnam's transition to modernity. Modernity in the Vietnamese context was marked by rapid social, cultural, and economic change. This included a profound departure from traditional practices, beliefs, and epistemologies; the creation of a market economy, and hence an openness to new ideas through the global circulation and exchanges of products, commodities, trends, and fashions; a booming printing press, albeit one punctured by political censorship;

and a corresponding heightened collective anxiety about the uncertainties of the modern era.[26] Observing the effects of French colonial modernity on the "soul" of a younger generation of Vietnamese at the time, the two brother poets Hoài Thanh and Hoài Chân remarked: "A strong wind from far away suddenly blew in this direction. In one fell swoop it shook the entire foundation of the past."[27] "The West," they explain, "has now penetrated the deepest part of our souls. We can no longer feel happy the way we used to feel happy, feel sorrow the way we used to feel sorrow, love, hate, be angry as before."[28] These modernist poets reveal something of the profound sense of disorientation and emotional intensity their generation felt, occasioned by the arrival of Western culture and the onslaught of modernity.

In many parts of the world, modernity was also marked by the growing influence of sexology, the theory of sex that emerged toward the middle of the nineteenth century in Europe and spread from there across the globe to Asia.[29] Sexology encompassed an array of disparate disciplinary fields, but especially medicine and psychiatry, that together sought to create a set of normative classifications of sexual practices, morphologies, and identities arranged on a spectrum from so-called normal to perverse. It was nineteenth-century sexology—also known as *scientia sexualis*, or sexual science—that inaugurated the dyadic categories of "heterosexuality" and "homosexuality"; promulgated the notion of sexual inversion, whereby a man or woman was "trapped" in the opposite-sexed body; and labeled certain practices, such as sodomy, masturbation, and cross-dressing, as "perversions"—deviations from a wholesome sexual norm. These categorizations have persisted far into the late twentieth century and arguably into the twenty-first.

When I first began this research project, I reasoned that because the 1920–1945 period represents the tail end of French colonization in Vietnam, when European culture would have exerted its strongest influence, I should be able to locate the so-called seeds of the pathologization of homosexuality in this period—that is, the conceptual frameworks, signifying practices, and vocabularies that contributed to its stigmatization in Vietnam's postsocialist period.[30] An examination of the cultural archive, however, took me in a different direction. As the episode in Khái Hưng's novella that opens this introduction illustrates, earlier discourses and traditions that existed before French or Western influence on Vietnam did not wither away after the twentieth century. Permutations, for example, of the premodern topos of gender crossing persisted through the 1930s. The practice of gender crossing did not appear in a cultural vacuum. Rather, it was a recurring trope in varied Southeast Asian and Sino-Vietnamese traditions that had longer histories in the region, traditions studied more closely in the first three chapters of this book. These traditions and histories were carried over in modern translation with the adoption of the romanized script. In fact, the new script led to an exhilarating period of linguistic and literary translation. While the period certainly saw the translation of French and European works, Vietnam's interwar period was also, in fact, the golden age of translation of Chinese fiction.[31]

"Translation" here ought to be understood not so much in the narrow sense of linguistic fidelity to an original as a creative process of cultural and epistemic negotiation, mediation, and innovation.[32] Like Vietnam's national classic, Nguyễn Du's *The Tale of Kiều*, some of the literary sources that *Queer Vietnam* examines are, at times, Vietnamese creative adaptations of East Asian literary works.[33] Others are translations of nineteenth-century *nôm* works that were themselves transcriptions of oral folklore. Still other times, they are translations of Chinese fiction adopted for Vietnamese political ends. Through these works in translation, premodern traditions that admitted greater gender and sexual variance persisted through the interwar period. Explaining the dramatic changes that took place in late colonial Vietnam, Peter Zinoman aptly described this period as exhibiting the coexistence of an "incongruity" between "traditional epistemologies" and "modernizing development."[34] As we will observe in this study, some Vietnamese intellectuals of the time demonstrated an acute awareness of this incongruity in their urban reportages, in which the practices of tradition and modernity jostled with each other in an uneasy cultural palimpsest.[35]

At the same time, the Vietnamese print public sphere received with inspired awe marvelous news emanating from abroad—especially from France—of the existence of dynamic "queer" bodies that seemingly defied comprehension. In the aftermath of World War I, France experienced the traumas of war in the face of enormous loss of life. This led to a natalist discourse and accompanying anxieties over the potential sterility and eventual obsolescence of French civilization—a "civilization without sexes."[36] Simultaneously, the interwar period in Paris was a socially decadent one in which challenges to sexual and gender norms were in the air.[37] This discourse of sexual subversion was amplified in the Vietnamese colony by frequent news stories of scientific experiments involving sex changes in animals and humans, occasioned by the advent of the emergent field of endocrinology. These French and European discourses on gender and sexual plasticity, rather than nineteenth-century sexology, dominated the Vietnamese public sphere.

In response, Vietnamese debated in the print public sphere the question of sexual and gender variance and the interrelated problems of kinship, desire, intimacy, and the grounds on which societal relations ought to be built. Some drew on the cultural resources of the Vietnamese classical past to interpret the explosive growth of "queer" stories arriving from abroad. Others envisioned radically new configurations of social and cultural organization. In a notable piece of imaginative fiction, for example, a Vietnamese writer by the name of Chung Anh described a futuristic world in which the sexual distinctions between male and female are transcended, the idea of the family superseded by new forms of kinship ties between and among a higher form of humans, a newly evolved "hermaphroditic" species. Whether they were premodern tales translated and adapted for various modern political ends or newly invented stories with futuristic sensibilities, a bevy of such wondrous narratives concerning queer subjects pushed the imagined frontiers of the human body.

In this context, we can better comprehend the relative status and place of nineteenth-century Western sexology in the Vietnamese public sphere. The "West" was not one homogenizing block. Sexology's influence was certainly already underway, traces of its pathologizing rhetoric evident in some Vietnamese sources. But it was in competition with Sino-Vietnamese and Southeast Asian traditions that had longer histories in the region, as well as a set of other French and European discourses on gender and sexual plasticity specific to the interwar period: demographic anxieties, emergent sexual emancipation movements, and the advent of reproductive science.

From this corpus of Vietnamese sources, we can draw certain key conclusions about the character and periodization of sexual modernity in Vietnam's early twentieth century. One key finding is that the diagnostic categories of nineteenth-century sexology, such as gender "inversion," had not yet garnered meaningful traction. There are historical reasons for this, chief among them that the French colonial state failed to effectively transpose Western medical models onto Indochina. Vietnam, instead, was still significantly influenced by premodern Sino-Vietnamese paradigms of the body, illness, and health. In fact, the contemporary Vietnamese term for "sex/gender" (*giới tính*) had not even been invented yet. There was no formal, uniform vocabulary to refer to the modern Vietnamese sense of sex or gender, which, according to a standard dictionary published in 2005, is defined as the "characteristics of the body and psychology [*cơ thể và của tâm lí*] that . . . distinguish males and females."[38] Instead, a variety of older terms were used to refer to the different composite elements of sex, gender, morphology, and desire.

Just as there was no formal term for "sex/gender" in the contemporary sense, neither was there a self-consciously "perverse" modern subjectivity. Historical scholarship tracing the development of modern sexual science has shown that diagnostic categories helped bring into being perverse sexual subjects, such as the "homosexual," whom European sexology labeled an "invert," trapped in the wrong-sexed body. Homosexuals, in turn, would come to embrace their stigmatized identity, organize as a collective, and form a "reverse discourse" around the same identity.[39] But in Vietnam, such developments came later. In the interwar period, more often than not, gender bore little to no correlation with sexual desire. Certainly, gender was connected to sexual desire insofar as the latter is often routed through cultural notions of gender. But unlike the figure of the homosexual "invert" in European sexology, acts of gender transgression in the Vietnamese archive were not decisive markers of homosexual desire. On the contrary, in some cases, men and women who transgressed gender boundaries did so within a historically distinct normative regime. Women characters who cross-dressed as men to fight in battle, for example, reverted to their former female selves upon returning home to serve as loving and devoted wives to their husbands. One principal reason for this peculiar Jekyll-and-Hyde transformation is that the demarcation between the public and private spheres in premodern Asia was simultaneously a gendered one: women who entered the androcentric public sphere could normatively do so only as "men." By the same token, male poets in the world of arts and letters would often write in a woman's voice, assuming female personae and female subjectivities, precisely because there was normatively no space for "real" women in this public sphere.

The persistence of premodern gender practices far into the early decades of the twentieth century suggests the need to rethink the prevailing historical periodization that has characterized scholarship on Vietnam's late French colonial period. In this body of scholarship, the interwar period was characterized by a transition from tradition to modernity. David Marr's seminal work *Vietnamese Tradition on Trial*, for example, demonstrates fundamental changes at the level of "political and social consciousness" among the Vietnamese intelligentsia, changes that call into question traditional modes of thinking and practices.[40] Other works stress the cultural dimensions of modern change. Nguyễn Văn Ký's *Vietnamese Society Faces Modernity* (*La société vietnamienne face à la modernité*) looks at the "three" agents of modernization—schools, science, and medicine—driving some of the transformations in the spheres of art, literature, journalism, bodily practices, and women's fashions. More recent works of scholarship have furnished even finer-grained portraits. Through an examination of the 1930s Self-Reliant literary group, Martina Nguyễn has identified a strain of "cosmopolitan nationalism" to which the group adhered, whereas others have examined innovations in modernist literary aesthetics by some Vietnamese writers in the wake of the collapse of the mandarin civil service system and the explosive growth of the modern Vietnamese language.[41] Finally, some scholarship has broached the subject of queer genders and sexualities during the late colonial period. Ben Tran touches on the question of queerness from the perspective of modernist literary aesthetics.[42] Likewise, Nguyễn Quốc Vinh has written an essay claiming the deviancy of "homoerotic desire" in Vietnamese literary sources during the French colonial period.[43]

While this body of scholarship remains important, *Queer Vietnam* suggests the need to rethink the meaning of "tradition" in asking after the more fundamental question as to who or what defines it. In the early twentieth century, Vietnamese modernist reformers depicted the nineteenth century and its legacy as a backward, feudal period in need of reform. Like their counterparts in the New Culture Movement in China (1915–1919),[44] Vietnamese modern reformers of the 1920s and 1930s conceived of themselves and their peers as radically departing from historical precedent, denouncing the pernicious effects of so-called Confucian traditional mores. Yet as some of the examples of gender transgression I have presented thus far suggest, the extent to which and the manner in which "traditional" Confucian ideas appeared in Vietnam's early twentieth century needs to be reconsidered. While it is true that modern ideas entering Vietnam in the early twentieth century led to significant cultural changes, it does not follow that Confucian ideas were entirely superseded. Nor does it follow that nineteenth-century Confucian ideas took the form that modernist reformers have presented them to be. In fact, in Chapter 3, we will examine cases in which advocates of the modern Vietnamese women's emancipation movement took inspiration from classical heroines who transgressed gender norms in the Confucian "tradition." Thus, it is not simply that there was a transition from one way of thinking to the other; rather, that tradition may have already existed, albeit uneasily, at the heart of Vietnamese modernity.

Queer Vietnam draws on popular print sources written in the modern Vietnamese vernacular that flourished beginning in the 1920s. Many of these are the same key sources that Vietnam studies scholars have relied on to reconstruct the cultural history of the period. They include newspapers, short stories, novels, hygiene manuals, popular sex manuals, grammar guides, personal letters, memoirs, dictionaries, reference works, other cultural works, and journals. In terms of geographic distribution, the major print sources from the northern, central, and southern regions were examined. In the north, the renowned journals included *These Days* (*Ngày Nay*), *Mores* (*Phong Hóa*), and *Science Journal* (*Khoa Học Tạp Chí*); in the central region, *People's Voice* (*Tiếng Dân*), the longest-running newspaper of the interwar period; in the south, *Women's News* (*Phụ Nữ Tân Văn*) and *Women's Bell* (*Nữ Giới Chung*). These newspapers and journals were often in dialogue with one another: as we will see, Vietnamese intellectuals engaged in fierce pen wars. Hence, the study's findings are based on some of the most significant print sources of the period from all three regions. Together, they form one of the liveliest periods of exchange among Vietnamese in the print public sphere. After 1945, however, this period of lively public debate was interrupted by the beginning of the First Indochina War.

To restore to public memory the forgotten history of variant genders and sexualities during this vibrant period of Vietnamese history, the first chapter illuminates the conditions that contributed to the period's sexual and gendered efflorescence. In particular, Chapter 1 reconstructs a milieu of cultural pluralism in which Sino-Vietnamese, Southeast Asian, and Western discourses coexisted as well as jostled with one another. It looks at the competition between Sino-Vietnamese and Western models of medicine, the absence of the contemporary formal Vietnamese term for sex or gender (*giới tính*), and the array of Sino-Vietnamese terminology that existed previously instead. The chapter concludes with an examination of male sodomy, showing that rather than being understood as a symptom of homosexual identity, "sodomy" was a semiotic sign of Vietnam's embeddedness in cross-cultural contact.

Chapters 2 and 3 each look at a specific form of gender and sexual pluralism. Chapter 2 suggests that men, especially among the scholar literati, could hold a wider variety of gender and sexual subject positions than modern and contemporary binary divisions of sex, gender, and desire typically allow. Specifically, the chapter demonstrates a persistent separation of sexuality from gender such that gender transgression need not signify male homosexuality, a key motif of the nineteenth-century sexological model. Instead, the men in the documents examined could assume plural forms of gendered and erotic subject positions.

Chapter 3 looks at a plethora of stories involving women who transgressed gender and sexual boundaries. Many of the stories were originally premodern tales that were translated into the modern Vietnamese vernacular in the early twentieth century but reinterpreted and redeployed by Vietnamese writers for a variety of different, and sometimes contradictory, political purposes. These include the reaffirmation of a lost Confucian tradition, the celebration of nationalistic sentiment, and the advancement of the modern women's emancipation movement. Regardless of the ostensible purpose for translating these premodern stories, they nevertheless furnished a rich cultural repertoire of female figures who transgressed the limits of gendered norms in the early twentieth century.

Chapter 4 shifts the study's attention to modern changes that scholars have already observed about the period to argue that gender plasticity represents a significant but overlooked variable. The modern transformation that shook Vietnamese society at the time simultaneously destabilized perceived traditional notions of gender. The return of a sizable number of Vietnamese students who studied abroad in France; news of the shifting changes in gendered norms taking place in Europe and elsewhere; and discoveries, experiments, and innovations in the natural sciences all combined to create an atmosphere that pushed the imagined frontiers of the gendered and sexed human body.

Taken together, these chapters show that a far livelier presence of "queer" subjects existed in Vietnam during the interwar period than has been supposed. *Queer Vietnam* simultaneously insists that any understanding of the question of variant genders and sexualities in Vietnam today would be incomplete without acknowledging this other, earlier gender history.

ONE

THE HISTORICAL
CONTEXT
A Milieu of Cultural Pluralism

IN A 1939 ARTICLE IN the *Science Journal*, a writer in Hà Nội described a female spirit medium (*bà đồng*) who lived next to his house. Each night, he wrote, she would make prayers to the female deities, playing music that sometimes, he acknowledged, was melodious and truly pleasant to the ears. But on other occasions she and her spirit devotees (*hầu bóng*) made a ruckus that disturbed the entire neighborhood. One day, he noticed the sounds from his neighbor had all but stopped. Curious, he went over to take a peek and saw that she was writhing in pain and feeling unwell with what appeared like an unusually high fever. That same night, he heard her, once again, making audible prayers for help from the female deities: "In the rituals of spirit possession [*lên đồng*], she danced, she jumped, she shouted, she screamed loudly, such that the whole neighborhood heard her voice." It did not take long before she worked a sweat, drenched as if having just "bathed," like a person who had undergone a "hot water bath." The next day, she claimed that she had recovered from her illness thanks to the female deities, but others believed that she was cured simply by having worked up a sweat. The writer concluded: "Who knows where the truth lies?"[1]

The story of this female spirit medium illustrates some of the key tensions of Vietnam's interwar culture. Scientific secular modernity, which understood itself as purified of myth, superstition, and unjustified belief, was certainly marching forth, sweeping through the French colony to make its mark on the Vietnamese people.[2] At the same time, rituals, practices, and traditions that would seem antithetical to modernity coexisted and, at times, competed with a disenchantment of science. The practice of spirit mediumship had been in homage to Princess Liễu Hạnh and her pantheon of female deities, a cult whose cultural presence in Vietnam can be traced to sometime in the sixteenth century and that exhibited a popular following in the early twentieth century, especially among Vietnamese women.[3] Some scholars point out that the unusual presence of powerful female figures is a characteristic that makes Vietnam straddle the line between Confucian East Asia and Southeast Asia.[4]

In the early twentieth century, French colonialists, Confucian literati, as well as Vietnamese nationalists and moderns singled out the practice of spirit mediumship for being rooted in what they framed as backward superstition, the result of ignorance and poor education.[5] Yet for many of its female devotees, the ritual practice furnished particular value and meaning. As we shall see, the practice opened up spaces not only for female community but also for gender- and sexual-variant practices that depart from the paradigms of Western secular science and Confucian morality. Its existence far through the late 1930s fore-grounds the complex relationship of gender, tradition, and modernity.

This chapter explores some of the premodern traditions, terms, and prac-tices, respectively, around sex/gender during the interwar period, when they commingled with nascent but not yet dominant Western influence.[6] The period, I argue, was a culturally pluralist milieu in which sexuality and gender were un-derstood in more varied and fluid ways than the scholarship has acknowledged.

THE PERSISTENCE OF SINO-VIETNAMESE
AND SOUTHEAST ASIAN TRADITIONS

The period of French colonization (1862–1954), while historically closer and more immediate to us today, must be placed in the context of Vietnam's longer history with East Asia. China ruled Vietnam approximately eighteen hundred years before France and had colonized Vietnam for far longer (111 BCE–938 CE).

Although the region that we call Vietnam today extends back to the be-ginning of the second millennium, the first independent Vietnamese polity appeared during the tenth century in and around the Red River delta, having declared independence from a northern Chinese state. From the tenth to the twentieth centuries, Vietnam itself experienced successive dynasties, of which the relevant ones for this discussion include the Lý (1009–1225), Trần (1225–1413), Lê (1428–1788), and Nguyễn (1801–1945). Of these dynasties, Buddhism dominated the belief systems of the Lý and Trần. In contrast, Neo-Confucian Sinitic culture and administration heavily influenced the Lê and Nguyễn. The influence of the Buddhist and Confucian traditions will become relevant when we later turn to an examination of Vietnamese sources on gender variance.

To appreciate the relative degree of Buddhist influence, the founding Lý dynasty was in many ways a creation of local Buddhists. An extended period of tribal warfare in the tenth century led local Buddhist leaders to broker a truce and to catapult to the throne the founding Lý emperor, Lý Thái Tổ, an orphan nurtured and raised in the Buddhist monastery. Soon after he assumed the throne, not only did Buddhist monks serve as political advisers but Buddhism became the standard measure of civilized behavior for royalty and subjects alike.[7]

The emperors of the Trần dynasty were also devout Buddhists and continued the legacies and achievements of the Lý clan. Unlike the Lý, however, the Trần dynasty introduced elements of Confucian culture in establishing an examination system modeled on the Chinese one. As a result, a growing class of Vietnamese literati cultivated an ideal of learning based on the Chinese classics since the thirteenth century.[8]

The rise of the Lê dynasty (1428–1788) in the fifteenth century was a consequence of political resistance against Ming imperial expansion in the fourteenth century. Prior to the Lê dynasty, Vietnam was in a tributary relationship with China. In such a relationship, as with other nearby Asian countries, Vietnam was a vassal state that had to pay homage to its Chinese suzerain. Between 1406 and 1407, for complex reasons that will not detain us here, the Ming breached this relationship by invading and occupying Vietnam. This period of Ming occupation brought with it an ever-growing transformation of Vietnam in the image of China. The Ming had already erected, however imperfectly, educational and administrative structures modeled on a Chinese worldview.[9]

By the time the Ming were expelled and the Lê dynasty was founded in 1428, the Lê emperors had decided to keep much of the imperial administrative and legal structures that the Ming had established, judging them to be effective and convenient forms of statecraft. For the next three and a half centuries, the Lê dynasty would adapt and modify the Chinese borrowings. It was during the Lê dynasty that the imperial examination system was once again renewed.

It was also during the Lê dynasty when the Vietnamese kingdom began to make significant territorial expansion southward. Although the major ethnic Vietnamese group, the Kinh, who resided primarily in the flat delta, had a long history of interaction with their neighbors—whether with the highland ethnic minorities or the indigenous groups located further south, such as the Cham and Khmer—as a result of demographic pressures, among other reasons, the fifteenth century marked aggressive territorial expansion.[10] This and later migration even farther southward would contribute to the increasing contact, and assimilation, of the Vietnamese with neighboring Southeast Asian cultures.

From the sixteenth to the seventeenth century, a parallel Vietnamese civilization was founded in the central region. With the approval of the then lord of the Lê dynasty, Trịnh Kiểm, Nguyễn Hoàng migrated in and around Huế, where the Cham civilization resided. From there he and his heirs would develop a political and economic center, a parallel Vietnamese civilization called Đàng Trong, or the Inner Region, that was distinct from the one based in the north. This frontier civilization was characterized by its ethnic pluralism and religious syncretism.[11] While Hoàng paid taxes to the Lê-Trịnh in the north, in the early seventeenth century, one of his heirs stopped doing so, sparking a series of north-south military conflicts.

By the late seventeenth century, Vietnam was politically divided by ruling clans. The Confucianized Trịnh family dominated the north, and the syncretic Nguyễn lords, the south. In 1771, this two-hundred-year political division came to a sudden end with the eruption of the Tây Sơn rebellion, a mass peasant upheaval led by three brothers. While the Tây Sơn brothers defeated the Trịnh lords in the north, Nguyễn Phúc Ánh, exiled in Siam (present-day Thailand), attacked the Tây Sơn. With the aid of French sailors, soldiers, and ecclesiastics, Nguyễn Phúc Ánh, later known as Emperor Gia Long, emerged victorious.[12] Having defeated the Tây Sơn brothers, he ushered in the founding of the Nguyễn dynasty in 1802, almost sixty years before the arrival of French colonization.

As the founder of the Nguyễn dynasty, Gia Long sought to unify the three

regions. He moved the capital from Hà Nội in the north to Huế in the central
region. From there, he and his heirs would build what remain today as the historical relics of a Sinicized imperial system. Several generations of Vietnamese
mandarins were trained under the "Great Tradition" of Neo-Confucianism.[13]
The nineteenth century represented, therefore, something of a historical cul-
mination of Vietnam's long relation to China and the East Asian Confucian
world. As a result, when we later discuss the influence of, say, the periods of
the Tang (618–907), Ming (1368–1644), and Qing (1644–1911) and their varied
cultural influences on twentieth-century Vietnamese authors, it is neither an
anachronism nor historical decontextualization.

Finally, the other significant sources of Sinitic culture and Confucian influence in Vietnam derive from the long history of immigration of the ethnic
Chinese. Since at least the sixteenth century, Chinese immigrants have come
to Vietnam as merchants, workers, and traders.[14] But toward the end of the seventeenth century, in the wake of the collapse of the Ming dynasty, a group of
ethnic Chinese called the *minh-hương*—Ming loyalists—fled their homes to
settle in central and southern Vietnam. This latter cohort of ethnic Chinese,
with their knowledge of the northern imperial court, would prove invaluable
to the Vietnamese kingdom in serving as cultural and political mediators to
Beijing.[15]

Insofar as nineteenth-century Vietnam emulated its northern neighbor and
participated in a shared East Asian classical culture, it simultaneously inherited
certain paradigms concerning the body, gender, and erotic life. Studies on the
question of gender in the history of medicine in China have suggested a radically distinct paradigm from the biomedical body that is arguably dominant
today. As Charlotte Furth has demonstrated, in such a paradigm, the signifiers
of bodily gender were captured in the dynamism of yin and yang, which Sinitic
culture understood not as binary oppositions that map onto heteronormative
imperatives. Rather, they viewed them as revealing the fluctuating, complementary forces that everyone, man or woman, possesses, depending on location and
context. Furth explains: "Unlike the 'one sex' model of classical European medicine, the body of classical Chinese medical imagination appears as genuinely
androgynous. Yin and yang name the 'feminine' and 'masculine' as aspects of all
bodies and of the cosmos at large. Such a logic would suggest room for variation
and flexibility at the boundaries of gender."[16] In classical European medicine,

the one-sex model espoused the belief that a woman's reproductive organs represented a lesser form of the man's, and hence, a woman is a lesser man.[17] It was not until sometime in the eighteenth century—the beginning of the modern period in the West—that the two-sex model emerged, in which the male and female reproductive organs became distinct, each with their own denominations.[18] The paradigm of classical Chinese medicine, however, profoundly differed from its European frameworks. In the Chinese model, androgyny was the gender ideal, a fusion of yin and yang that evidenced far more bodily variation and flexibility. The question of sexual reproduction centered on that delicate equilibrium— neither excess nor deficiency—in the balance of yin and yang. Furth explains: "Thus even though human males were not pure yang and human females not pure yin, anomalies which impaired generative function were transgressive, distorted configurations of yin yang influences."[19] Perturbations of this delicate balance were signs of potential illness or disease, departures from the "androgynous ideal of health."[20] In such a dynamic system, accounts of spontaneous sex change in the human or animal world were not beyond the realm of possibility or rational explanation. Moreover, unlike the nineteenth-century Western sexological model, medical authorities did not consider instances of gender transgression symptoms of homoeroticism or same-sex sexual identity. Instead, they were interpreted as the creative and expansive possibilities of the cosmos.[21]

In the early twentieth century, this East Asian cosmology did not wither away. While the French may have succeeded in forming the political and material geo-body of Indochina,[22] they were less successful in other areas, such as medicine. Despite the creation of a modern French colonial state and the relentless wheels of modernization, Sino-Vietnamese traditional medicine persisted.[23] The French colonial state certainly attempted to use medicine as a "civilizing" tool of control, proclaiming the superiority of Western medicine as the engine of progress. Denouncing the so-called backwardness of indigenous, non-French, or non-Western forms of healing, colonial authorities instituted the indigenous health policy Assistance Médicale Indigène in 1905 to regulate—at least in theory—the medical industry in demarcating a strong distinction between so-called scientific Western medicine and traditional Vietnamese ones. Yet despite the colonial state's attempts at regulatory control, the influence of Sino-Vietnamese medicine continued to manifest itself in the cultural domain. Sino-Vietnamese ideas about gender and the body were popularized in part through sexual hygiene manuals. For example, in the preface of one hygiene manual, the editor observes that the treatments for sex-related health problems in Vietnam can often be found in "Chinese medicine books" (*sách thuốc Tầu*). But with the displacement of classical Chinese by modern Vietnamese, few people can now access these older books, rendering them effectively "useless" (*cũng như không*). For this reason, the hygiene book in question would be of great utility to the public: it was edited and translated into modern Vietnamese by an "erudite sinologist" (*nho học uyên thâm*) and who possessed "cursory" (*thiệp liệp*) knowledge of Western medical science to boot.[24] The editor's preface suggests that while Western medical science was slowly gaining a cultural foothold, its imprint in the cultural domain was still uneven. The influence of Sino-Vietnamese traditional medicine persisted, by way of translation, into the modern Vietnamese vernacular.

Another example of the continued influence of Sino-Vietnamese medicine recurs in another hygiene manual. In explaining the detrimental effects of masturbation, the manual noted that the problem with such a practice is the lack of a "balance" between yin and yang found in sexual intercourse. The manual states: "People who masturbate [*thủ dâm*] usually have the mistaken belief that it is akin to sexual intercourse but do not realize that sexual intercourse entails the balance [*điều hòa*] of yin and yang [*âm dương*], allowing the free circulation of blood pressure, whereas masturbation only has yang pressure and so cannot promote fluid balance."[25] Such an explanation in a manual whose purpose is to serve as a "moral guide" to heterosexual couples is striking in its quaintness. In the West, since the dawn of the Enlightenment in the eighteenth century, masturbation had been believed to pose a profound moral problem, an unnatural defilement of both body and imagination, an antithesis of Enlightenment ideals of rationality, restraint, and autonomy.[26] By the nineteenth century in the West, masturbation was linked to "every conceivable sexual deviance," including homosexuality.[27] Yet instead of recapitulating the prior modern Western view of masturbation, the hygiene manual insisted on an explanation unmistakably grounded in the Sino-Vietnamese paradigm.

The prior reliance on the Sino-Vietnamese paradigm reflected the overall trends in medicine of the time. By the 1930s, the French colonial state conceded that it was unable to effectively transpose a Western medical model onto Indochina. The colonial state certainly succeeded in establishing vaccination campaigns against smallpox, instituted urban sanitation programs, and introduced medicines against infectious diseases.[28] These achievements, however, need to be situated in the context of the colonial state's professed limitations. A number of practical constraints hampered the widespread dissemination of Western medical models in Indochina: inadequate budgets; shortages of facilities, personnel, and medicines; and limited knowledge of tropical diseases.[29] These limitations may partly explain the increase by the late 1930s in reports of sorcery in Indochina, underscoring the simultaneous limits of the administration's efforts to inculcate in the indigenous population rational medical beliefs.[30] Moreover, in the context of such limitations, some hygiene manuals saw themselves as accessible alternatives to medical experts, aiming to democratize education about matters pertaining to sex, gender, and sexuality.[31] Acknowledging the lack of "widespread" (phổ thông) and "authoritative" (chân chính) knowledge about sexual matters in Vietnamese society, the preface of a two-volume sexual hygiene manual explains: "It is hoped that these volumes will help everyone in society, regardless of their background, rich or poor, high class or humble, old or young, male or female." The manual's title, however, is illuminating: "East-West Medicine (Occidental and Sino-Vietnamese Medicine and Love)" (Đông-Tây Y-Học [Médecine Occidentale et Sino-Annamite et de l'Amour]).[32] The manual, in other words, is a fusion of Western medicine and Sino-Vietnamese "love" conceptions. Like the prior hygiene manuals, modern Western medicine had not yet achieved cultural hegemony but intermingled with existing ones: traditional medicine had not withered away. Rather, it continued to serve as a paradigm in and through which to explain health, love, and disease.

A paradoxical consequence of the practical limitations in transposing Western medicine onto Indochina was the increasing focus on Southeast Asian local practices and beliefs. The French colonial state, in fact, shifted toward a process of "nativizing" colonial health care. This process entailed the "Vietnamization" of medical personnel and the continued critical role of traditional practices, albeit under the encouragement and oversight of French colonial authorities.[33] In this context, it is not surprising that Vietnam's first female and Western-trained medical doctor, Henriette Bui, began turning to traditional Chinese medicine in the mid-1930s upon opening her own private practice.[34] The process of nativization extended to maternity and childbirth practices, as well. Vietnamese midwives in urban centers delivered a mixed form of maternity service that adhered to certain French rules of hygiene while retaining Vietnamese cultural birthing rituals and practices derived from traditional Chinese medicine.[35] In rural areas, traditional practices that had preexisted French occupation continued to prevail. The coexistence, at times intermingling of both French and local health practices, is what some have called "medical pluralism."[36]

Moreover, throughout the nineteenth and early twentieth centuries, another set of beliefs coexisted with, if not rivaled, the Nguyễn dynasty's emulation of Confucian cosmology and sociopolitical institutions. Alongside the solemnity of official Sinitic discourse existed the syncretic values of Southeast Asian popular religions and rituals that conferred an unusually high status on female deities relative to elsewhere in Confucian East Asia.[37] Vietnam had long been known for its female deities. In Buddhist shrines, the veneration of the female deity Quan Âm Thị Kính (Guanyin, in China), the goddess of mercy, popularized in Vietnamese literature and theatrical performance since the sixteenth century and onward as having disguised herself as a monk, symbolized a female deity to whom a woman could wish for a problem-free birth or pray for an ailing child's recovery.[38] Despite its professed Confucianism, the early Nguyễn dynasty embraced a variant of Mahayana Buddhism,[39] known to have been more tolerant of gender variance than its Theravada counterpart, exemplified in the dynasty's acceptance of local holy mother cults. One female deity in central and southern Vietnam, where the Nguyễn dynasty ruled, was Po Nagar. This Cham goddess, who became localized as Thiên-Y-A-Na, represented a syncretic merging of Mahayana Buddhism with local indigenous beliefs. In the country's north, the most notable female deity since the late sixteenth century is Lady Liễu Hạnh, known in Vietnam as the daughter of the Daoist Jade Emperor but who, in the Chinese version, had no female offspring. Lady Liễu Hạnh is the leading female deity in the popular religion of the Three Palaces or Four Palaces (depending on different traditions). Three or four mothers reign over the palaces: the Heavenly Domain, the Earthly Domain, the Water Domain, and the Domain of Mountains and Forests.[40] In the seventeenth century, Daoist sorcerers attempted to vanquish this female deity, only to witness epidemics and natural calamity thereafter, leading the Trịnh lords to pay homage to her and confer on her official recognition.[41] In the nineteenth century, the goddess and her religion were forbidden by the founding Nguyễn emperor Gia Long (1802–1820) but later rehabilitated under the rule of Đồng Khánh (1885–1889), a cult follower and benefactor.[42]

In the early twentieth century, the continued influence of this popular religion was documented in several sources. In 1909, Henri Oger, a French colonial administrator in Indochina, published a multivolume book filled with snapshots of Vietnamese cultural life. He had commissioned a team of artists and wood-carvers to fan out into the city of Hà Nội and the surrounding regions. Much like ethnographers, these artists documented the material culture and practices of the Vietnamese of the time.[43] In its 4,200 drawings—of weddings, funerals, rituals, worship, fortune-telling, commerce—Oger's book demonstrates the conspicuous presence of spirit mediums in everyday Vietnamese life. For example, a drawing of princess Liễu Hạnh (fig. 1.1) makes an appearance, as does an illustration of a female spirit medium engaged in ritual as a follower

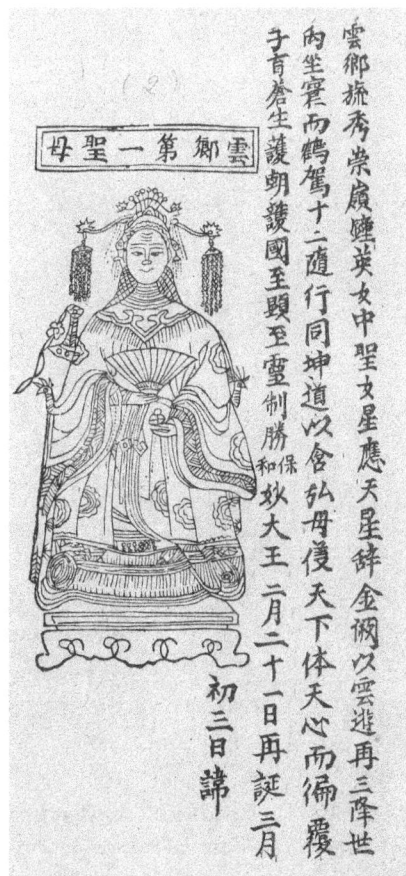

FIGURE 1.1. An artist's sketch of the female deity Princess Liễu Hạnh. From *Technique du peuple Annamite* (*Mechanics and Crafts of the People of Annam*), by Henri Oger (1909; republished 2009).

kneels before her (fig. 1.2). Yet another drawing displays the costumes of male and female spirit mediums (fig. 1.3).[44] Still another drawing depicts a procession of women. At the center are written in Sino-Nôm characters: a "group of female spirit mediums greeting the deities" (fig. 1.4). On the basis of these drawings, the practice of spirit mediumship clearly continued to play a visible part of Vietnamese cultural life.[45]

In the interwar period, the influence of spirit mediums was vividly depicted in literary reportage, a distinctively modern phenomenon that was a form of investigative journalism.[46] In one reportage titled "Serving the Spirits" ("Hầu Thánh"), the author Lộng Chương recounts the story of Mrs. Hàn Sính, a wealthy businesswoman who becomes involved with spirit mediums.[47] She is married and has a son, who studies law abroad in France. Despite what would outwardly appear to be a successful family, Mrs. Hàn Sính is deeply unhappy be-

FIGURE 1.2. An artist's sketch of a female spirit medium and a devotee kneeling before her. From *Technique du peuple Annamite* (*Mechanics and Crafts of the People of Annam*), by Henri Oger (1909; republished 2009).

開光　愛童　翁童揲香蓮遶　360

四百

FIGURE 1.3. An artist's sketch of a female and male spirit medium. From *Technique du peuple Annamite* (*Mechanics and Crafts of the People of Annam*), by Henri Oger (1909; republished 2009).

聖迓童要各　龍亭　571

FIGURE 1.4. An artist's sketch of a procession of female mediums greeting the spirits. From *Technique du peuple Annamite* (*Mechanics and Crafts of the People of Annam*), by Henri Oger (1909).

cause no matter which physician she consults or which herbal remedy she tries, she cannot seem to bear a daughter. One day, a female friend suggests that Mrs. Hàn Sính seek the help of the female deities. And so begins the protagonist's sojourn into the world of spirit mediumship. She spends extended periods of time visiting temples and along the way befriends a group of other women devotees. To prepare for the rituals, Mrs. Hàn Sính buys expensive ritual costumes, paraphernalia, and other spirit offerings. The story reaches a climax when she discovers that her husband conceived an illegitimate child while she was away. Upon discovering this infidelity, in her mixture of rage and grief, she grows ever more engrossed in the world of spirit mediumship and forgets her Confucian obligations as a dutiful wife and mother.[48] In an attempt to rescue his marriage and family, Mr. Hàn Sính calls upon the aid of a friend, Mrs. Tư, whom his wife had once admired for being "upright, Confucian-educated, and honest" (*đứng đắn, có nho học, và trung trực*).[49] Mrs. Tư tries to persuade Mrs. Hàn Sính to return home, but to no avail. By the story's end, Mrs. Hàn Sính has left her husband and is living with another man, Ký Sìn, a spirit medium musician. They bear a son together. Ký Sìn, however, is an opium addict who is wasting away his increasingly deteriorated body and the family's hard-earned fortunes.[50]

The moral of the story is not difficult to fathom. Simply put, the superstitious belief in spirit mediumship threatens the Confucian family and, hence, the basis of the Vietnamese social order. This message is made clear throughout the narrative, when the intrusive narrator, as well as various characters, repeatedly criticize the practice. The women involved are described as experiencing "madness" (*diên dồm*) and an ecstatic "loss of self" (*quên cả mình*).[51] The narrator describes the money spent on the extravagant rituals as akin to "throwing money out the window."[52] Mrs. Hàn Sính's irrational devotion leads to her being duped out of her own fortunes by scheming, unscrupulous opportunists. Finally, followers of this belief are perceived as benighted souls who have yet to see the light of scientific reason. One of the characters, the son of Mrs. Tư, maintains that "people can still believe such nonsense because their minds are still dark, and their minds are still ignorant." The narrator continues: "He hopes that one day, people can use science to explain illusory things, and reeducate people."[53] In short, as one scholar aptly summarizes: "The story of Mrs. Hàn Sính's downfall is meant as a cautionary tale, one that details the disastrous effects that superstition can have on family life and society."[54]

Yet despite its disparaging attitude, "Serving the Spirits" furnishes a rare window into the spaces of possibility for gender and sexual variance during Vietnam's interwar period. While scholars have alluded to this reportage for its coverage of spirit medium rituals at the time, its depictions of variant gender and sexual practices remain understudied.[55] A closer reading reveals an emphatically queer and enchanted world that transgresses both heteronormative and Confucian normative regimes. For example, in describing the world of the female devotees, the reportage depicts instances of female friendships, some of which are clearly homoerotic. In one scene, two women, Mrs. Đào and Mrs. Châu, form bonds described as something akin to those of a "husband and wife." Mrs. Đào is a widow, and Mrs. Châu is a popular spirit medium. Describing Mrs. Đào's relationship to the other woman, the narrator explains:

> She [Mrs. Đào] has already "bonded" [kết căn] with the medium Châu! Could it be that her broken love and affection [tình âu yếm] had planted a sadness and regret in her heart, forcing her to seek the caress and affection of a strange love [tình yêu kỳ dị] with another woman? Because remarriage in her case is an impossibility in our harsh society and education system, which does not allow her to arbitrarily indulge her concerns. So she had to give her meaningless love to the medium Châu. Because the two of them have "bonded" with each other, meaning to put it simply, the two of them have already become husband and wife.[56]

In the Confucian context, the major problem this scene of female same-sex eroticism and practice would elicit is not the notion of immorality or abnormality, as in the Christian West. Rather, the problem lies in the potential obstruction that such female desires could pose to Confucian obligations. Admittedly, the yin and yang cosmology, according to which a blending of the male and female symbolized an androgynous ideal, would lend itself to a tolerant view of variation in sexual behavior and gender roles.[57] Although no sex act would thus be singled out as unnatural in such a cosmology, the ideal of reproductive success was still the normative arbiter.[58] In a Confucian paradigm, society might overlook female same-sex eroticism and practice, but only so long as they do not violate the norms of marriage and reproduction. These norms partly explain the reportage's derisive tone toward Mrs. Đào. The world of spirit mediumships has led her, even as a widow, to a point at which she has "forgotten her vocation [thiên chức] as a woman and especially as a mother."[59]

To complicate matters even further, the pronouns that the characters use to refer to each other are cross-gendered. So the women refer to certain other ones as "mister" or "sir." In the case of the relationship between Mrs. Đào and Mrs. Châu, the reportage does not reveal how they address each other, except that the former clearly assumes the role of wife and the latter that of husband. The use of cross-gendered pronouns appears elsewhere in the reportage, as well. For example, in a scene where the women gather for a meeting, one of the women, a female spirit medium named Mrs. Hàng Bồ, addresses the main protagonist, Mrs. Hàn Sính, using gendered pronouns. The passage proceeds as follows:

> And she [Mrs. Hàng Bồ] called on Mrs. Hàn Sính:
> —Hey "mister" [ông], why are you so indifferent, letting the rosy-cheeked guest miss you so much, will you come over here to talk to this aunt [mợ]?[60]

In the Vietnamese address system, everyone is connected to everyone else in a web of relations based, in part, on gender, status, and age differentiation. The pronouns of address are those within the kinship system. So someone outside of one's kin may still be called "brother," "sister," "uncle," or "aunt." The word for "mister" or "sir" (ông) is generally used to refer to a gentleman or an elderly man. Yet, Mrs. Hàng Bồ employs this masculine pronoun to address Mrs. Hàn Sính. At first, it is not clear whether the use of the masculine pronoun is an isolated incident, exclusive to Mrs. Hàn Sính, perhaps due to some special feature that she exhibits, such as her appearance or elevated status in the group as a wealthy businesswoman.

The reportage suggests, however, that the use of the masculine pronoun is ubiquitous among the group of women. In another scene, Mrs. Hàn Sính and a female companion, Mrs. Tư Yên Phụ, visit the house of Mrs. Năm Khách to plan their religious pilgrimage together. The host quickly calls her servants to offer the guests some tea. Addressing Mrs. Hàn Sính and the female companion, the host states: "Ah, I was just about to invite you two 'sirs' [ông] to dinner today. I've been wishing for a long time to have the opportunity to invite you 'sirs' [các ông] to eat that Chinese-style snake stew, it's so delicious."[61] The narrator underscores the queer uses of gender pronouns by placing them within quotation marks, which suggests that the gendered pronouns are not to be taken literally but instead function as conventions of an alternative, parallel kinship system. As the reportage unfolds, it becomes clear that this parallel kinship

system turns out to be that of the supernatural realm of the spirits. The masculine pronoun used to address some of the women indexes the gender of the spirit
that each woman represents: each woman is merely a vessel—a medium—in and
through which the spirit is ritually incarnated. In another scene, Mrs. Tư Yên
Phụ is called a "prince" or "master" (*bố*) by a servant woman named "Uncle"
Đức (Cậu Đức)—an "old woman, wrinkled, toothless, her head tied with a red
square protruding forward."[62] The narrator explains this peculiar system of address: "'Uncle' Đức addresses [Mrs. Tư Yên Phu] in this way because Mrs. Tư
has a spiritual bond [*căn*] with a great mandarin [*quan lớn*], whereas 'he' [*cậu*] is
spiritually connected only to small princes [*các cậu*], meaning at the lower level
of the progeny. 'He' very much admires Mrs. Tư because she once bonded with
an Imperial Prince [*ông bố*]. So even though 'he' is old, 'he' still considers Mrs.
Tư like his biological father [*bố đẻ*]."[63] In this passage, the standard markers
of age and gender differentiation in the kinship address system are scrambled.
Even though the servant woman is older, in this context she is ranked in an inferior position to the two younger women, one of whom, in turn, apparently plays
the role of the servant's "father." All three women adopt masculine pronouns
to boot.

A sketch of the imagined hierarchical structure of the pantheon can help
elucidate this interpretive conundrum. In this alternative structure, six hierarchical ranks exist: the Mother goddesses are at the top, while in descending
order are the Five Mandarins, Twelve Ladies, Ten Imperial Princes, Twelve
Princesses, and Small Princes.[64] Given that the old servant woman has been
possessed by only the lower-level spirits—the "small princes" (*các cậu*)—she is
therefore at the bottom of the hierarchy, inferior to both Mrs. Tư and Mrs.
Hàn Sính, who have had contact with higher-level spirits, such as the "imperial
princes" (*ông hoàng*). In light of this structure, we can now also understand why
Mrs. Hàn Sính and Mrs. Tư were previously addressed as *ông*. The word *ông* by
itself means "mister" or "sir," but *ông hoàng* means "imperial prince." So, in the
context of this supernatural world, Mrs. Hàn Sính and Mrs. Tư were previously
being addressed as the spiritually incarnated forms of the "imperial princes"
(*ông hoàng*), but most likely through an abbreviated form (*ông*). This alternative
kinship structure also explains why all three women adopt masculine pronouns,
reflecting the gender of the spirits that possess them and that they embody.

This intricate universe and its hierarchy of gendered deities open up spaces for gender and sexual variance. The reportage's bracketing of the Vietnamese words of address, as in "uncle," "sir," and "he" to refer to the women, simultaneously underscores the artificiality of the gendered mode of address, its untethering from the standard Vietnamese kinship system, and its referentiality to another supernatural world that—like a palimpsest—is, nevertheless, lived out in *this* world. The parallel kinship system means that the gender attached to a person in this earthly world need not be either fixed or permanent. In this supernatural realm, as we have seen, the women can adopt—indeed, performatively embody—other gendered roles through the various spirits by which they have been possessed or with which they have been in contact. These roles may confer on them a higher or lower status, and hence empowerment or disempowerment, than what they would normally assume in their earthly lives.

There is some debate as to the extent to which the women participants have "agency" in the practice of spirit mediumship and hence the gender that they embody. If they have no agency in relation to the spirits they represent, then it would seem that this ritual is a scene of constraint, even bondage, rather than an alternative to Vietnamese society's patriarchal gender norms. The anthropological scholarship, however, on spirit mediumship has problematized the narrow notion of agency, understood in the sense of a bounded autonomous self. It suggests instead the need for a more expansive notion, one based on a distributed and relational agency that encompasses the deity who needs the human body, the spirit medium who embodies the deity, and the ritual community without which neither deity nor spirit medium could be sustained.[65] Consistent with the ethnographic findings, the cultural archive of the interwar period on spirit mediumship supports this more expansive, complex notion of agency. In a reportage about this practice serialized in nine parts in the journal *Phong Hóa* (Mores), for example, the investigative writer Trọng Lang describes the case of a woman who fell ill and then turned to the practice of spirit mediumship for relief. The reporter explains: "She recovered like a person recovering from a cold. From that day on, according to her request, twice a year, the Tenth Imperial Prince would enter her once. To chew betel, drink wine, wear new red and blue clothes, and bestow good fortune with famous writings . . . She now belongs [*của*] to the Tenth Imperial Prince and of the other Princes. According to the teachings of the Spirits and of Spirit Mediums, she is forbidden from marrying another man."[66]

At first, the female spirit medium would appear to have little agency. After her first experience in which the Tenth Imperial Prince (Ông Hoàng Mười) possessed her body, the reporter notes that she not only "belongs" to him and the other male spirits but is also forbidden to marry another man. Despite the rhetoric of ownership and bondage, however, it is noteworthy that in the prior scene, it is the woman who chooses when to summon the male spirit medium. Once he possesses her, she assumes all the male privileges of the Tenth Imperial Prince. Moreover, it is not clear how fixed the marriage prohibition is. The reporter notes that the woman in question eventually married another man in the earthly world anyway. In fact, in another reportage from the same series, Trọng Lang describes the case of a married couple, a female spirit medium and her husband, and the asymmetrical power dynamics between them. In this relationship, according to Lang, the woman in her mortal form is tolerable. When she is possessed by the spirits, however, she feels empowered, even sadistic, punishing her husband "like a smart dog that slowly sits, with two hands grasping the legs . . . sitting there even though mosquitoes bite him, until the spirit [the wife] lets him go."[67] As one critic states, the scene describes the case of a "henpecked" husband, whereby power and status in a Confucian Vietnamese family are reversed.[68] It is no wonder that the literatus Phan Kế Bính not only denounced this spirit medium practice but also compared it to the freewheeling styles of European women.[69] The temporary reversal of the normative social order is what Bataille has called a "limited" transgression, a finding consistent with Olga Dror's conclusion in her historical study of the meanings of the princess Liễu Hạnh cult.[70] Believing that this female deity represented not state ideology but "popular aspirations," especially by Vietnamese women, Dror maintains that the cult opens up carnivalesque spaces in which people enact new modes of relationships that are contrary to the prevailing societal hierarchy.[71]

Thus, the extended example of spirit female mediumship during Vietnam's interwar period illustrates the many kinds of gender- and sexual-variant practices that some women could embody beyond a heteronormative paradigm.[72] In short, these examples all underscore the highly syncretic character of Vietnam's early twentieth century. Both Sino-Vietnamese traditions and Southeast Asian popular religious practices coexisted, intersected, and at times competed with one another. These "cross-currents" and "intermingling" temper any claim to the dominance of the nineteenth-century Western paradigm in this period and its rather fixed conceptualizations of sex, gender, and desire.[73]

THE VOCABULARY OF SEX/GENDER

Further evidence of the limits of the Western paradigm derives from the vocabulary of sex and/or gender that prevailed in the early twentieth century. In reconstructing the terms that the Vietnamese print public sphere employed, this study demonstrates that, unlike in Japan and China, the modern Western sexological vocabulary had not yet succeeded in fully penetrating Vietnam. Instead, the period still witnessed the discernible persistence of premodern Sino-Vietnamese sexual vocabularies and cosmologies, even as the influence of modern medical-scientific vocabulary and its accompanying epistemic paradigms were already underway.

Here it is worth clarifying what is meant by the terms "sex" and/or "gender." In conventional English usage, "sex" typically denotes one's anatomical assignment at birth and "gender" the cultural meanings associated with femininities and masculinities. A growing body of scholarship in feminist, queer, and trans studies, however, has challenged any such easy distinction, insisting that "sex" may already be a form of "gender." For Foucault, for example, the term "sex" in the West was a "fictitious unity," a historical condensation of anatomy, physiology, psyche, desire, and more.[74] Indeed, the positivist presupposition of a bodily facticity untouched by cultural determinants is now untenable. Philosophers of science working at the intersection of biology, genetics, sociology, and anthropology have shown that, given the advances in the natural sciences in the past half century, it is now more reasonable to understand the biological as codetermined by sociomaterial conditions that, in turn, shape the meanings of sex and/or gender itself.[75] To acknowledge these complex debates, I provisionally use the designation "sex/gender" as a heuristic device to show their potential historical separation and/or interconnectedness. Whether they are perceived as distinct, the same, or multiple, I follow where the historical evidence leads me to trace the vocabulary in the Vietnamese documentary sources. Finally, the analysis that follows must, of necessity, temporarily set aside the issue of how meaning can dynamically change in pragmatic real-life contexts. The terms we will examine can admittedly be used differently as they move from one context to another or within multiple frames of a single context. Nevertheless, the recuperation of the Vietnamese vocabulary for sex/gender in the early twentieth century is a critical step in historicizing this critical concept.

To grasp the interpretive historical problem at issue, let us begin with an example from Vũ Trọng Phụng, an author renowned for his stories about sex and
prostitution. In the 1930s, among the several literary works that he produced,
Phụng published the novel *To Be a Prostitute* (1936), based on his ethnographic
research on the sex industry in Hà Nội. This novel, along with much of his literary corpus, however, was censored during the high communist period, from
the 1950s to the mid-1980s. Vietnamese critics rehabilitated Phụng's works in
the late 1980s and onward beginning with the country's "open door" policy.[76]
In the 2005 republication of Phụng's novel *To Be a Prostitute*, the late Hà Nội
critic Hoàng Thiếu Sơn included a preface, written shortly after the open door
period in 1986, explaining the enduring contemporary significance of Phụng's
novel. Citing the prevalence of the AIDS epidemic in Vietnam in the 1990s, Sơn
concurs with the novel's didactic purpose: "Our schools must realize that sexual
education [*giáo dục giới tính*] is very necessary. How can one not see this to be
so when the AIDS disease is like a wildfire spreading through the plains, threat-
ening the lives of humanity's future? Yet it is not until now that our schools
have sexual education [*giáo dục giới tính*] when the 'water has already risen to
our feet.'"[77] The term for "sex" or "gender" that Sơn uses is *giới tính*, the contemporary term in Vietnam for "sex/gender." This is the term that he repeatedly
employs throughout the preface, including the third subheading, which states:
"In Sex Education 'One Must Teach Children since Early On" (*Trong Giáo Dục
Giới Tính Phải Dạy Con Dạy Thuở Còn Thơ*).

Yet it is remarkable that Vũ Trọng Phụng never uses the term *giới tính*. It
appears nowhere in the novel itself or in the author's preface that he included
in the story's initial publication in 1936. In that preface, Phụng—like the contemporary critic Sơn—proposed that Vietnamese society promote some form of
sexual education. Such an education was necessary, according to Phụng, because
he worried that Vietnamese society was falling into a state of sexual chaos.[78]
The author explains: "What is more unreasonable than to accept that various
modern activities including theaters, cinemas, modern dresses, dance halls,
perfumes, cosmetics create the conditions for people to increase their *sexual
activity* [*cái dâm*] yet to refuse to accept simultaneously the need to promote
sexual education [*giáo dục cái sự dâm*]?" This passage not only suggests Phụng's
pedagogical motivations that animated his social realist novels but also reveals

the historical character of the vocabulary for sex/gender. While both Sơn and Phụng support the idea of sex education, each uses a different vocabulary to refer to sex/gender. It may be difficult to discern the difference in translation, but the interpretive problem hinges precisely on the different uses of the word "sex/gender" italicized in the prior passages. Sơn employs the contemporary term *giới tính* (*giáo dục giới tính*),[79] whereas Phụng uses the term *dâm* (*giáo dục cái sự dâm*). Is *giới tính* simply a synonym for *dâm*? Is *dâm* another way in Vietnamese to denote "sex/gender" as it is understood today? In short, are these terms transhistorical in meaning? Answering these questions requires the task of historical reconstruction.

It turns out that the two prior terms for sex/gender—*giới tính* and *dâm*—are historically and conceptually distinct. Briefly, *giới tính* is a contemporary notion that unifies morphology, desire, and psyche into two discrete genders. In contrast, *dâm* is the Vietnamese romanization of the pre-twentieth-century character for *yin* (婬), meaning "lust," "lewdness," "excess," and a term associated with moralism, not medico-scientific classification. Given his fears of widespread sexual chaos in Vietnam, Phụng may have envisioned a sex program that would eventually discipline people's pleasures and desires, as he was groping for something akin to the contemporary regime of gender dimorphism. Yet he was unable to marshal the precise language to do so. In a 1937 letter, Phụng translated the French *éducation sexuelle* as the "education of male female copulation" (*nam nữ giao cấu giáo dục*), thus emphasizing sexual acts, a profound departure from the contemporary meaning of sex understood as *giới tính*.[80] Phụng's terminology, then, hints at a fundamental difference in the understanding of sex/gender in Vietnam's early twentieth century.

The Absence of the Contemporary Term for Sex/Gender

To understand the profound historical difference in the meanings of sex/gender in early twentieth-century Vietnam, we first must consider the contemporary vocabulary. The standard Vietnamese term for sex/gender today is *giới tính*. As defined by a Vietnamese dictionary published in 2005, *giới tính* refers to the "characteristics of the body and psychology that . . . distinguish males and females."[81] *Giới* (界) means "limit," "boundary," "demarcation," but it can also mean "group," "kind," or "domain." *Tính* (性) implies one's sexual character or disposition. Together they constitute the contemporary Vietnamese term that organizes bodies into two discrete normative genders, male and female, each with its respective morphologies and psychologies.

Such a powerful term that labels a large swath of today's demographic population is historical, however. It nowhere appears in standard reference sources from the late nineteenth to the first half of the twentieth century. The term appears neither in P. J. Pigneaux and J. L. Taberd's 1838 Annamite-Latin dictionary, nor in Trương Vĩnh Ký's 1884 French-Annamite dictionary, nor in a 1931 Hà Nội reference manual.[82] Nor is it present in Trần Trọng Kim's 1940 grammar book.[83]

The closest approximation in the early twentieth century to the contemporary term *giới tính* is captured in the phrase *nữ giới* (female kind). The pioneering women's journal *Nữ Giới Chung* (*Women's Bell*), first published in 1918, displayed on its front cover the equivalent title in Sino-Vietnamese characters: 女界鐘 (fig. 1.5). The character 界 for the Vietnamese term *giới* in no way denotes sex or gender as it does today; rather, it more closely means "kind," "group," or "world" in the sense of the general domain to which one belongs, such as the "world of arts and letters." Đào Duy Anh's Sino-Vietnamese dictionary (*Hán Việt Từ Điển*), while containing no entry for *giới tính*, nevertheless displays an entry for *giới* (界), which it defines as "domain, limit, means" (*cảnh-địa, hạn, cách*).[84]

Had the term *giới tính* been a universal, transhistorical word to designate sex/gender, it ought to have appeared minimally in some of the major reference manuals. Its absence from them suggests that the term has a history and that the Vietnamese must have historically employed a different vocabulary to refer to sex/gender, or understood it differently than they do today, or both. The complex history of the contemporary term *giới tính* is beyond the scope of this study, but the issue of which terms were used instead during the interwar period is relevant. Thus, the contemporary term for sex/gender—that precise paired combination of *giới* and *tính*—is, in fact, a recent invention with little discernible precedent in the early twentieth century. As we will examine toward the end of this chapter, the second term—*tính* (性, *xing*)—also lacked cultural traction.

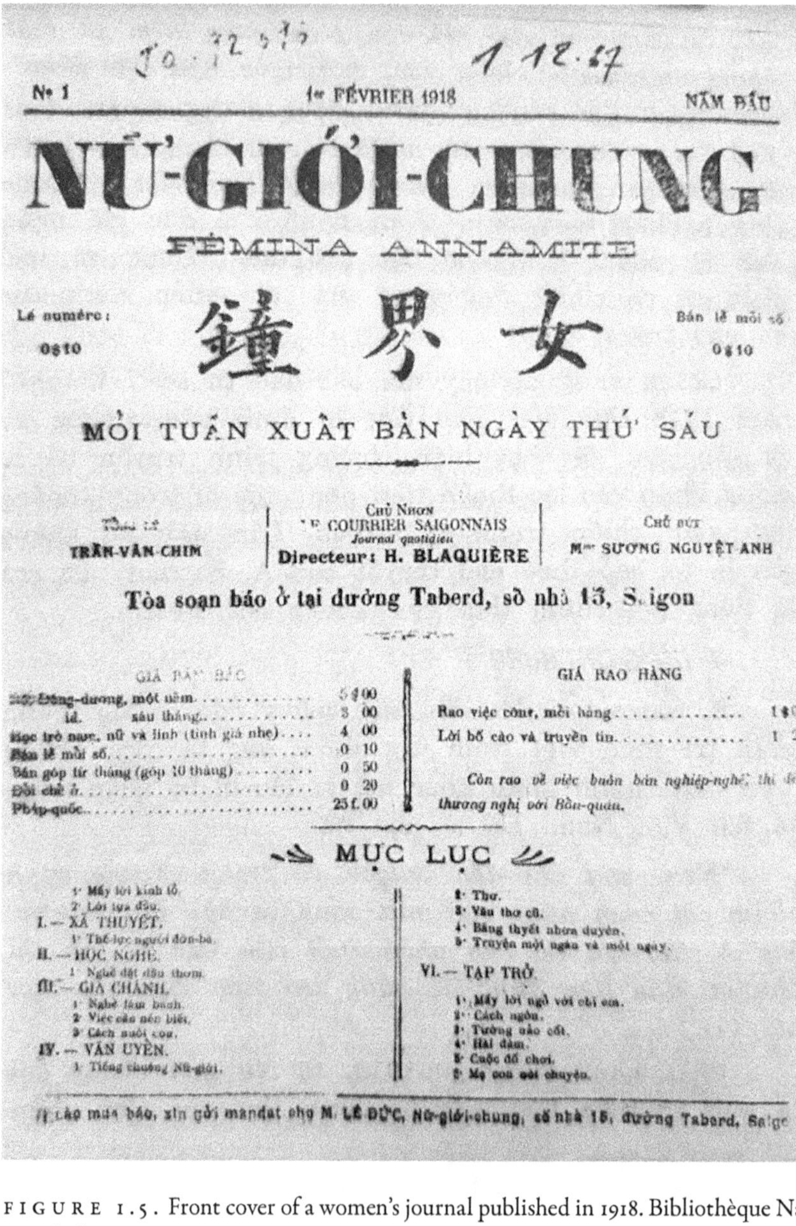

Nº 1 — 1er FÉVRIER 1918 — NĂM ĐẦU

NỮ-GIỚI-CHUNG

FÉMINA ANNAMITE

Lé numéro:
0$10

鐘界女

Bán lẻ mỗi số
0$10

MỖI TUẦN XUẤT BẢN NGÀY THỨ SÁU

Chủ Nhơn
LE COURRIER SAIGONNAIS
Journal quotidien
Directeur: H. BLAQUIÈRE

Tổng lý
TRẦN-VĂN-CHIM

Chủ bút
Mme SƯƠNG NGUYỆT ANH

Tòa soạn báo ở tại dường Taberd, số nhà 15, Saigon

GIÁ BÁN BÁO

Đông-dương, một năm	6$00
lẻ, sáu tháng	3 00
Học trò nam, nữ và lính (tính giá nhẹ)	4 00
Bán lẻ mỗi số	0 10
Bán góp tứ tháng (góp 10 tháng)	0 50
Đổi chỗ ở	0 20
Pháp-quốc	25 f. 00

GIÁ RAO HÀNG

Rao việc công, mỗi hàng	1$0
Lời bố cáo và truyền tin	1 2

Còn rao về việc buôn bán nghiệp-nghệ thì đi thương nghị với Bổn-quán.

🙠 MỤC LỤC 🙡

1. Mấy lời kinh tế.
2. Lời tựa đầu.

I. — XÃ THUYẾT.
   1. Thể-lực người đờn-bà.

II. — HỌC NGHỆ.
   1. Nghề dệt dầu thơm.

III. — GIA CHÁNH.
   1. Nghề làm bánh.
   2. Việc cần nên biết.
   3. Cách nuôi con.

IV. — VĂN UYỂN.
   1. Tiếng chuông Nữ-giới.

2. Thơ.
3. Vận thơ cũ.
4. Bảng thuyết nhơn duyên.
5. Truyện một ngàn và một ngày.

VI. — TẠP TRỞ.
   1. Mấy lời ngỏ với chị em.
   2. Cách ngôn.
   3. Tướng mạo cốt.
   4. Hài đàm.
   5. Cuộc đố chơi.
   6. Mẹ con nói chuyện.

Ai đặng mua báo, xin gởi mandat cho M. LÊ ĐỨC, Nữ-giới-chung, số nhà 15, dường Taberd, Saigon

FIGURE 1.5. Front cover of a women's journal published in 1918. Bibliothèque Nationale de France.

The Plural Terms for Sex/Gender

A historical examination of the vocabulary for sex/gender in the late nineteenth and early twentieth century suggests a range of potential terms. Unlike the contemporary regime that has narrowed the diversity of sexual and gendered subjects in recognizing only two discrete morphologies and psyches, the terms and meanings to designate sex/gender in this earlier period were, as we shall see, far more capacious than has been supposed, and certainly more so than the contemporary one. One reason for this phenomenon, hinted at in the case of Vũ Trọng Phụng, is the lack of a formal consensus and formalization of the terms for sex/gender. During this time, the modern romanized Vietnamese language was still inventing, searching, and assaying a vocabulary for talking about new concepts. Abstract terms such as "society," "culture," "civilization," and "nation," among others, were neologisms imported from elsewhere in East Asia to Vietnam through a complex process of linguistic translation and modernization. While scholars have studied some of these other terms, few, if any, have looked at the vocabulary for sex/gender in the Vietnamese context.[85]

One term that Vietnamese sources employed to refer to sex/gender was *dâm* (婬, 淫, *yin*). This is the term that, as noted, Vũ Trọng Phụng uses in the 1936 preface to his novel *To Be a Prostitute*. Đào Duy Anh's *Sino-Vietnamese Dictionary* defines *dâm* as "obsession over wine and beauty" (*ham tửu sắc quá độ*). It lists, among other entries, the combinations associated with debauchery or licentiousness (*dâm dục* and *tà dâm*).[86] Likewise, a 1931 Hà Nội dictionary defines *dâm* as "1. To be enraptured 2. Intoxicated in matters of beauty [*sắc dục*]."[87] An article in the journal *Southern Wind* (*Nam Phong*) that was evaluating the status of modern Vietnamese language listed in a footnote the paired term *dâm đãng* (淫蕩) in the context of pornographic literature.[88] These definitions— all consistent with the meaning of the term *dâm* in its pre-twentieth-century East Asian context—allude to sexual excess, serving as a moralistic warning.[89] Such a moralistic connotation is distinct from a medico-scientific regime of pathologization.

Another term that merits attention and is often associated with sex/gender is *dục*. By itself, it refers to carnal desire. Its character could be 慾 or 欲, with the latter having replaced the former in the People's Republic of China today.[90] In his *Sino-Vietnamese Dictionary* Đào Duy Anh lists the Vietnamese word and its Sinitic character "欲 Desire—Greedy—Longing" (欲 Muốn—Ham—Lòng

Muốn). But this term in Vietnamese is rarely used by itself and is almost always paired with another term, such as *lòng dục* (yearning) or *dâm dục* (sex/gender, 淫欲). In its glossary of new Sino-Vietnamese vocabulary in the early twentieth century, *Southern Wind* furnished the following paired combinations: *dục vọng* (欲望) to denote "desire, hope" and *vật-dục* (物欲) to mean "instinct," "impulse," "passion."[91] In short, the term *dục* denotes various forms of desire or longing. The term *dục* bears mentioning here because it is the paired complement to two critical terms that we will examine toward this chapter's conclusion: *tính dục* (性欲) and *tinh dục* (情欲).

Still another term that Vietnamese sources employed to designate sex/gender was *giống*. Unlike the previous terms, whose meanings come from Chinese, this one is derived from *nôm*, the demotic script that borrowed Chinese ideographs to transcribe the Vietnamese language.[92] The term appears in Trương Vĩnh Ký's 1884 French-Annamite dictionary in translating the French terms *sexe* and *sexuelle*: "種 species, gender or type" (*loại, giống, thứ*); "belonging to a species, gender, type (man or woman, male, female)" (*thuộc về loại, giống, thứ* [*dàn ông hay là dàn bà, đực cái, trống mái*]).[93] This is the same term that an 1898 French-Vietnamese dictionary defined for the term "sex": *giống*.[94] The word *giống*—gender or sex—denotes a naturalistic classification of the animal world of which humans are a part. It is the one term that endures historically through the second half of the twentieth century. Trần Trọng Kim uses the same term to designate the idea of gender in his 1940 grammar book.[95] It is also a term that lacks any reference to psychology, as evidenced in the above 1884 source and other subsequent sources. Yet *giống* is less utilized in today's public discourse in reference to human sex/gender, having been superseded by the term *giới tính*.

Furthermore, in the early twentieth century, *giống*'s meaning was not limited to sex/gender. Rather, it functioned more expansively to refer to any division of the natural world. In the entry in Trương Vĩnh Ký's dictionary, the other definition listed is "species" or "type." This is the same definition that Aubaret's Vietnamese-French grammar (1867) furnishes for *giống*: "type, species, seed" (種 *genre, espèce; semence*). The definition of *giống* in the sense of "kind" or "type" is further reinforced in a 1928 hygiene manual in which the term functions as a classifier for microorganisms such as bacteria: "the class of bacteria" (*giống vi trung*).[96] The biological associations captured in these definitions are related to another meaning that the term *giống* would later assume: "race." Early modern Vietnamese textbooks used the term *giống* to refer to the "white race" (*giống trắng*) or the "yellow race" (*giống vàng*). The idea of race was connected to Vietnamese debates in the early twentieth century regarding theories about social Darwinism and national survival.[97] Hence, given the many different meanings that *giống* could assume, the term was not a universal referent to label people's sex/gender and, in some contexts, denoted racial exclusivity. The word's chameleon-like character underscores its imprecision—indeed, its instability—and suggests that it would be a poor candidate as a precise term to scientifically classify and mark people's sex/gender.

Finally, another term that Vietnamese sources employed to refer to sex/gender is *sắc*, the Vietnamese equivalent of the East Asian term for *se* (色). When used alone, the term generally refers to beauty or the world of appearances. Đào Duy Anh's Sino-Vietnamese dictionary defines sắc (色) to mean "Fertile. Countenance—the countenance of a beautiful woman. Landscape" (*màu mỡ. Dung mạo—Sắc con gái đẹp. Phong cảnh*).[98] Rocha explains that in premodern East Asia, the term *se* implied lust, temptation, or seduction and could be used in combination with other terms to form, for instance, the phrase "pornographic novel" (*seqing xiashuo*, 色情小說).[99] Génibrel's 1898 Annamite-French dictionary combines it with other terms such as *dục* (longing, desire) and displays this entry: "Sắc dục: Luxure, volupté; Nữ sắc: Fornication; Nam sắc: sodomie, pédérastie; Thủ sắc: masturbation; Mê sắc: Adoné au vice impur; Viện sắc: s'abstenir des voluptés charnelles."[100] In this entry, *sắc dục* is translated into French to mean *volupté*—or sensual pleasure. The word *nam*, which means male, coupled with *sắc*, leads to a French translation for sodomy (*sodomie*) and pederasty (*pédérastie*)—male-to-male activity. Finally, the last entry is *s'abstenir des voluptés charnelles*—restraining oneself from carnal pleasures. In this context, the word *sắc* shares the same meaning as the word *dâm*: "wanton desire." Both words point to a sexual activity or relation, but that is not quite the same as a principle of sexual identity or a regime that links anatomy, physiology, and psyche. A sexual hygiene manual published in 1931 confirms this meaning of sex as practice. In listing the ten cardinal habits for a hygienic life, the manual advises its readers to practice "sex" in moderation: "Whenever one engages in excessive sex [*sắc dục*], one may weaken one's health, not digest effectively, weaken one's muscles and bones."[101]

In short, in the early twentieth century, the Vietnamese evinced a plurality of terms and meanings to designate sex/gender. One reason for this is that there appeared to be no formal consensus on a standardized term for sex/gender, complicating any claim that a modern sexual regime organizing and disciplining people's identities had been consolidated.

The Absence of Sex and Predominance of Desire

Further evidence that the Western scientific vocabulary for sex/gender had not yet fully penetrated Vietnam during the interwar period is the relatively lukewarm reception of the modern Chinese concept of sex: *xing* (性) in Chinese and *tính* in Vietnamese. China's Republican period in the early twentieth century experienced a profound epistemic shift. Whereas *xing* in its premodern classical sense previously meant "character" or "natural instinct," its meaning in China by the 1920s came to embody the biological idea of sex, which came to replace earlier and more plural notions of gender and sexuality.[102] A similar phenomenon transpired in Japan during the Meiji Restoration in the middle of the nineteenth century.[103] One would have expected that, like in China, a parallel phenomenon would have taken place in Vietnam. Yet the historical evidence suggests otherwise: the linguistic and conceptual transformation of sex embodied in the modern Chinese concept of sex, *xingyu* (性欲), had not yet gained traction.

Vietnamese reference sources predating the twentieth century certainly captured the older sense of the term *tính*. For example, Génibrel's 1898 Annamite-French dictionary defines the term as follows: "Nature, natural, character. Disposition or natural quality. What comes from nature. Penchant (natural)."[104] This excerpt captures only the main definition for *tính* in an otherwise lengthy entry with several examples of paired word combinations. Génibrel lists two-word combinations with *tính* that merit discussion. The first is *tính mê dâm dục*, which he defines as "lust, lewd, debauchery" (*la luxure, luxurieux, débauché*). A literal translation would be "disposition of lustfulness." The "lustful" component stems from a compound term we have already examined: *dâm dục* (婬欲), meaning "licentiousness." But *tính* still means "character" or "disposition." Another noteworthy combination is *đồng tính*, which the manual defines as "of the same family." This definition is astonishing because the term's contemporary meaning is "homosexuality" or "same-sex sexuality." Yet nowhere is "homosexuality" listed in this entry in Génibrel's dictionary. The noticeable absence of the contemporary meaning of *đồng tính* suggests that *tính* had not yet come to mean "sex" or "sexuality."

The meaning of *tính* in the modern biological sense of "sex" or "sexuality" does admittedly appear in Đào Duy Anh's Sino-Vietnamese dictionary, published in 1932. In the entry for *tính dục*, the manual states: "the aspect of desire [*tính-dục*] in people's character [*tính người*]—carnal desire [*nhục-dục*] in male-female relations (sexual desire) [*désirs sexuels*]."[105] The same entry lists the translation for the French term *éducation sexuelle* (sexual education) as *tính giáo dục*.[106] Hence, the manual employs the Vietnamese equivalent of the modern Chinese term for sex: *tính*. Based solely on Đào Duy Anh's manual, then, *tính* appears to be synonymous with the new concept of *xing*, understood as sex in the Chinese context.

Furthermore, the term *tính dục* also appears in a lay medical journal titled *Y Học Tân Thanh: La nouvelle voix de la médecine* (The New Voice of Medicine), published in 1938 (fig. 1.6). In explaining Freudian sexual theory, the article uses the term once in the title heading for its translation from French of the term for "sexual education" (*éducation sexuelle*): *tính dục học*.[107] Yet this term is not repeated in the rest of the article. In translating novel concepts such as "sexual instinct," "sexual repression," and "sexual education," the article resorts to an older vocabulary. The word for "sexual instinct" is at times translated as *dâm tình* (sexual love) or *dục tình* (desirous love). The word for "sexual activity" in Vietnamese is expressed through a metaphoric euphemism: "fired incense" (*hương lửa*). To convey "sexual education," then, the article's author often translated it with the euphemistic expression: the "education of fired incense" (*giáo dục hương lửa*). In other words, even in this article where the modern translation of the concept of sex/gender—*tính*—did surface, its usage was infrequent and its influence rather lukewarm.

Indeed, despite the appearance of the modern term for sex in these documents, the bulk of other Vietnamese sources—reference manuals, grammar and language textbooks, sexual hygiene guides—do not employ the term. Consider, for example, another source, a Vietnamese dictionary published in 1931 that defines the term *tính* as follows: "性. The natural character [*bản-nhiên*] that the Heavens [*trời*] endow: Good character. Evil character."[108] The entry clearly furnishes the older meaning of *tính*. Other paired combinations that the entry lists are all associated with the disposition of animate or inanimate beings,

F I G U R E 1 . 6 . Front cover of a medical journal in 1938. Bibliothèque Nationale de France.

such as *tính cách*: "性格. The individual character of a being that has become an immutable fixed form."[109] The notion of *tính* understood as sex/gender appears nowhere in the entry. Thus, even though Đào Duy Anh in his Sino-Vietnamese dictionary, as previously noted, listed *tính* in the modern sense of "sex," the fact that another reference source published in the same period in no way lists the modern definition suggests that it had not sufficiently penetrated Vietnamese linguistic and cultural usage.

Other sources bear this point out. Chinese-Vietnamese instructional language textbooks that include the ideogram for *tính* (性) do not list a definition understood as "sex." Instead, they provide only the classical definition understood in the sense of character or disposition. This was the case with a text-book published in 1920, another in 1924, as well as others published in 1928 and 1943.[110] Because the purpose of many of these textbooks was to revive an earlier epoch of Confucian learning based in Sino-Vietnamese, it is perhaps not surprising that they list only the classical definition of *tính*. Yet the fact that these texts circulated for as long as they did in the print public sphere suggests that they most likely served as a countervailing cultural current, diluting the effective promulgation of the modern scientific discourse of sex/gender.

The unpopularity of *tính* as the modern term for sex was not limited to Chinese-Vietnamese language manuals, however. Sexual hygiene manuals published during the period likewise very rarely employed the term *tính* in the modern sense of "sex." An examination of more than two dozen different manuals suggests the remarkable absence of *tính*. Consider, for example, a manual titled *The Sexual Education of Males and Females*.[111] In addition to being published as late as 1939, the manual represents the most "Westernized" of the sexual hygiene manuals examined in this study. It delineates the latest Western theories about sex and sexual reproduction from France and Germany, with diagrams of the male and female reproductive systems. Yet the terms the manual uses for one's sex/gender are those we have previously discussed. For example, in a section urging its readers to practice sexual moderation, the manual states, "Male and female sex [*giao-cấu*] is a natural activity to continue the race [*nòi-giống*], but it should be maintained with restraint [*tiết-độ*]."[112] The term for "sex" in the sense of sexual activity in this passage is *giao cấu*, the same term that the writer Vũ Trọng Phụng employed in a 1937 letter translating from the French *education sexuelle*. Other terms referring to sexual intercourse that the manual employs include *dâm dục*, *mại dâm*, and *giao hợp*. The vocabulary for "male" and "female" include *nam giới* (male kind) and *nữ giới* (female kind).[113] These are terms that all have pre-twentieth-century Sino-Vietnamese roots. Like the Vietnamese novelist Vũ Trọng Phụng, the manual never uses the contemporary term *giới tính* for sex/gender, much less *tính* for "sex." In fact, the absence of this key term is most evident in the editor's "Address to the Readers," in which he explains that the manual's scope and purpose is to serve, among other things, as a form of *éducation sexuelle* (sexual education), which he translates into Vietnamese as *khoa loại dục*. *Khoa* means the science or study of some subject; *loại* means "kind," "species," or "type"; *dục*, as previously discussed, means "desire" or "longing." Literally, then, the editor has translated "sexual education" into Vietnamese to mean the "science of species desire"—in other words, this 1939 manual filled with Western ideas about sex/gender, sexuality, disease, and health never even uses the Vietnamese translation of the modern Chinese "sex": *tính*. Instead, it employs a variety of other pre-twentieth-century terms. Had *tính* proved a prevalent, or even standardized, concept in Vietnamese cultural discourse of the time, we would expect it to appear more frequently in sources, and especially in sexual hygiene manuals. The term's absence in certain key texts suggests that *tính* as "sex" had not achieved cultural hegemony in the early twentieth century, much less a foothold in the Vietnamese sexual lexicon.

Instead of *tính dục* (性欲, *xing yu*), another term that Vietnamese sources frequently employed in the context of sex or sexual activity was *tình dục* (情欲, *qingyu*). While the difference in romanized Vietnamese is barely perceptible, hinging on a single diacritical mark, the Sino-Vietnamese ideograms are markedly different. If *tính* in the classical sense signified "disposition" or "character" and held only a tenuous connection to sex/gender, the term *tình* is more closely associated with the affective dimensions.

Génibrel's 1898 dictionary defines *tình* to mean "passion, sentiment (of the soul)."[114] Likewise, the journal *Southern Wind* included the term in its Sino-Vietnamese glossary and defines it thus: "That which one personally longs for (*ham mê*).—Desire, Passion, Concupiscence."[115]

The idea of *tình dục* in the sense of passion has a history. Scholars of Ming-Qing China (fourteenth to nineteenth century) have noted the phenomenon of the "cult of *qing*" that underscored the centrality of sentiment (*qing*) and desire (*yu*) that pervaded much of the cultural texts of the time. As a response to Neo-Confucian orthodoxy's focus on reason (*li*) and character (*xing*), the Wang Yangming school of thought elevated *qing* as sentiment to the status of basic human nature. The enshrining of *qing* to such a status, in turn, led to a profusion of Chinese literary and cultural discourse on the supreme importance of sentiment.[116]

Recent scholarship suggests that the Wang Yangming school of Neo-Confucianism traveled to Vietnam in the nineteenth century, especially the south, and from there developed its rhizomatic roots and exerted its influence.[117] The historical itinerary of the Wang Yangming school to Vietnam may partly explain the discourse of sentiment and desire captured in the term *tình dục* in the Vietnamese translation of the idea of sex/gender.

Vietnamese sources from the early twentieth century appear to have absorbed and continued this concept of *tình dục* in their translations of the modern discourse of sex and sexuality. For example, Đào Duy Anh's 1932 Sino-Vietnamese dictionary, one of the few Vietnamese sources from the period that furnishes a definition of *tính* as "sex," defines the term as follows: "The aspect of desire [*tình-dục*] in people's character [*tính người*]—carnal desire [*nhục-dục*] in male-female relations (sexual desire) [*désirs sexuels*]."[118] In this entry, the author relies on an older concept of desire captured by *tình dục* to help explain the modern concept of sex captured by *tính dục*. Together with other pre-twentieth century terms already discussed, *tình dục*, and not *tính dục*, was a frequent term that Vietnamese sources employed to refer to desire associated with sexual activity.

Evidence from sexual hygiene manuals further supports the proposition that the older vocabulary of desire prevailed over the modern one for "sex." For example, a 1924 sexual hygiene manual addressed to married heterosexual couples never uses the term *tính dục* but employs *tình dục*. In a section subtitled "On the Question of Sex [*giao cấu*] in the Postpartum Period," the manual gives advice to women who have just given birth: "Those who are in the postpartum period . . . that is a period in which the activity of sex [*tình dục*] is prohibited, so as to allow for the body to recover; the refrain from sexual intercourse [*giao hợp*] should be from eight to nine weeks."[119] It is clear from context that *tình dục* here means "sex," or some kind of sexual activity, evident by the terms *giao cấu* and *giao hợp*, both of which mean sexual intercourse. Similarly, a 1929 manual on sex and pregnancy never employs *tính dục*.[120] Instead, it uses other terms, such as *giao cấu*, along with *dâm dục* and, most important, *tình dục*.[121] Another manual published in 1932, again, never uses *tính dục* but employs *tình dục*.[122] In the preface, the editors introduce the manual's purpose in providing the latest knowledge concerning sexual hygiene from Euro-America (*Âu-Mỹ*). Explaining the need to be more open about sexual matters, they state: "Sex [*tình dục*] is the natural inborn character [*thiên tính*] of humanity much like hunger and thirst, without which humanity would perish."[123]

As a final example, the earlier-cited 1939 sexual hygiene manual that presented Western theories of sexuality never uses the term *tính* to mean "sex." It does, however, employ *tình dục* in the sense of sexual desire or activity. For example, in the section "On the Origins of Sexual Desire [*tình dục*]," the manual enumerates different Western theories explaining the reasons for the libido: "Before the first century, Hippocrates was the father of European medicine. He investigated the origins of sexual desire [*tình dục*]. He said that the source of human sexual pleasure [*khoái-lạc của sự tình-dục*] emanates from the cerebrospinal cord."[124] In this excerpt, the editors repeatedly refer to "sex" or the "sexual" with the term *tình dục*. Thus, like the prior sexual hygiene manuals examined, this one adopts a pre-twentieth-century vocabulary denoting desire or sentiment to articulate the modern concept of sex.

Finally, perhaps the clearest piece of evidence showing the unpopularity of the modern Chinese term for "sex" is that the Chinese neologism for a biological "woman" (*nüxing*) never gained traction in Vietnam's early twentieth century. The idea of woman in the sense of a sexed subject became popularized in China beginning in and around the 1920s.[125] This new idea of woman was captured in the neologism *nüxing*, a conjoining of the words for "female" (*nü*, 女) and "sex" (*xing*, 性). Since the Ming period in the fourteenth century, the most dominant Chinese term for "woman" had been *funü* (婦女), a term that in no way marked feminine biology. Instead, this older term signified the "collectivity of kinswomen in the semiotics of Confucian family doctrine."[126] Conjoined by the kinship terms *fu* (married woman) and *nü* (unmarried woman), *funü* is defined by the Confucian protocols specific to the subject position. As a critical response to Confucianism, the neologism *nüxing*, by contrast, emerged as a "foundational womanhood beyond kin categories," grounded, in part, by the authority of the then-emergent sexual sciences and the common physiological ground that one shares with others outside the kinship group.[127]

In Vietnam's early twentieth century, however, the dominant terms to connote "woman" remained largely confined to an older Vietnamese and Sino-Vietnamese vocabulary. Consider, for example, the terms that Vietnamese sources used to describe the iconoclastic figure of the "New Woman." This was a figure who departed from Confucian traditional mores in embracing modern Westernized styles of dress and living habits, a topic that we will return to later. Yet the vocabulary that the Vietnamese employed to describe this "New Woman" included terms such as *tân nữ giới, phụ nữ tân tiến, tân phong nữ sĩ,* and *gái tân phong*.[128] Regarding the first term, *tân nữ giới,* the word *tân* means "new," and *nữ giới* means "female kind," which we previously saw in relation to the journal title *Women's Bell* (*Nữ Giới Chung*, 女界鐘). Together, the term simply means "new female kind." The modern idea of "sex" appears nowhere in the Vietnamese vocabulary to refer to the "New Woman."

Regarding the second term, *phụ nữ tân tiến*, *phụ nữ* means "women" and *tân tiến* means "new" or "modern." *Phụ nữ* is the Vietnamese equivalent of the Chinese *funü*, which defines a woman on the basis of her subject position and relations in a Confucian kinship system. The term *phụ nữ* also is in the title of one of the most significant, forward-looking intellectual journals of the period: *New Women's News* (*Phụ Nữ Tân-Văn*; 1929–1935). Thus, the description of the "New Women" is based on a word—*phụ nữ*—with premodern roots. The fact that the premodern Sino-Vietnamese term *phụ nữ* persisted through the 1930s, even to describe the iconoclastic figure of the "New Woman," suggests both the lack of dominance of the modern sexological vocabulary and the enduring influence of the older Vietnamese one.

Other terms Vietnamese sources employed to refer to the "New Woman" are *tân phong nữ sĩ* and *gái tân phong*. The first derives from the name of an eponymous novel written by the southern Vietnamese writer Hồ Biểu Chánh (胡表政; 1884–1958) titled *New Styled Women* (*Tân Phong Nữ Sĩ*).[129] The story tells of a heroine, Tân Phong ("New Wind" or "New Style"), who wishes to imitate her counterparts in Euro-America in opening an all-women's school and who runs a Sài Gòn newspaper titled *The New Woman* (*Tân Phụ Nữ*). The novel's title combines "new style" (*tân phong*), "female" (*nữ*), and "learned" (*sĩ*). The latter combination is listed in the journal *Southern Wind* in its glossary of new Sino-Vietnamese vocabulary, which defines *nữ sĩ* thus: "女士. A young woman [*con gái*] of letters or with education."[130] The "education" in question is a modern Western-style education. Finally, the other linguistic variation to refer to the "New Woman" is *gái tân phong*. In one of the novel's scenes, a female journalist interviews a male medical doctor about the differences, if any, between a single woman and a married woman. The female journalist introduces herself and her colleagues working at the paper as follows: "We are modern educated females [*gái tân học*] who have decided to band together create a newspaper to understand how the 'Modern Woman' [*Tân Phụ Nữ*] has opened up paths of progress and equality for the female kind [*phe nữ lưu*]."[131] The passage is striking in that it reveals another linguistic variation in referring to the new woman captured

in the phrase "modern educated females" (*gái tân học*). In the Vietnamese vernacular, the word for "female" is *gái*, and the words for "modern education" are
tân học.[132] This linguistic variation in referring to the iconoclastic New Woman
recurs in other Vietnamese print sources.[133] The implication is that the New
Woman is one who has received a Western education and imbibed its modern
values.

In none of the Vietnamese variations of the term referring to the iconoclastic
New Woman does the word *tính* in the modern sense of "sex" appear. Instead, as
we have observed, the Vietnamese sources continually employ older terms with
premodern Vietnamese and Sino-Vietnamese roots. Hồ Biểu Chánh's *New
Styled Women*, published in 1937, is representative of the Vietnamese sources.
In the scene in which the female journalist interviews a modern medical doctor
about potential differences between a single and married woman, it is ironic
that not once do any of the characters ever employ the modern word for "sex/
gender," particularly its modern Chinese equivalent as captured in the word
tính. Indeed, the modern sense of this word is entirely absent in the novel.

In Vietnam, unlike in China, therefore, the term *nüxing* ("woman," *nữ tính*)
in the sense of a sexed female subject failed to gain substantial traction in the
print public sphere of the early twentieth century. This finding is consistent
with the fact that the key term *tính* itself hardly appears in many of the popular
sexual hygiene manuals translated into Vietnamese during this time. It is also
consistent with the findings of scholarship on the uneven influence of French
medicine on Indochina: local practices and knowledges more often than not
prevailed. In essence, the influence of premodern discourses on sex/gender persisted for far longer than the current scholarship has acknowledged.

A PERIOD OF CULTURAL PLURALISM:
THE CASE OF SODOMY

Further evidence of the uneven reception of Western sexology can be gleaned
from the representation of male sodomy. In France during the interwar period,
male "sodomy" had collapsed into the category of "homosexual" identity. In
Vietnam, however, "sodomy" was not a symptom of this identity but a semiotic
sign of Vietnam's embeddedness in cross-cultural contact and the complex potential hierarchies that follow from such explosive interactions.

In the Western tradition, the word "sodomy" from biblical times bears, in fact, little relation to its sexual connotation today. Scholars now believe that the meaning of the biblical tale of the two cities of Sodom and Gomorrah in which God rained down fire and brimstone on the inhabitants is more ambiguous: the reasons for the Almighty's punishment may be related less to sexual activity than to the "sins" of pride, greed, luxury, and inhospitality.[134] The sexual meaning associated with the word came only later during the Middle Ages. The etymology of the English "sodomy" has its roots in the Medieval Latin *sodomia*, a term coined to condense, semantically, a series of pejorative associations that encompassed such vagaries as "unnatural" sexual acts, the "unmentionable vice," or acts that involve the "rubbing, touching, or other improper actions" that lead to "wasted" semen.[135]

Such fine historical distinctions—between "sodomy" and the "sins" of Sodomites—are important. Insofar as the Bible remains a powerful source of cultural authority, the choice of one interpretation over another can have immense consequences. Foucault himself suggested that sodomy's meaning shifted at a particular moment in European history from a juridical notion to one that was bound up with a nineteenth-century invention of a homosexual "personage."[136] So, on this account, "sodomy" ought not to be confused with "homosexuality" understood as an identity. Whatever historical relation that may exist remains open to interpretative reconstruction. Before reconstructing the Vietnamese meanings of sodomy, let us first examine the two historical sources of influence on Vietnam in the early twentieth century: namely, the Sino-Vietnamese tradition and the French-European one.

The basis for early twentieth-century Vietnamese law was the Gia Long Code, which had been formalized in 1812. The founding Nguyễn emperor, Gia Long, borrowed liberally from Chinese laws of the late Qing dynasty (1644–1912), to the extent that, as Paul-Louis-Félix Philastre put it in 1876, describing the code's section on "fornication": "The law and the commentary are the texts corresponding to the Chinese code without any modification."[137] Well into Vietnam's French colonial period (1858–1954), the Gia Long Code served as the basis for colonial administrators' translations of Vietnamese laws, and onto it were later superimposed French laws, including the Napoleonic Code and the Civil Code of 1931 for Tonkin, or North Vietnam.[138] The code's assessment of sodomy, and that of the Qing laws that preceded it, both shaped and reflected the way that modern Vietnamese understood sexual practices and identities.

The age and endurance of the Qing legal system make it a good place for us to begin: no law singled out male homosexual relations, let alone outlawed them.[139] But the Qing legal system did seek to maintain and propagate a hierarchically masculinist social order, whose rankings of perceived power shaped the perception of sodomy. No stigma was conferred on the penetrant, regardless of the gender of the penetrated.[140] If, however, the recipient were male, he suffered a loss of masculinity; Qing culture associated him with the feminine. The ideogram for "sodomy" (雞姦) reinforces this hierarchical gender relationship: it suggests lewd activity associated with domestic fowls, the characters for which, in turn, refer to an ambiguously gendered condition. Sommer explains: "The origins of the term *ji jian* are not clear. In Qing legal sources, a logograph meaning 'chicken' is used to represent the sound *ji*. This usage appears to be a later substitution for an obscure logograph, also pronounced *ji*, which, according to the late Ming scholar Yang Shiwei, meant 'to use a male as a female' (*jiang nan zuo nü*). The essence of the term is the gender inversion imposed on a male who is anally penetrated."[141] The femininely gendered condition of the penetrated male brings us to another key point regarding Qing legal culture. The laws on sodomy applied, in principle, equally to males and females and to hetero- and homosexual relations. To the extent that sodomy surfaced in Qing legal discourse, it was almost always inside of discussions about other criminal offenses, such as rape or murder. Criminal cases involving sodomy (*ji jian*; 雞姦) in no way singled out homosexual relations but rather were subordinated to the larger category of "illicit sex" (*jian*; 姦).[142]

One indication of the enduring traces of the prior Sinitic cosmology in early twentieth-century Vietnam appears in the varied definitions of sodomy itself. The word for sodomy in Vietnamese is *kê gian*, the equivalent of the Chinese *ji jian*. Let us look at an example. In his Sino-Vietnamese dictionary, Đào Duy Anh defines the term as follows: "A male with a male or with a female who have sex [*gian dâm*] at the anus like chickens; this practice is widespread in civilised countries (sodomie)."[143] I want to emphasize three key points here. First, note that sodomy is not singled out as an exclusively homosexual activity ("a male with a male or with a female"). Second, in the prior entry, it is no coincidence that the Vietnamese term used here for "sex"—*gian dâm*—implies committing adultery or engaging in some form of "illicit" sex. Finally, the allusion to "chickens" would seem rather odd, even gratuitous, without the context of the ideogram for "sodomy" and its transregional linkage with Sinitic culture. These points all reinforce the fact that, whether in the Qing Code or the Gia Long Code derived from it, Sino-Vietnamese prohibitions against sodomy in no way singled out homosexual relations but were a category subordinate to a more general rubric. The fact that a sexual practice is not attached to an identity suggests that both are less fixed at this time in Vietnam's history than they would later become. But there is another countervailing culture in this period that exerted a powerful influence: the French.

Beginning in 1858, when France first invaded present-day Đà Nẵng, it sought to remake colonial Indochina in its own image.[144] What that image would have meant regarding sodomy, then, is worth examining. Since the Enlightenment, French law had shifted away from its theological basis to become more secular. Public transgressions concerned the authorities, but private life was a relatively protected space. Even though French society largely considered sodomy morally repugnant, it fell into this private domain, and so the Constituent Assembly of 1791 abolished antisodomy laws. Neither the Napoleonic Code (the civil laws) nor the penal codes that followed outlawed sodomy. In short, in revolutionary and Napoleonic France, the state did not generally consider sodomy a legal problem.[145]

The French state did regulate sexual practices in other ways, though. Like the codes of the Qing and Gia Long, French law contained a general "indecency" provision under which sodomy could be prosecuted. Since at least the eighteenth century, the semantic distinction between "sodomy," understood as anal intercourse, and "pederasty" (*pédérastie*), understood as male homosexual relations, had begun to erode.[146] While pederasty implies, historically and etymologically, the "love of boys," its meaning in France increasingly came to signify, generally, men who had sexual relations of any kind with other men.[147] Thus, while "sodomy" may have been decriminalized, "pederasty" was not: it continued to be regulated and policed.[148] In addition to the indecency laws, the French state also enacted various regulatory measures to guide proper moral and gendered conduct of its citizens.[149] Finally, the medical pathologization of sexuality and sexual "perversions" took on greater prominence by the middle of the nineteenth century and onward, coinciding with the rise of psychiatric institutions.[150] In short, while sodomy was not criminalized, various forms of regulation did constrain sex and sexuality, and these attitudes accompanied French colonialists when they came to Vietnam.

French law extended to the parts of Indochina that it controlled, which meant that the law's relative indifference to sodomy generally carried over into this new context. French colonial authorities were far more preoccupied with the problem of heterosexual prostitution. The arrival of French soldiers in the colony increased the demand for sex workers. Prostitution, considered a victimless crime, was legal in the French colony, as it was in France. French colonial authorities, however, did seek to regulate it.[151] The aim was less to support the well-being of the locals than to maintain the health of French soldiers and French expatriates. The motivations for these stringent regulations were as much a question of public health as the preservation of white prestige. By regulating sex, the authorities could then control miscegenation.[152]

In fact, they strictly defined a "prostitute" as a woman, excluding homosexual prostitution from the definition.[153] Official records in the colonial archive demonstrate some attention to homosexual relations or male-male sex work, but it is relatively scant.[154] For example, in a report on the problem of prostitution in the Vietnamese colony, the French authorities noted: "It is known today that the 'houses of boys' [les maisons de garçons] are as numerous as the 'houses of girls' [les maisons des filles]. Our large cities contain all varieties of prostitution and there is satisfaction for all sexual appetites."[155] Despite this brief acknowledgment, however, non-heterosexual practices fell outside their official regulatory gaze, likely because they did not threaten to erode white prestige.

Vietnamese language sources mention sodomy much more frequently. And on the whole, the Vietnamese idea of sodomy was not tethered to a homosexual identity. Rather, it served as an anxious sign of Vietnam's embeddedness in cross-cultural contact and the complex potential hierarchies that follow from such explosive interactions. Admittedly, some Vietnamese authors did make the conflation between act and identity. This is most apparent in the writings by the Vietnamese author Vũ Trọng Phụng. Throughout the 1930s, Phụng engaged in pen wars with his contemporaries, accusing his peers of adulating Western culture: "Do you men realize that in Germany millions of people practice the vice of sodomy [kê gian] (pédérastre) and in France such big names like Gide, Rostand, and Verlaine are all leaders of this practice?"[156] By posing this question, Phụng implies that his peers seem blind to the West's shortcomings, namely the "vice" of sodomy, which he considered "filthy" (nhơ bẩn) and "impure" (ô uê). He places in parentheses next to the word "sodomy" the French term *pédérastre*—the person, as opposed to the act, *pederastie*—to imply that the two are one and the same. Thus, for Phụng, "sodomy" is a marker for "pederasty," a conflation of practice and identity that is consistent with French beliefs. In examining the evidence for his claims, it is apparent that he drew on French sources that, paradoxically, render him closer to a certain conservative strand of Western culture that he so adamantly opposed.[157] The case of Phụng—and his negative conflation of sodomy and homosexual identity—represents strong evidence of Western influence.

An examination of a wider set of cultural documents during this time, however, suggests that sodomy was less tethered to a homosexual identity than to the swirl of culture in Hà Nội. Consider the definition that Đào Duy Anh provided in his Sino-Vietnamese dictionary. I have already examined the term's Sinitic influences, but it contains additional details that warrant further explication: "A male with a male or with a female who have sex [*gian dâm*] at the anus like chickens; this practice is widespread in civilized countries (sodomie)."[158] A conspicuous detail stands out here. In parenthesis is the word *sodomie*, a French word in an otherwise Sino-Vietnamese dictionary. This Francophone word provides a linguistic and cultural translation of the Vietnamese *kê gian*. The author thus presupposes that the reader can grasp the French term to aid in comprehending the unfamiliar Vietnamese one. The presence of the French could simply imply, among other things, the prevalence of the French language in the colony—not that the practice of sodomy derives from, or is exclusively practiced by, the French. But some Vietnamese writers, including Vũ Trọng Phụng, would make this erroneous deduction. Either way, the idea of sodomy in the prior example traverses multiple languages, illustrating how "sodomy" is a sign of Hà Nội's cross-cultural contact.

The prior definition's assertion that sodomy is widespread in "civilized" countries is worth lingering over, for the term "civilization," especially in the 1930s, was vexed. French cultural prestige rendered many Vietnamese intellectuals insecure about their own cultural heritage. While some considered Vietnam a civilized country, others attempted to measure up to impossible standards by various means, such as reforming the romanized national language; still others sought to displace their anxieties onto various Others.[159] In short, depending on their cultural baggage, Vietnamese readers of the time could interpret "civilized countries" to be descriptive, aspirational, or both—whatever the case, Đào Duy

Anh's definition implied a cultural hierarchy. Is Vietnam also considered "civilized"? Is this "widespread" practice something that Vietnam and its people ought to emulate? Of course, others like Vũ Trọng Phụng satirized Western ideals, as in the *Dumb Luck* scene depicting "Mr. Civilization" effeminately primping over himself.[160] The inclusion of this seemingly minor but historically pregnant word—"civilized"—discloses the tense, anxious, relentless activity of comparison among some emergent Southeast Asian nations, what Benedict Anderson has called the "spectre of comparisons."[161] In other words, sodomy is not simply sexual activity. Instead, it is simultaneously a semiotic and historical sign of Vietnam's cross-cultural contact with other "civilized countries."

Further evidence of sodomy as a sign of cross-cultural exchange appears in the Vietnamese reporter Trọng Lang's "The Wretched of Hà Nội" (1938), an investigation of the then-thriving sex industry. In one scene, the reporter depicts an encounter with a world of male prostitutes who engage in sodomy: "In all of Hà Nội, almost 90 blokes engage in the 'So' practice (*kẻ gian* [*sic*]) discreetly circling around in search of work at the hotels or resting houses. Ninety 'ignoble and base' and 'immoral' blokes have made us Annamese ashamed and disgraced before the Westerners. These blokes do not cater to us Annamese because we do not like this kind of activity . . . they only receive Western clients, especially the Black Westerners [*Tây Hắc*] with their protruding lips and curled hair like a snail."[162] In this passage as well, sodomy becomes imbricated in a web of complex transcultural processes. Three key points stand out. First, note the inclusion in the original of *kẻ gian*, the Sino-Vietnamese term for sodomy, in parentheses after the use of the argot "So," apparently a broken version of the French *sodomie*. Importantly, the narrator never calls the male prostitutes "homosexuals" or "pederasts"; the French term *pédérastre* is never invoked. Instead, the narrator parenthetically uses a Sino-Vietnamese term to aid his implied readers to understand a Francophone-derived argot referring to "sodomites." He thus reverses the linguistic direction that Đào Duy Anh used in his definition of sodomy. In both cases, sodomy is a nodal point for the multilingual transfer of meaning between Vietnamese, Sino-Vietnamese, and French.

Second, this passage reveals how racial, gendered, and sexual identity are intertwined formations. Sodomy is associated with "Westerners." It is the "Westerners," according to the reporter, who enjoy these practices, not the Vietnamese men ("These blokes do not cater to us Annamese because we do not like this kind of activity"). Later in the reportage, the author comments that he will never forget the sight of the male brothels catering exclusively to "Western-European men" (*đàn ông Âu-Tây*)—a "painful humiliation" for those with a "mustache."[163] To be a Vietnamese man, then, one cannot exhibit a propensity for this kind of sexual activity because it would be a masculine humiliation. Through the complex circuits of disidentification—the psychic expulsion of that which the subject is not—the reporter reinforces his unconsciously constructed identity: at once racial, gendered, and sexual. Sodomy, then, is perceived as a foreign imposition—a violation of the integrity of this identity—borne of the transcultural contact between different subjects under empire.

Third, the narrator provides evidence of interracial male same-sex sexual relations. Specifically, the passage reveals relations between male "Annamese"— the historical term for Vietnamese—and black French subjects residing in Indochina: the "Black Westerners." These subjects were most likely soldiers who traversed the French empire and intermingled with the locals therein.[164] Their interracial relations were triangulated by way of French empire and complicate the Vietnamese term for "West" or "Westerner" in showing its racial, gendered, and sexual stratification: "Westerner" need not mean whiteness and heterosexuality. In all cases, "sodomy" is not synonymous with "homosexuality" as a coherent modern identity but is the nexus of a dynamic array of cross-cultural relations that are riven by hierarchy and power.[165]

Indeed, the meaning of "sodomy" during this period is conceptually distinct from a "homosexual" identity. Because of the modern Western tendency to associate sodomy with homosexual identity or other non-procreative sexual activities, it may be difficult to grasp other potential meanings associated with sodomy. To help us discern some of the distinctions in the Vietnamese context, let us consider another definition that Đào Duy Anh furnishes, namely the meaning of homosexuality (*đồng tính luyến ái*) in the same reference manual: "A male loving a male, or a female loving a female (amour homosexuel)."[166] Whereas "sodomy" is defined as a practice akin to that of domestic fowls and is apparently widespread in so-called civilized countries, "homosexuality" is here associated with the vocabulary of "love." Recall, too, that in Đào Duy Anh's reference manual, sodomy was not understood as exclusively a homosexual proclivity or even a sign of homosexual identity.

It is possible that the amorous discourse associated with homosexuality could be related to the "free love" movement that some Vietnamese youth promulgated at the time to revolt against traditional societal strictures. Writers of the New Poetry Movement and the Self-Reliant Literary Group insisted on a break from traditional family conventions that they believed were "feudal." Instead, they produced works of literature that inspired introspection and the exploration of one's feelings.[167] The positive connotations associated with the meaning of "homosexuality" stand in stark contrast to the rather ambiguous meaning of "sodomy" in Đào Duy Anh's entry. It is ambiguous because it is unclear how best to reconcile the reference to domestic fowl and to "civilized" countries. I have suggested that the origin of the former reference derives from the Sino-Vietnamese tradition and the latter to the discourse of the French civilizing mission. In short, whereas "homosexuality" appears to be linked to a local movement concerned with free love, "sodomy" is tethered to a hybrid discourse that is a confluence of cross-cultural, transregional exchanges.

This distinction between sodomy and "homosexual love" helps in interpreting a rape scene in Vũ Trọng Phụng's short story "Stratagems" (Thủ Đoạn). Published in 1931 in Hà Nội, the story depicts a scene in which a big boss, presumably French, asks one of his male Vietnamese servants to find him a female prostitute. Unable to find one quickly enough for the man's immediate needs, the servant is forced to serve as the boss's sexual receptor. The ensuing dialogue translated into English from broken French and Vietnamese follows:

> —What do you say then my friend ... Where is the decent *femme* [woman] who is supposed to come here tonight? ... I am very bored this Saturday night ... !
> —I have found one, but she is busy with her sick son ...
> —You lie ... ! I see that you're lying ... !
> —But no! I found one, I swear to you ... Only an incident prevented her from coming.
> —Well, you are going to recommence your role ...
> —Oh my God, *mon Dieu* ... !
> —What? You are not content ... then.
> —We've done it so much that I'm completely sick ... and don't feel *plaisir* [pleasure] anymore. *L'excès en tout est mauvais.* [Excess in anything is always bad].

—Then you shouldn't ask for anything anymore . . . eh! Nothing more . . .
Now . . . be nice, okay? Only one more time . . . Whenever you can contact
the decent *femme* I will stop. Come on, one last time, please . . . You do
not accept?[168]

The servant succumbs after the boss threatens him with loss of private property.
The scene concludes with a voyeuristic allusion to other male servants who witness the spectacle by peeking through a crevice in the door. The episode ends
with the statement: "Oh! What a heavenly scene!" (*Ôi! Cảnh thần tiên!*). We
do not know from whose perspective the concluding statement is issued—the
narrator, servants, implied reader, or the author. If the latter, we can reasonably infer irony in the statement.[169] By depicting an instance of sodomy during
a same-sex rape, Vũ Trọng Phụng may have intended to convey any number of
things, such as the violation of Vietnam by French colonial rule, the emasculation of Asian men, or the uncivilized nature of the French themselves. For the
purposes of our discussion, the scene helps to underscore the tenuous relationship between sodomy and sexual identity. Consider, for instance, the lack of any
reference to the term "homosexuality" and the absence of a unified homosexual
psyche or identity. The boss, at first, wanted a female prostitute. In her absence,
the male servant became the effeminized substitute: "Whenever you can contact the decent *femme* I will stop," the boss comments. After the act of violation,
the male servant returns home, infuriated, and begins to abuse his wife physi-
cally, as if to regain, symbolically, the prestige of his masculinity. The narrative
focuses on the horrific effects of colonial violation on a presumptively heterosexual Vietnamese man. In so doing, the act of sodomy in this scene represents
less a sign of a coherent homosexual identity than an allegory of the violence of
the French civilizing mission.

Finally, let us circle back to the earlier cultural debate on sodomy, namely the
pen wars between Vũ Trọng Phụng and his contemporaries in the early twentieth century. Recall that Phụng ridiculed his peers for their adulation of Western
culture and their ignorance of the "millions" in Germany and France who practice the "vice" of sodomy. Whatever empirical evidence may exist in support of
his claim, it is clear that sodomy is not an exclusively "Western" phenomenon.
Likewise, time and again sodomy was not synonymous with homosexual identity but was understood as a sexual practice intertwined with complex cultural

meanings arising from the explosive interactions of different languages, peoples, and cultures.

CONCLUSION

The chapter has looked at the domains of tradition, language, and practice, respectively, to reconstruct something of the available meanings of gender and sexual identities in Vietnam during the interwar period. In each of these domains, premodern paradigms coexisted and, at times, competed with the not-yet-dominant Western models of science and medicine to contribute to a milieu of heightened cultural pluralism.

In the realm of tradition, Vietnam at the time still experienced the powerful presence of Sino-Vietnamese and Southeast Asian local beliefs. These traditions coexisted with Western science to create, for example, what some scholars call "medical pluralism," the intermingling of both French and local health practices. In the realm of language, the period demonstrated a variety of terms to denote sex/gender, many of which showed unmistakable traces of their premodern Sino-Vietnamese roots. No single formal term yet existed to capture today's word for "sex/gender" (*giới tính*) that united the disparate elements of gender, morphology, desire, and psyche into binary oppositions. Finally, the chapter concluded with a case study of sodomy to demonstrate that the practice was less a sign of male homosexual identity than of Vietnam's explosive interactions with other cultures.

These prior conditions all point to the thesis that Vietnam's interwar period was a *queer* one—in the positive sense of exhibiting greater spaces for gender and sexual pluralism than the current scholarship has acknowledged.

TWO

THE VARIETY OF MALE
GENDERS, RELATIONS,
AND PRACTICES

ONE OF THE PROFOUND EFFECTS of the inversion paradigm in nineteenth-century European sexology—and its eventual global dispersion and translation—was the conceptual linking of gender to sexuality. If "gender" is understood as the cultural practices, manifestations, and assumptions associated with femininity and masculinity, and "sexuality" is defined, minimally, as the character of one's choice of erotic object, then the inversion paradigm contributed to the linking of cultural norms of gender to sexuality. This effect was nowhere more manifest than in the figure of the male homosexual and, by logical extension, the male heterosexual.

In this paradigm, the male homosexual was embodied in the effeminate figure of the gender invert. This figure was "inverted," or manifested "inversion," to the extent that he exhibited feminine attributes. The inverted attributes could manifest themselves through the possession of either bodily attributes or a feminine "soul." The feminine attributes could express themselves corporeally, whether through the invert's perceived effeminate voice, dress, or behavior. Moreover, in this inversion paradigm, the body could normatively appear "male," yet the soul, feminine. The idea of the feminine soul derived from the lawyer Karl Heinrich Ulrichs, who posited in the 1860s that male same-sex attraction derived from having a "female soul enclosed in a male body."[1] Because he believed that sexual desire was defined as attraction between opposite genders, male and female, it was impossible that same-sex desiring males, what he called Uranians, could fall in love with each other. The Uranian who possessed the female soul and male body could be attracted only to another person who was male in soul and body. In all cases, the male homosexual was by now tethered to a femininely gendered disposition.

The implications of the prior schema yoking gender to sexuality (and vice versa) are profound, for it was the nineteenth-century sexological revolution that produced the contemporary Western conception of homosexuality and heterosexuality. This opposition, seemingly so commonsensical today, led to a minimum of two consequences. First, the invention of the "homosexual" was a singular achievement in that it linked sex, gender, desire, practice, and psyche into a unified identity. The figure of the "effeminate male homosexual sodomite" aligns these aforementioned disparate elements together, creating what Foucault once called the homosexual "personage."[2] Second, in crafting such gendered sexualities, the inversion paradigm created normative identities to which people could and should aspire. In that schema, if the nineteenth-century homosexual was inextricably bound to gender and psychic deviance, the male heterosexual conversely symbolized normative masculine plenitude. In artificially linking these disparate elements into a unified whole, the sexual regime rendered deviations from this uniformity to be either unthinkable or a "perversion" of the natural order of things.

By assigning to each individual a gendered and sexual identity, the new nineteenth-century system defined what people were, thereby foreclosing other possibilities. It made it seem as if it had exhausted the kinds of genders and sexualities available to people. It effectively blinded people to other visions, trapping them in a black box, incapable of seeing what is outside.

The inability to imagine and see other possible genders and sexualities is arguably the most profound consequence of nineteenth-century sexual science. So powerful is this gender and sexual system, which persists to this day, that it has become nearly impossible for some to see it as historical singularity, that is, as belonging to a particular time and place, as representing only one way of organizing gender and sexuality and as reflecting something of the limits of its time. In European history, for example, before the 1700s, the idea of the man who had sex with other men would not have been a sign of either inborn or acquired effeminate "homosexuality." Rather, in traditional European culture from the twelfth to the seventeenth centuries, the figure of the sodomite purportedly had sex with both women and boys and embodied the "most daringly masculine of men."[3] It was, by contrast, the figure of the "fop," who was perceived as effeminate yet sexually desired other women. With the legacy of nineteenth-century typologies yoking male homosexuality with gender deviance, twentieth-century readers who observed the figure of the fop in Restoration plays mistakenly confused the figure for an effeminate homosexual who disliked women.[4] In reevaluating the fop, scholars of eighteenth-century British culture succeeded in correctly separating gender from sexuality, even as they acknowledge in other cases the interconnections between the two.[5]

Although much of this history has been well documented in the Euro-American context, scholars are gradually filling in the gaps in knowledge about other cultures and societies, especially in Asia, where the gap is particularly glaring in the case of Vietnam. As of this book's writing, not enough scholarship has yet been produced on the history of gender and sexual variance in Vietnam.

Drawing on the aforementioned theoretical insights on the divergence and convergence of gender and sexuality in different times and places, this chapter seeks to ask the following questions: What is the meaning of male same-sex sexual relations during this period? Is it identical to the nineteenth-century figure in Europe of the male homosexual who was associated, if not conflated, with the practice of sodomy, gender transgression, and psychiatric pathology? Did Vietnamese culture in the early twentieth century associate the male homosexual with these attributes? As this chapter demonstrates, in Vietnamese popular culture and modernist literature of the time, male same-sex relations were not yet coterminous with these predicates, especially that of gender deviance. Instead, men could assume a variety of genders, desires, and sexual practices irreducible to a homosexual identity, even as each could and did intersect with the other.

The chapter reconstructs these diverse subject positions in foregrounding those that surface in the Vietnamese cultural archive. The chapter is divided into three main parts. The first two parts look at figures and tropes within the Sino-Vietnamese tradition that may potentially be less familiar to a Western audience. These figures include the eunuch mandarin, who, contrary to some of the prevailing scholarship, this chapter argues is actually associated with masculinity. The chapter then turns to an examination of the variety of subjectivities and practices that the male scholar gentry could assume within the Sino-Vietnamese tradition that did not necessarily imply homosexual relations as defined by nineteenth-century sexology. These include the practice of feminine comportment by male scholars who desired women, the activity of female impersonation in poetry, and the discourse of intimate male friendships. Finally, the chapter concludes with a study of a scandal that exploded in the Vietnamese press involving a man who dressed as a woman to live in a nunnery. Apart from revealing the social limits of gender transgression—and the circumstances under which Vietnamese society deemed such transgressions unacceptable— the scandal further underscores the conceptual separation in this period of gender transgression from male homosexuality. In each case, the chapter maintains that Vietnamese culture in the early twentieth century had not yet fully absorbed the discourse of nineteenth-century sexology and its typologies, even as the discourse's influence was admittedly already underway. Ultimately, the study illuminates the plural forms that male genders, desires, and relations could symbolically take in Vietnam's early twentieth century.

THE MASCULINE FIGURE OF THE EUNUCH MANDARIN

A figure that endured through Vietnam's early twentieth century was that of the eunuch mandarin. The body of the eunuch is in some sense already a departure from heteronormative standards of biological reproduction. In the scholarship thus far, the eunuch mandarin appears to be a site of gendered contestation. Some late twentieth-century secondary sources based on French primary sources associate the figure with an effeminate, even homosexual, disposition. As we will see, however, despite this biased perception in some of the French sources, in Vietnamese sources of the interwar period, the eunuch was, at best, associated with masculinity and admiration and was, at worse, an object whose bodily condition ought to elicit compassion, not animus.

Before looking at evidence in support of the relative acceptance of the eunuch's body, let us first look at some opposing claims. In *Life inside the Nguyễn Imperial Court* (*Đời sống cung đình triều Nguyễn*),[6] Tôn Thất Bình paints a picture of the eunuch as an effeminate and emasculated object of ridicule. To reconstruct this picture, he relies on some French and Vietnamese sources. We will look at each in turn. A key French source on which Bình relies derives from the observations of Michel Duc Chaigneau, who resided in the Nguyễn imperial court in the early nineteenth century. Chaigneau published *Souvenirs de Hue, 1867* (Memories of Hue, 1867), from which Bình draws to demonstrate the eunuch's physiological and morphological abnormality.[7] For our present purposes, I present an excerpt from the original French translated here in English:

> At that moment, a character entered without a sound and a lowered head who altogether seemed to me a skeleton in clothing; he resembled enough like a woman and dressed in men's clothing but was neither one nor the other: it was the head of the eunuchs whom the king had sent to introduce me to the queen. This poor man was one of the ugliest types that I had ever seen: its figure, petite and emaciated, resembled by its color and by its wrinkles to an apple forgotten in the attic for several months; his eyes were hollow and expressionless, his nose flat, his chin pointed and adorned with a wart covered with some hairs, the only beard he possessed; his tuckled-in mouth indicated that the unfortunate man no longer had those little bones so necessary for chewing. As for his voice, it was quite feminine and shrill. He wore a large turban, which made his face even smaller, a short blue tunic and white silk pants. This man was probably not aware of his unfortunate situation, for, as he left the room, he walked waddling and giving himself a certain air of an important man.[8]

Although the passage furnishes valuable details about what a Vietnamese eunuch during the early nineteenth century might have looked like, it is not without normative judgments concerning gender embodiment. To Chaigneau, the eunuch exhibits an ambiguous morphology. Chaigneau observes that the eunuch "resembled enough like a woman and dressed in men's clothing but was neither one nor the other." He also notes that the eunuch was hairless and possessed a voice that was "quite feminine and shrill."

It is unclear, however, whether these normative judgments concerning the eunuch's gender are representative of how the Vietnamese imperial culture of the time would have perceived the eunuch. For the Frenchmen who arrived in today's Vietnam, the cultural signs that demarcated the genders were far from transparent. In his study of French colonial constructions of Vietnamese genders, Frank Proschan demonstrates that Frenchmen for the most part misread Vietnamese bodies, perceiving the male as "androgynous, effeminate, hermaphroditic, impotent, and inverted and, conversely, the Vietnamese female as virile and hypersexualized."[9] While Proschan's study focuses primarily on sources since the 1880s, Michel Duc Chaigneau's work, from 1867, is still within the appropriate historical ballpark. Indeed, the French belief concerning the gendered ambiguity of the eunuch is consistent with the views of other European colonial explorers that Proschan studies. To them, the eunuch mandarin lacked the "graces of the sex to which they do not belong nor the vigor of the sex given them by nature."[10] These perceptions of the eunuch mandarin, as Proschan acknowledges, may very well have coincided with the complex processes of colonialism, exoticism, and Orientalism, whereby the Asian male is feminized. This Orientalist discourse is something that we will have to exercise care in distinguishing from the gendered ambiguity that the Vietnamese discursive public sphere itself witnessed in the early twentieth century as part of a global historical trend (I later demonstrate this in chapter 4). Thus, Chaigneau and his observations concerning the Vietnamese eunuch mandarin more likely reflect European Orientalist ideology than the eunuch himself and the gendered semiotics of the Nguyễn imperial court.

Another source that Tôn Thất Bình relies on to reconstruct a portrait of the eunuch mandarin is Vietnamese classical drama (tuồng). He does not cite the names of any specific dramas but offers an excerpt of a "representative dialogue" (một giai thoại tiêu biểu) showing the eunuch mandarin's negative popular image, due in no small part to the notorious figure of Lê Văn Duyệt. Born with a congenital condition, Duyệt first served as a eunuch to the founding Nguyễn emperor, Nguyễn Ánh, later known as Emperor Gia Long. Duyệt would later ascend the imperial ranks, serving as the emperor's commander in battle. When Gia Long died, Duyệt encountered power struggles with the court's heir, Emperor Minh Mạng, who impugned the eunuch's reputation and passed various measures to weaken the eunuch's influence. Duyệt's tarnished name was not formally cleared until the reign of Tự Đức (1847–1883), and only posthumously.[11] It is in this broader historical context that Tôn Thất Bình recounts a joke in a classical drama in which wedding guests indirectly poke fun at the eunuch couple during their wedding ceremony. The joke is in the form of a poetic pun that questions how, as "half-male and half-female" (á nam á nữ), the eunuch couple can achieve sexual satisfaction, presumably because they lack genitalia. It is Bình who employs the language of "half-male and half-female" to characterize the eunuchs. Although the author appears sympathetic to their plight, he remarks how the joke demonstrates that the "masses" (*dân gian*) in and around the imperial capital of Huế were wholly "unsparing" (*không tha*).[12]

Tôn Thất Bình's reconstruction of the eunuch figure raises, then, two key questions. The first is related to the terminology to describe eunuchs. Did the imperial court of the time perceive eunuchs as "half-male and half-female"? Or is this a denomination that Tôn Thất Bình anachronistically ascribes to them? The second question is related to the popular Vietnamese attitude toward eunuchs. Was the cruel joke representative of Vietnamese attitudes in the late nineteenth and early twentieth centuries? Or is it a function of the soured imperial relationship between Emperor Minh Mạng and Lê Văn Duyệt? Given that Tôn Thất Bình does not cite the name of the drama from which he recounts the joke, it is difficult to evaluate these questions on the basis of Bình's documentary sources alone.[13] Nevertheless, as we will see, the answer to the first question is complex, given the overlapping historical meanings of the eunuch figure in the early twentieth century, a period during which premodern and modern ideas coexisted. The answer to the second question is that, whether of premodern or modern origins, interwar period sources evince a relatively sympathetic portrait of the eunuch mandarin.

One Vietnamese-language source that alludes to the eunuch and can help elucidate this interpretive problem appears in the translations of Pu Songling's *Tales of the Strange*, a well-known collection of eighteenth-century Chinese stories of the uncanny. The stories were serialized in different Vietnamese venues of the early twentieth century, including the journal *East Wind* (*Nam Phong*), edited by the man of letters Phạm Quỳnh and published in multivolume anthologies. One story, "Fate of a Female-Contaminated Lad" (*Duyên chàng lại cái*) was based on Pu Songling's *Qiao niang* [巧娘].[14] The story recounts the life of a seventeen-year-old boy born with deformed genitals and a diminished penis size. The translation is noteworthy in revealing the Vietnamese vocabulary for expressing the boy's congenital condition, and so can help us clarify the interpretive problem regarding the cultural perception of nineteenth- and early twentieth-century Vietnamese eunuchs.

Indeed, the difference in the titles of the Vietnamese and Chinese versions is illuminating. The title of the Chinese version—"Qiao niang"—literally means "cunning girl," referring not to the male protagonist but to a "tragic" woman in

the story who dies of sadness for having married an impotent husband. In ghost
form she meets the said boy and magically rehabilitates his deficient genitalia so
that the two can engage in sexual intercourse. The Vietnamese title removes the
woman's name and replaces it with a description of the male character's eunuch
condition. In fact, the Vietnamese text even contains a footnote explaining the
title: "*Female contamination* [*lại cái*] refers to a male whose penis [*ngọc-hành*]
does not function, who cannot reproduce; it is a person who is impotent in the
bedroom [*vô dụng về việc phòng*]. The result is a man who has become female
[*người cái*]. The Chinese term is *Thiên hôn*, the northern Vietnamese term is
Nại cái."[15] In the Chinese version of the story, the boy is referred to as a "natural eunuch" [*tian yan*, 天 阉].[16] In the Vietnamese version, the term has been
equivalently translated as "female contamination" (*lại cái*), denoting a man's
reproductive incapacity, as in the case of eunuchs. In contemporary Vietnamese, the slang term for an effeminate male homosexual is "female-contaminated
shadow" (*bóng lại cái*).[17] The contemporary Vietnamese term collapses sex,
gender, and sexual orientation into one, whereby the male homosexual is associated with an effeminate gender disposition. Both the contemporary slang
and the historical passage contain the phrase "female contamination," but they
presuppose radically different sex and gender paradigms. In the passage, "female
contamination" denotes not so much a male's choice of erotic object or gender
comportment as his reproductive inability. Indeed, the story makes clear that
the male teenager is attracted to the female sex. When one of the female characters asks whether he is aroused by "beautiful girls" (*gái đẹp*), the boy states: "The
blind certainly do not forget to look, the lame-footed do not forget to walk.
Even though I do not have that [reproductive genitalia], does it mean that I do
not desire?"[18] As already noted, after his genitalia are rehabilitated, the teenager engages in sexual intercourse with the female ghost and, by the end of the
story, bears her a child and even gets married. Toward the story's conclusion,
the Vietnamese text refers to him as the "husband contaminated by the female"
(*anh chồng lại cái*).[19] Hence, the expression "female contamination" has nothing
to do with the male teenager's choice of erotic object or gender comportment,
as implied in the contemporary Vietnamese slang, but rather pertains to the
eunuch's reproductive incapacity. By the definition based on reproduction, even
infertile heterosexual men can be deemed "female contaminated."

The idea of male deficiency is consistent with the historical milieu in which

Pu Songling wrote his *Tales of the Strange*. In her study of Ming-era medical texts, Charlotte Furth notes that the "natural eunuch" belonged to the category of the "false male," where "false" is understood in the sense of being functionally impotent. This category encompassed a wide range of character types, including the castrated; the leaky, who released uncontrolled or excessive semen; the coward, who refused to engage with the enemy; and the changeling, whose body is both male and female. The "changeling" was classified as male but associated with hermaphrodites and their erotic capabilities. The "natural eunuch," in contrast, was defined as a "male whose beard does not grow" or "whose yang is impotent and of no use."[20] So the natural eunuch, as in the case of the story's protagonist, is distinct from the changeling or the hermaphrodite. This distinction calls into question the perceptions of the French in nineteenth-century Vietnam who found the eunuch mandarin an object of disgust in virtue of the latter's perceived effeminacy. It also complicates Tôn Thất Bình's description of the eunuch mandarin as "half-male, half-female" (*á nam á nữ*). Furth notes that male gender identity in the late Ming period was not easily compromised by observations of the sexually "strange," because they could be explained away through the then prevailing medical theories.[21] Insofar as the Nguyễn imperial court of the nineteenth century strove to imitate Beijing and its millennia of culture, the eunuch mandarin figure as translated into Vietnamese in the early twentieth century captures the traces of this earlier cosmological framework. In short, the eunuch was not necessarily an object of cultural derision by virtue of his so-called bodily deficiency.

Other Vietnamese language sources further corroborate the notion that the eunuch figure was not necessarily an object of derision. One group of sources that support this claim comprises the biographies of Lê Văn Duyệt. A biography published in 1924 depicts Duyệt's eunuchism as a kind of congenital condition. The document states: "Due to the deformity [*tật*] of eunuchism [*ẩn cung*] (1) Nguyễn Ánh placed him in the role of a eunuch."[22] In the footnote is an explanation of the three different kinds of eunuchism in the imperial palace: "People who are '*ẩn cung*' help in the emperor's inner palace and can be divided into three kinds: (1) *Yêm-hoạn* (閹宦) the customary way to call a lid atop the penis [*chỗ âm dương*]; (2) *Tầm-hoạn* (蠶宦) (hence the meaning of the word "silkworm" [*tầm*]) means that the penis [*ngọc-hành*] is the size of a silkworm. The general's [Lê Văn Duyệt's] eunuchism [*ẩn cung*] is apparently of this kind;

(3) *Cung hoạn* (宮患) is a regular person but whose genitalia is missing."[23] This passage focuses primarily, and matter-of-factly, on the physiological conditions of the eunuch, consistent with the rest of the document. In no way does it associate eunuchism with the inferior status of effeminacy or emasculation. Instead, it notes that despite feelings of "self-consciousness" (*thẹn*) in his youth about the congenital condition, Duyệt was otherwise a brilliant military strategist who helped Nguyễn Ánh defeat his adversaries, the Tây Sơn brothers, in key battles: "Whenever confronted with the Tây Sơn enemy he was always able to win. On the battlefield, he fought courageously; anyone who witnessed it was impressed using it as a model to encourage the whole army."[24] As this document suggests, Duyệt's eunuchism has little to no bearing on his military prowess.

A similar portrayal of Lê Văn Duyệt appears in another source. In his biography of this famous figure, Ngô Tất Tố acknowledges the eunuch's congenital condition but otherwise presents him as exhibiting characteristically "masculine" attributes.[25] In describing the eunuch, Tố writes: "For time immemorial heroes portrayed in books are generally tall, with erect backs, whose countenances appeared grand. By contrast, as for Duyệt, his size was small, his face was not particularly handsome. Yet, he was quick-witted and ferocious, talented and healthy. He had a stubborn disposition, disliked books and preferred studying only martial arts [*chỉ thích học võ*] . . . the truth is that Duyệt met Lord Nguyễn only due to his *ẩn cung* condition that the Heavens had gifted [*phú cho*] to him. Due to this condition, he was assigned the role of a eunuch mandarin."[26] The passage is notable for two reasons. First, while Duyệt may not possess the typical physical endowments of Vietnamese heroes as portrayed in history books, in no way does the author depict Duyệt as any less masculine or as somehow not belonging to this mythologized heroic tradition. On the contrary, the eunuch is portrayed as displaying an early interest in martial arts, a possible retrospective explanation as to how he would later become Emperor Gia Long's general. Elsewhere in the book, the author states that while Duyệt may have assumed the role of a "eunuch" (*hoạn quan*), he exhibited a disposition that was "aggressive," "imposing," and "fierce" (*bạo tợn; uy phong; dữ dội*) that struck "fear and awe" [*sợ và nể*] in the later emperor Minh Mạng.[27] This tendency to canonize Duyệt and other commanders under Gia Long was apparently a consistent pattern in books by the literati of the early 1920s, even despite Duyệt's widely known eunuchism.[28] Ngô Tất Tố alludes to this condition, referring to it as heaven's "gift" or "endowment" (*phú cho*). The

THE VARIETY OF MALE GENDERS, RELATIONS, AND PRACTICES   69

language that the author adopts in the document therefore suggests that Duyệt's congenital condition has little bearing on his perceived masculinity. On the same page in a note, the author clarifies the meaning of the term *ẩn cung*: "That is to say, not having testicles [*ngoại thận*]." This clarifies a question surrounding the practice of eunuch castration: namely, what exactly is "castrated"? Is it the penis, testicles, or both? While this may seem like hairsplitting minutiae, this question has significant implications on the cultural meanings of masculinity. Scholars have suggested that between the sixteenth and twentieth centuries in Western culture, the anatomical measure of manliness centered on the scrotum, not the penis. The fixation on phallus size did not emerge until after Freud's conceptual preoccupation with penis envy. The shift from a cultural regime of the scrotum to that of the penis simultaneously designated a shift from a focus on status and reproduction to libidinal desire as the principle for assigning meaning to sexual activity.[29] In the case of Vietnam, Freudian theory did not enter the Vietnamese public discourse until the 1930s, and then only in an uneven manner.[30] As a member of the literati, Ngô Tất Tố and his biography of Duyệt from 1938 most likely reflect the former paradigm of status and reproduction. Duyệt's case demonstrates that, though his anatomical condition deprived him of reproductive capacities, the same cannot be said of his status in the imperial court or perceptions of his masculinity in the eyes of this and other biographers.

Some Vietnamese documents did associate the eunuch in ways that departed from this premodern paradigm, hinting at the influence of a modern framework propagated by medical science. Consider an article published in 1931 on the decline of the Chinese imperial eunuchs. The article furnishes a perspective on the plight of eunuchs in search of work after the collapse of the Chinese imperial system and the rise of a market economy. The opening statement notes: "The human species is divided into two dispositions (*sexe*), the male and female. Yet strangely enough, there is occasionally the hermaphrodite [*phi nam phi nữ*]." The article continues, "This hermaphrodite according to the East Asian political regimes helped to assist the king, better known as the eunuch [*kêu là hoạn-quan hoặc thái giám*]."[31] The writer then recounts the impact of eunuchs in various Chinese imperial intrigues, noting how influential they became—sometimes dangerously so. After explaining the circumstances of the eunuchs, the writer immediately stresses, "Whatever the case, they are still a species of our humanity [*giống người với ta*], and we should be aware of their painful plights."[32]

Two things are noteworthy about this document. First, the eunuch figure is now one and the same as the hermaphrodite, understood as half-male and half-female. This conflation of the eunuch with the hermaphrodite derives, in part, from the paradigm of medical science which in the early twentieth century reached its ascendancy in neighboring China. The author of the prior Vietnamese article acknowledges from the outset that he learned of the predicament of the eunuch mandarins from a Chinese reportage.[33] Scholars of Chinese queer genders and sexualities have revealed the ways in which the dominance of the medical science paradigm fundamentally restructured Chinese understandings concerning sex in the early Republican period. In his study dedicated to the eunuch figure in modern China, Howard Chiang demonstrates the profound epistemological shift in the meaning of the eunuch with the rise of medical science. Medical science altered the very grounds by which Republican China perceived and understood the sexed and gendered body. With the collapse of the mandarin system in the early twentieth century, premodern categories such as the "natural eunuch" (*tianyan*) clashed with new ontological concepts deriving from medical science. Ideas in biology, sexology, and endocrinology combined to structure the conception of "sex" such that the eunuch mandarin became perceived as one and the same as the hermaphrodite.[34]

Unlike China, however, in Vietnam the medical science paradigm had not yet achieved hegemony during the same period. While medical science was certainly growing, it was still only one among other rival paradigms. As noted in chapter 1, while modern medical science reached the shores of what was then French Indochina, much of it was still in its nascent stages. This context is important to keep in mind when interpreting the prior document that conflates the eunuch with the hermaphrodite. Vietnamese documents that rely on early Republican Chinese sources reflect this medical science paradigm.

The second point about the document is its relatively sympathetic attitude toward the eunuch figure. The article in no way suggests that the imperial eunuchs deserve to suffer or be social outcasts by virtue of their bodily conditions. The article stresses the commonality of the eunuchs by referring to them as a part of the "species of our humanity" (*giống người với ta*). I have retained the genitive form of the Vietnamese expression in translation because the original text does not simply state that the eunuchs are a part of the "human species." Rather, the Vietnamese text stresses the eunuchs shared humanity with the implied reader. *Giống* means "species"; *người* means "human"; *với ta* means "with or like all of us": the eunuchs are a human species like all of us or together with all of us—they are a "species of our humanity." Further evidence of this sympathetic tone is captured in the article's comparison to the situation of Vietnamese eunuchs: "Like our country during the time of the emperors, eunuchs were housed in the palaces by the hundreds. According to custom, they were called '*ông bộ*.' It was said among the common folk that in whichever village was born an *ông bộ* the palace officials had to be informed immediately; officials would pay to help raise the child until it was time to take the child to the palace to become a servant [*đầy-tớ*] of the royal house, from there to serve until old age and death."[35] The passage reveals that eunuchs were not only accepted in premodern Vietnam but also highly prized. So valuable were the "natural eunuchs" that palace officials even financially supported villagers in which children were born with dysfunctional or ambiguous genitalia to groom them to later serve the royal palace. Such a comparison to premodern Vietnam normalizes the figure of the eunuch, not as some freak of nature but as an integral component of the cultural order of things. The broader point here is that the attitude toward the eunuch figure is characterized not so much by stigma as by sympathy—indeed, even by great esteem. Such a portrayal of the eunuch grounded on Vietnamese sources complicates the earlier picture of the eunuch figure based on French sources as an object of derision and, simultaneously, underscores the persistence of premodern East Asian cultural notions in Vietnam's early twentieth century.

THE SCHOLAR GENTRY'S WORLD

Another core group of documents in the Vietnamese cultural archive concerns the variety of sexual and gendered positions that a scholar-gentleman could assume, especially as depicted in literary sources. The mandarin civil service examination in Vietnam persisted far into the early twentieth century and did not end until 1919, much later than in Republican China, which abolished its exams in 1905. So, despite the decline in the institution, there were still candidates studying and preparing for the exams. A substantial cohort of scholarly officials born in the previous century but who lived to witness the present one also continued to participate in Vietnamese public life.[36] In the realm of literary and popular representation, the scholar-gentry figured prominently in the Vietnamese archive. This figure, however, did not embody a single archetype but a constellation of many kinds of literati within the East Asian repertoire that surfaced in the Vietnamese cultural discourse.

Among the gendered positions that a scholar-gentleman could assume included, first, what I call the "feminine man," a man whose gender comportment resembled a beautiful woman but who simultaneously desired women; second, cases of male writers who assumed female personae; and finally, cases of male-male friendships that could, in some cases, be homoerotic in character.

The Feminine Man: Fluid Gender Crossings in Literary Works

A conspicuous figure in the Vietnamese sources, especially in literature, is that of the "feminine man" who desired women. In the nineteenth-century sexological model, the consequences of which we still live with today, the juxtaposition of "feminine" and "man" in the same sentence would seem to immediately call into question the man's sexuality: Is he homosexual? Bisexual? He most certainly cannot be a "straight" man, by heteronormative standards, as evidenced by some of the nineteenth-century French sources concerning the ambiguously gendered eunuch mandarin. Yet in excavating the Vietnamese cultural archive, one is able to discern the historical figure of the "feminine" man whose appearance seemed to rival that of a woman, yet who was simultaneously endowed with so-called masculine attributes. Consider, for example, the martial arts novel *Righteous Heroes of Wind and Moon* (*Hiệp Nghĩa Phong Nguyệt*). Published in four volumes in 1931, the story tells of the love between a noble knight, Thiết Trung Ngọc, and his beloved, Miss Thủy Băng Tâm. In the story, the former rescues the latter from another man, a sinister rival who, in turn, seeks vengeance upon the knight by slandering his name and poisoning him. In the end, the knight overcomes the obstacles that stand in the way of being with his beloved and succeeds in marrying her. In the opening scene, the novel depicts the hero as follows:

> A long time ago . . . there was a baccalaureate graduate with the surname Thiết and given name Trung Ngọc, who appeared of great beauty with a handsome countenance, pale complexion and who looked just like a beautiful woman [*một cô mỹ-nữ*], and for this very reason the neighborhood people would call him the-beautiful-woman-Thiết [*Thiết-mỹ-nhân*]. According to custom, people with such a beautiful appearance should have a temperate demeanor, walk and

move with gentleness, speak and act with softness. But such was not the case with the baccalaureate graduate Thiết. While his appearance and countenance were beautiful, his personality was tough; his speech, strict and honest; his conduct, respectable. Additionally, he also possessed extraordinary martial skills coupled with literary talent. Whenever he saw an injustice, he would step in to intervene, and nobody could stop him.[37]

How are we to interpret this seemingly strange conjunction of a man with feminine appearance, even to the point of being called a "beautiful woman," yet who exhibits romantic interest in other women and whose personality—the "tough" demeanor, "strict and honest" speech, the "extraordinary" martial skills—would, by heteronormative standards, best be described as "masculine"? It appears that the story presents us with another matrix of gender and sexuality, another historical regime, distinct from the one that nineteenth-century European sexology has bequeathed us.

The aforementioned novel was originally a Chinese martial arts story published sometime in the early Qing dynasty. Although written by a Chinese author with the pseudonym Danh Giáo Trung Nhân (名教中人), the story was translated into *nôm*, the Vietnamese demotic script, in the nineteenth century with the title "The New Story of the Well-Matched Couple" (*Hảo cầu tân truyện diễn âm*, 好述新傳演音),[38] and from there to be translated again into the modern Vietnamese vernacular in the early twentieth century. The story belongs to the scholar-beauty romance genre, a genre that grew in popularity in the late Ming dynasty (1368–1644) and the early Qing (1644–1911).[39] As a response to the Ming-era erotic novels, the scholar-beauty romance often celebrated the values of chastity, chivalry, virtue, and wit in depicting a comedy of errors between a male scholar and beautiful lady.[40] The gendered practices of the woman in the relationship are examined in the next chapter. For the purposes of this chapter, it is noteworthy that, in such stories, the man in the relationship was often an "effeminate scholar-poet."[41]

Because today's gendered language of "effeminacy" may not be analytically supple enough to capture the context at hand, it is important to understand the historical and cultural meanings of the key term "femininity." The contemporary sex/gender paradigm inherited from nineteenth-century European sexual science has created a binary division, according to which masculinity is a male heterosexual preserve and, conversely, male homosexuality is defined by overt forms of femininity.[42] In such a paradigm, the "heterosexual" male is the marker of masculine plenitude, devoid of any traces of femininity. Yet such a rigid distinction between femininity and masculinity lacks a cultural analogue in the East Asian context.

As Martin Huang has demonstrated, in Ming and Qing literature, the idea of masculinity was intertwined with cultural notions of femininity.[43] Signs of femininity in no way detracted from a man's "masculinity." In such circumstances, masculine men strived to appear as "feminine" as possible. While potentially strange to some contemporary readers today, these practices were once considered the norm. Indeed, based on the modern homosexual/heterosexual paradigm, one might deduce—erroneously—that these practices in men are all signs of "homosexuality." Huang, however, draws a distinction between "femininity" and "effeminacy." Whereas the former could culturally enhance a man's erotic appeal, the latter diminished it.

Huang demonstrates that this culturally gendered notion of beauty—the attractiveness of the feminine man—was widespread and not limited to scholarly literati. Rather, the idea encompassed other professions typically considered "masculine" by contemporary standards, such as martial warriors. "Even in the few scholar-beauty novels that emphasize the martial prowess of the male protagonist," Huang explains, "the men's feminine beauty is presented as a masculinity to be celebrated with great enthusiasm."[44] One implication of this gendered cultural system is that, unlike the modern sexological paradigm, same-sex eroticism is neither the cause nor the effect of feminine behavior, and vice versa. Rather, during the Ming and Qing dynasties, feminine and masculine were not absolute opposites but components of a gendered continuum.

To help illuminate the distinctiveness of this gendered system, it may be instructive to look at another story in which a man does cross-dress as a woman. If the beauty of the feminine man rivals that of a "real" woman, one might reasonably wonder how, in this alternative gender regime, it is possible to distinguish, if at all, between a feminine man and woman? The story *The Rowdy Hero* (*Anh Hùng Náo*; 英雄鬧, *yīngxióngnào*) furnishes some clues. Published in a four-part series in 1925 in the Vietnamese press, the historical romance takes place during the reign of Zhengde (正德; 1491–1521), the eleventh emperor of the Ming dynasty. The complex plot recounts the tale of a group of heroes whose mission is to save the emperor from attempted regicide. Two of the main characters are the hero, Tang-Đại, and the heroine, Sở-Vân. In the course of the story, both characters cross-dress: Tang-Đại disguises himself as a supposedly innocent countryside woman to seduce and kill a villain whose Achilles' heel is a fondness for women. Sở-Vân, by contrast, unbeknownst to her fellow peers, cross-dresses as a man throughout the novel. In so doing, she/he is able to valiantly protect the emperor by deploying acumen and martial skill. The question of women cross-dressing as men is discussed in the next chapter; here, we concentrate on the hero, Tang-Đại, and his act of cross-dressing.

But before turning to a discussion of Tang-Đại's cross-dressing, it is worth considering the relative quality and quantity of *The Rowdy Hero*'s print circulation. It is noteworthy that the story appears in a range of different sources and genres. Vũ Đình Long, playwright, literary editor, and a translator of this story, explains that he based it on the Chinese work *Eight Swords, Seven Knights-Errant, Sixteen Righteous Ones* (*Bát kiếm, thất hiệp, thập lục nghĩa*).[45] He published his translation of *The Rowdy Hero* in two parts: the first half comprises a five-volume set that narrates the story up to the episode in which Tang-Đại assassinates the villain.[46] The second set, of which there are only two extant volumes, narrates the story of Sở-Vân and the question of her cross-dressing.[47] Selected episodes of *The Rowdy Hero* also circulated in the press. In a three-part series, the newspaper the *Civilizing Daily* (*Khai Hóa Nhật Báo*, 開化日報) published a short story titled "Heroes Who Get Married" (Hào Kiệt Kết Duyên).[48] While the title is different, the story is, in fact, *The Rowdy Hero*—with the same plot, setting, and characters. The question of gender identity is the focus of theatrical versions adapted to the then-emerging genre of reform theater (*cải lương*) and apparently performed live in Sài Gòn and Hà Nội. On the evening of Saturday, April 9, 1927, the Cầu Muối Theater in Sài Gòn performed a rendition of *The Rowdy Hero* in which Sở -Vân saves the emperor and Tang-Đại is in "disguise as a female [*giả gái*]."[49] Likewise, in the entertainment section of a Hà Nội newspaper, the *Hà Thành Ngọ Báo*, advertised the performance of *The Rowdy Hero* on Wednesday, December 3, 1929: "Tang-Đại dresses as a woman, a woman from the countryside [*đàn bà nhà quê*] . . . Sở-Vân dresses as a man, a male hero [*đàn ông anh hùng*] with all the military talents [*tài thao lược*] to rescue the Ming emperor from danger."[50] Finally, the theatrical version was also published in book form with a title highlighting the tale's gender-crossing theme in both Vietnamese and Chinese: *Tang-Đại Disguises as a Female* (*Tang-Đại Giả Gái*, 桑代野奶) (fig. 2.1).[51] This latter book was reportedly a bestseller. Publishers at the time typically aimed to sell about one thousand copies to make a profit. *Tang-Đại Disguises as a Female* sold an astonishing five thousand copies.[52] So popular, in fact, was the story of the *Rowdy Hero* that Thạch Lam, a key member of the Self-Reliant Literary Group, observed that Vietnamese youths, both males and females, would role-play the story's main characters.[53] Given its relatively widespread circulation and popularity, the Vietnamese audience of the time must have been cognizant of the story's gender-transgressive theme and, implicitly, the cultural semiotics of this alternative gender regime.

The semiotics of this gender regime are most apparent in the episode in which the hero Tang-Đại disguises as a woman in a plot to assassinate the villain. In the scene before the assassination, the hero makes the necessary preparations to dress in disguise. When he has finished changing his clothes, he makes a grand appearance before his coconspirators. The novel provides a description of the hero's womanly appearance thus: "Everyone stared at Tang-Đại: his silky, smooth hair had a gold hairpin on it, several lush apricot flowers were hanging, and a pair of silver flowers fell from his ears. He was wearing a new outfit, obviously a country girl going to a festival. Plus, he was walking quietly, under two pairs of curled eyelashes with sparkling amorous eyes, making anyone who sees them get intoxicated."[54] No sooner does the hero cross-dress as a woman than one of his coconspirators jokes that Tang-Đại looks almost like a real woman, except for one problem. Namely, his feet appear too "humongous" and "slightly difficult on the eyes" (*đôi chân to tướng, khi khó coi một chút*).[55] In response to this criticism, the hero amusingly replies: "Please don't laugh at me! I am just a country girl, so my parents cherished my childhood and did not force my feet to be bound [*bó chân*]. But I think, the bigger the feet, the more stable it is to stand, right?"[56] Based on this episode, a key cultural sign of a "woman," at least an aristocratic one, is her petite feet. Prevailing from at least the thirteenth through the nineteenth century, the fixation on petite feet hails from the long-standing Chinese practice of binding women's feet. In such a system, the sign that would give away Tang-Đại's disguise is not his genitals but the fact that he possesses unusually "large feet."

The episode of *The Rowdy Hero* brings into high relief the complex intersection of gender, culture, and history. It underscores the extent to which gender,

戾 改 鱉 縱

TUỒNG HÁT CẢI-LƯƠNG

(Đã có diễn khắp lục-châu được công-chúng
hoan-nghinh rồi.)

Diễn theo truyện Anh-Hùng-Náo, lúc Tang-
Đại chạy vào am Từ-Vân cho đến lúc Tang-
Đại phải Giả-Gái cùng là Lạc-thu-Hà, mẹ
con gặp gỡ, v. v. Tuồng Tang-Đại Cầu-
hôn nối theo sẽ in.

Giá mỗi cuốn : 0 $ 50

MUA SỈ CÓ HUÊ-HỒNG

Cấm đem đi hát hoặc rút
bài bản trong nầy mà làm
của mình, khi nào không
có phép người chủ bổn
cho.

IN LẦN
THỨ NHỨT
4.000 cuốn
PAR M. FÉLIX
MỘNG-TRẰN

Ex-Rédacteur
TẬP-ÍCH-BÁNG
Fournisseur principal des
pièces Cải-lương aux Théâtres
Modernes.

Bureau de Rédaction.
PHONG-THẠNH, (Bạc-liêu)

Cuốn nào không có con dấu ký tên
Mộng-Trằn là gian.

SAIGON
IMPRIMERIE Jh. NGUYỄN-VĂN-VIẾT

Juin 1925

TANG-ĐẠI GIẢ GÁI

F I G U R E 2 . 1 . Front cover of a drama: *Tang Đại Pretends to Be Female.* Bibliothèque Nationale de France.

its constitution, and its meaning are highly cultural and historical. In so doing, it simultaneously illuminates the extent to which the figure of the "feminine man" in "The New Story of the Well-Matched Couple," while potentially very strange to a contemporary audience, is logically coherent in the culture-inflected gender system of its time. Rendered into the modern Vietnamese vernacular in the early twentieth century, both stories crystallize in literary form an earlier alternative gendered regime, of which Vietnamese audiences back then would have been cognizant.

The reason Vietnamese publishers translated these stories, however, was not likely to preserve, much less promote, this alternative gendered regime. Rather, the purpose was to increase the number of literary works available to the grow-ing Vietnamese urban middle class who was hungry for entertainment and, above all, to promote greater literacy in the then-nascent romanized modern Vietnamese script. Nevertheless, in making these premodern stories available and accessible in the early twentieth century, Vietnamese publishers simulta-neously contributed to translating this earlier gendered practice across tem-poral and cultural distance. In so doing, the works—along with ones we have examined and others we still will examine—furnished a greater imaginative space for gender and sexual variance available to the Vietnamese than does the nineteenth-century European sexological model.

In the next chapter, we revisit the question of foot-binding and gender identity, but through the opposite case: that of a woman seeking to cross-dress as a man. For now, let us continue with the question of men who impersonate women in a slightly different context.

Female Impersonation, or Femininities without Women in Poetry

If the idea of the "feminine man" may strike some contemporary readers as strange, this idea assumed another configuration in the case of poetry. In the early twentieth century, Vietnamese society debated whether women could openly enter the world of letters. While a noncontroversial point today, the issue at the time led to vociferous debate. In response to this proposition, one male author voiced his opposition. In the article "The Rebuttal by Mr. Thế Phụng on the Question of Women and Literature" (1929), published in the *New Women's News*, the author claims that women are innately incapable of producing great works of literature. While the author's justification illuminates the misogynistic sexual norms of the earlier generation, it also furnishes clues to another set of prevailing norms of gender and sexuality:

> The male poet has to impersonate being a woman [*giả một người đàn bà*] in order to speak of himself. To do otherwise would be, first of all, impertinent [*trơ trẽn*] behavior and a deprivation of pleasure [*mất thú*]. Second, we cannot expect strong talented men [*trượng phu hào kiệt*] such as Mr. Khuất Nguyên [Qu Yuán], Đỗ Phủ [Du Fu], and Bạch Cư Dị [Bó Juyì] to be lamenting and sobbing. If they lose their appearance [*mất cái vẻ*] as strong talented men [*trượng phu hào kiệt*], nobody would pity them, and so they naturally must entrust [*ký thác vào*] women with this role, because when women sob and lament, there is grace and charm, which makes it easier for people to feel pity [*tội nghiệp, xót thương*].[57]

The passage is a response to Phan Khôi, the father of the New Poetry, who asserted that women should be allowed to produce literature because they could then reflect more mimetically their own sentiments and, in so doing, exceed their predecessors, the male Tang poets. But Mr. Phụng, the author of the passage, disagrees. In particular, the author considers female impersonation by male authors to be both welcome and expected. Because poetry is about illusion, semblance, and creation (*tạo hóa*), this author considers performance in drag part and parcel of poetic production. Mr. Phụng has us consider the case of theater and asks, rhetorically, what its point would be if people saw on stage real people perform their "real" selves? "If a real 'exquisite woman' [*giai nhân thiệt*]," he explains, "came to talk to me . . . she would be most unpleasant to my ear, and I would be wholly untouched" [*nghe có khoái tai, động lòng đâu*]. He continues: "But if the 'exquisite woman Do Phu [Du Fu]' opens his mouth, he would immediately stir in me pity and compassion [*ngậm ngùi*]."[58] According to the author's logic, having "real" women—however "real" may be defined—convey their own sentiments would deprive the presumptively male reader of pleasure. But if the actress in question is not a "real" woman, what, precisely, is the object of Mr. Phụng's desire? Is the pleasure the result of the actor's theatrical talent? Or the cultural fantasy of the image of the delicate woman? Or Do Phu's adept performance in drag? Or a proto-homoeroticism?

Suppose that the pleasure by Mr. Phụng and like male audiences was a direct response to the actor's talent. It would also follow that the gender of the performer is moot. Any talented actress could also be a source of pleasure. Indeed, men or women could perform this role, and the pleasure would stem from whoever best approximates the fantasy of the feminine ideal. But women cannot be engaged in articulating this ideal. The author's logic denies women this role because, for Mr. Phụng, in the androcentric world of arts and letters, only men can and should undertake such performances.

The use of the feminine as a figure for various political guises has an extensive cross-cultural history, as does criticism of the practice. Feminists in the West have long criticized this appropriation, claiming that in usurping the female subject position, male writers efface female sexuality or enact a "transvestite ventriloquism," producing a disjunction between gender and authorship.[59]

Some scholars have pushed the critique even further, challenging the premise that femininity and masculinity are the essential expressions emanating naturally from the binary sexes. Female biological sex need not express an essential femininity, just as masculinity need not flow naturally from male sex. There is no logical reason for either, except an arbitrary, though no less powerful, cultural apparatus that insists on a unity of sex, gender, practice, and desire. If femininity is not an essential attribute emanating from woman per se, we can interpret Mr. Phụng's commentary as a cultural construction of male femininity. Just as queer scholars have constructed cultural histories of "masculinities without men,"[60] so the passage exemplifies a case of "femininity without women." This interpretation may sound strange to some, but the idea is more plausible—even warranted—when coupled with the fact that the author banishes women from the domain of cultural production. The femininity that Mr. Phụng desires is, in his own terms, without "real" women.

This interpretation of a "femininity without women" is bolstered by the cultural and historical context. In the East Asian context, to which Vietnamese culture was intricately connected, literary female impersonation represents a complex cultural performance. In his study of literary texts from the Han to the Tang periods, Paul Rouzer calls such gendered performances "articulated ladies"—performances that enable male members of the literati to create cultural "fantasies of power and victory" or "laments of failure" before the emperor, court ladies, and fellow officials.[61] He emphasizes that the meaning of gender roles in such cultural performances are distinct from those based on a "physicality" of the empirical natural sciences; they are connected instead to a complex web of relationships within a Confucian cosmology. Hence, the articulation of gender in such performances cannot be equated with the "real" position of women in society.

While Rouzer is interpreting texts produced during a much earlier period in Chinese history, the practice of male writers assuming feminine personae persisted in Vietnamese culture. From at least the eighteenth through the early decades of the twentieth century, this practice was widespread among male Vietnamese poets. In the poem "Plaint inside the Royal Harem" (*Cung oán ngâm khúc*), for instance, Nguyễn Gia Thiều (1741–1798) assumed a female voice to compose his famous lament of a concubine who had lost favor with the emperor.[62] Likewise, in the 1930s, Xuân Diệu, an icon of the New Poetry movement, assumed a feminine voice in the poem "Words of a Concubine" (*Lời Kỷ Nữ*). Nguyễn Văn Vĩnh, famed cultural reformer and translator of Western literature, likewise employed the feminine pen name Đào Thị Loan.[63] The journalist and poet Nguyễn Vỹ took on the female name Miss Diệu Huyền.[64] These male poets, consistent with the views expressed by Mr. Thế Phụng that initiated the discussion on female impersonation, all appropriated the female subject position as a part of their literary craft, a craft that was culturally and historically rooted in the premodern Sino-Vietnamese practice of female gendered performance among male literati.

The Discourse of Male Friendship

Another group of documents underscoring the variety of sexual and gendered positions the male scholar-gentry could assume belong to what I call the premodern discourse of intimate male friendships. The Chinese classical discourse of male friendship (*bạn tri âm*) existed in premodern Vietnam and endured through the French colonial period, albeit in translation. The *Vietnamese-English Dictionary* published by the National Institute of Linguistics defines the concept *bạn tri âm* as "friends who fully understand each other; bosom friends."[65] That concept reveals an even more provocative history of "friend" (*bạn*), "knowledge" (*tri*), and "music" (*âm*). This history can be traced to the story of Boya and Zhong Ziqi. Boya is a masterful musician, and Zhong Ziqi, a listener. The latter is able to understand the former through his music. As Boya plays his zither and contemplates the nearby mountain, Zhong Ziqi is able to grasp his friend's thoughts. When Zhong Ziqi dies, as the story goes, the musician ceases to play the instrument because there is no one left to understand his music or, by extension, his thoughts.[66]

Although this tradition hails from the premodern period in China, the term *tri âm* itself travels and surfaces in classical and modern Vietnamese literary culture to encompass intimate friendships in general. Before turning to cases of male friendships, let us first look at how Vietnamese literate culture adopted this term. The *Tale of Kiều*, for example, invokes this concept in the episode where the eponymous heroine meets her male lover Kim Trọng for the first time. She states, "Wind's held me up, rain's kept me back—I've hurt your [*tri-am*] feelings much against my wish."[67] This concept surfaces again in another context related to this epic poem. In his memoir, *Poulo Condore Archipelago before March 9, 1945,* Trần Văn Quế notes that, to ease their confinement in the island, the prisoners read the *Tale of Kiều* and invoked this classic idea of friendship. Quế writes, "Kiều was the prisoners' soul mate [*tri âm*]. As talented and exemplary as she is, Kiều also had to go through many ups and downs, just like themselves!"[68] In the modern period, Madame Nguyễn Đức Nhuận named one of her editorials "A Letter from a Soul Mate [*Bức Thư Tri Kỷ*],"[69] referring to the intimate nature of the letter to her readers, even though its topic was mostly about the daily difficulties of running a periodical. Ms. Nguyễn Thị Kiêm invokes this idea of intimate friendship to defend the social and cultural role of women. Whether as wives or mistresses, according to Nguyễn, women were a benefit to renowned writers, including John Stuart Mill, Alphonse de Lamartine, and Alfred de Musset. Behind each man, she implies, was a woman—a "kindred spirit" (*bạn tri âm* or *bạn tri kỷ*)—without whom he would not have succeeded.[70] Hence, despite its origin in describing male scholarly friendship, the idea of *bạn tri âm* (or *bạn tri kỷ*) took on a variety of connotations over time and circulated as a general coinage. Whether used to describe men's mistresses, premodern and modern romances, one common denominator persisted: a deep bond between the two parties involved.

The term's classical notion of intimate male friendships, however, achieved its paradigmatic embodiment in the work and life of Xuân Diệu. Known as Vietnam's poet laureate, he was most famous for his bold innovations in the New Poetry movement (Thơ Mới). Writing on topics about love and desire, the poet employed the discourse of male friendship to express same-sex erotic relations. For example, in his first anthology *Poésies* published in 1938, Xuân Diệu composed one of his renowned poems, "Love of Men," dedicated to Rimbaud and Verlaine. In this poem, Xuân Diệu writes: "I remember Rimbaud and Verlaine, / fellow poets of dazzling bacchanal spirit, / intoxicated by strange rimes, infatuated with friendship."[71] If the topos of classical male friendship seems less clear in this Vietnamese homage to two archetypical French homosexuals, the connection is explicit in Xuân Diệu's two other works. In "The Words of Boyin" (*Lời Bá Nha*) and "Boyin and Zhong Zhiqi" (*Bá Nha, Trương Chi*), Xuân Diệu transforms the two legendary male friends into lovers who, in turn, are transformed into music.[72] The creative powers of music and melody, like the two "kindred spirits," intertwine so intensely that they stir the surrounding wildlife, reminiscent of the Western myth of Orpheus taming nature with his lyre. Within Boyin's "heart" is forever the image of Zhong Zhiqi, who is transformed into song. During this time, what is clear is that poets and writers felt comfortable using this classical discourse to speak of male homoerotic desire.

Indeed, this classical discourse of male friendship surfaces in the memoirs and letters between Xuân Diệu and his lifelong male companion, the poet Huy Cận. When the Hà Nội Writers Association published a two-volume book on Xuân Diệu written by Huy Cận, titled *Memoirs of Two* (*Hồi Ký Song Đôi*), the cover featured both men in the center. Not only does the memoir convey their deep affection for each other; it depicts the life they shared in Hà Nội and recounts the "insufferable" (*buồn đứt ruột*) experience of separation when Xuân Diệu left for a teaching post elsewhere.[73] While the work includes numerous letters and poems that Huy Cận and Xuân Diệu exchanged while apart, the author barely mentions Huy Cận's two wives. The publishing house and Huy Cận seemed hardly squeamish in displaying public affection between men—at least among poets. The author even refers to them as a couple—"Huy Xuân"— two "kindred spirits" (*bạn tri âm*).[74] The acceptance of this affection suggests the persistence of this earlier scholarly male tradition.

The classical discourse of male friendship is most clear in Huy Cận's writings. When Xuân Diệu died, Huy Cận and his son were still in Paris. On his return home to catch the funeral procession, which he would eventually miss, Huy Cận dreamed of a poem about his friend, a poem he included in the memoir: "Oh Diệu! Only recently, the two shores of Yin-Yang [*Âm dương*] have separated, when will they unite again? Huy Xuân met serendipitously, half a century together, and they still have not satiated their feelings of *tri âm*."[75] In the chapter "Xuân Diệu and I," Huy Cận writes: "This life and world of poetry have granted me a dear friend, given me the spirit . . . and feelings of *tri âm* from Xuân Diệu."[76] I have left the term in the original to underscore the persistence of this classical concept and its profound influence on the self-identity of these poets. The openness of Huy Cận and Xuân Diệu about their relationship reveals the extent to which the discourse of male friendship in the classical tradition endured through the late French colonial era, and beyond. Their relationship provides some indication that, in such a context, Vietnamese culture did not suppress men's desire for each other.

During the interwar period, the rhetoric of *bạn tri âm* constitutes one way in which Vietnamese culture understood male same-sex relations. Those relations could, historically, have been erotic in nature. Given the prior cultural context, it should be clear that this form of friendship is emphatically not what Nguyễn Quốc Vinh calls a "dynamics of displacement," a covert mechanism for expressing what Vinh claims would otherwise be "deviant" homoerotic desire.[77] The fact that "same-sex desire" assumes another form in varying historical contexts suggests that it is intertwined with other cultural formations distinct from its modern Western configuration, which during this period in Vietnamese history had not yet fully congealed.

The Case of a Cross-Dressing Nun: Gender Transgression Is Distinct from Homosexuality

In an article dated April 30, 1940, the *New Hà Nội* (*Hà Nội Tân Văn*) newspaper featured a story about Diệu Lý, a man who, "disguised" as a nun, lived in a convent for almost twelve years. Nguyễn-Văn-Bá changed his given name to the feminine "Diệu Lý" (or "Hồ-Thị-Ly") upon entering the convent. Diệu Lý would never have surfaced in the limelight had it not been for a traffic accident. After a motorbike collision, she was sent to the hospital and placed in the women's ward. A doctor who was inspecting her broken leg discovered that "she" was in fact a "he."

The vocabulary of fraud, impersonation, and disguise dominated press coverage in both Hà Nội and Sài Gòn, where news of the event first broke. The front page of the daily newspaper *Sài Gòn* announced, "Nguyễn-V-Bá disguised [*đội lốt*] as a nun and took the name of Hồ-Thị-Ly," followed by the subheading, "Unmasking the Nun." Another article by the same newspaper asks, "What is strange about the Long-Vân Temple?"[78] The *New Hà Nội* featured another article: "Behind the Back of the Buddha." The newspaper also shows a cartoon of one nun asking the others, "After the Diệu Lý affair, we nuns will have to inspect each other to avoid the misfortune of fraudulent exchanges."[79] On the May 18 cover page of the Hà Nội journal *These Days* (*Ngày Nay*), a farcical picture appeared of Diệu Lý standing before the sangha, the Buddhist community. Exposed, ashamed, and humiliated, her mustache remains intact (fig. 2.2). The heading states: "After the Diệu Lý Affair, a man pretending to be a woman, the sangha discusses whether to have monthly inspections of monks and nuns."[80]

FIGURE 2.2. Front page of the journal *Ngày Nay* (These Days): a man cross-dresses as a nun. From *Ngày Nay*, no. 208, May 18, 1949.

In each case, at issue was not the question of religion per se. Given that the scandal took place at a Buddhist temple, it was astonishing that not one newspaper or journal, not even the socially progressive *These Days*, mentioned the legend of Quan Âm Thị Kính, the Buddhist goddess of mercy who cross-dressed as a monk. Although the stories are not identical, they share structural and thematic parallels. By invoking this religious legend, the media could have linked the continuity of this event with a prior myth and produced a far more sympathetic narrative that conveyed some sense of "compassion" consistent with Buddhist principles. Indeed, the media was not even interested in Diệu Lý's supposed moral lapse in following the Buddhist precept of the Eightfold Path of Right Speech, the equivalent of "thou shall not lie."

Instead of a focus on the violation of religious precepts, the target was alleged sexual exploitation. In this view, because Nguyễn-Văn-Bá is male, he must have pretended to be a nun to exploit this community of women. This was the insinuation by almost every other news article. One reporter covering the scandal posed the following question: "In the twelve years he lived with a pack of nuns, how often did this fake nun achieve moments of bliss?"[81] A month after the affair had transpired, in fact, the writer Tú Mỡ crystallized this essential point in his satirical poem "Breaking Commandments."[82] But this insinuation also presupposes that Nguyễn-Văn-Bá was a straight man. The fact of his cross-dressing failed to function as the overt sign of his gender inversion, the predominant belief in nineteenth-century European psychiatry of the pathology that inflicted homosexuals.

Indeed, if Nguyễn -Văn-Bá was acting in bad faith, he certainly performed his female gender role exceedingly well. For twelve continuous years, the media admitted, Diệu Lý lived peacefully, blissfully, and surrounded by a paradise of women—if only it had not been for that traffic accident. This male heterosexual fantasy, however, seemed implausible to at least one female writer. In an article entitled "The Head Monk Muôn Intended to Deceive Nobody," Như- Hoa voices her dissent, pointing out that none of the parties involved could have predicted being in the limelight.[83] In the case of Diệu Lý, the head monk knew of her cross-dressing and, in fact, welcomed and encouraged it. After all, he was the one who christened her "Diệu Lý." The only "duped" audience, as it were, was the nuns themselves. Some speculated that Diệu Lý and the head monk conspired to exploit the community of nuns. The female writer Như-Hoa remained skeptical. This reporter quotes Diệu Lý's parents, who had commented, "Our child is mad [điên]; expressing compassion, the head monk merely brought him to the monastery to help cure him."[84] This writer hints at an alternative explanation and defends Diệu Lý's "insanity." If living in a peaceful monastery surrounded by nuns, she claims, is tantamount to madness, then she, too, wants to be "insane in this way." Despite the parent's vocabulary of pathologization, Như-Hoa suggests that Nguyễn-Văn-Bá may represent a case of a man who disidentifies with his socially prescribed gender—is this the possibility of a transgender person? The writer does not explicitly arrive at such a conclusion. Unlike other reporters, however, she leaves the question unresolved and declares that "the Buddha is the Buddha of all humanity."

The news coverage of this scandal helps demonstrate the disjuncture between gender transgression and male homosexuality in late French colonial Vietnam. Like many of the cases examined thus far in this chapter, the practice of men cross-dressing as women evoked neither the idea of homosexuality nor that of gender inversion.

CONCLUSION

This chapter has documented some of the plural forms of male genders, relations, and practices in Vietnam's early twentieth century to demonstrate that nineteenth-century sexology had not yet monopolized the cultural discourse. To demonstrate this point, the chapter examined the figure of the eunuch mandarin to argue that, contrary to some of the prevailing scholarship, this figure is associated with masculinity. The chapter then examined the variety of genders and practices that the male scholar-gentry could assume in the Sino-Vietnamese tradition that did not necessarily imply male homosexual relations as defined by nineteenth-century sexology. These include the practice of feminine comportment by male scholars who desired women, the activity of female impersonation in poetry, and the discourse of intimate male friendships. In each case, rather than the dominance of nineteenth-century sexual science, we observe instead the persistence of the Sino-Vietnamese cultural paradigm that permitted greater spaces for a variety of male genders, desires, and relations.

Finally, the chapter concluded with a study of a scandal that exploded in the Vietnamese press involving a man who cross-dressed as a woman to live in a convent. This exceptional case reveals the circumstances under which Vietnamese society restricted gender transgression, in this case, when there are allegations of sexual violation. Most important, the case study drives home the point that the vocabulary of sexology failed to yield any cultural traction: under no circumstance did the Vietnamese press employ the sexological vocabulary of gender inversion or homosexuality to describe the activity of cross-dressing.

The Sino-Vietnamese paradigm that underwrites much of the gender and sexual pluralism described thus far was not without its exclusionary problems. The paradigm was patently androcentric, privileging the male aristocracy at the expense of women and other subjects. Furthermore, as some scholars suggest, certain strands of the premodern Sinitic-based paradigm may be compatible with some of the stigmatizing impulses of the European sexological model.[85] The Sino-Vietnamese paradigm, therefore, should not be romanticized as some lost ideal to be recuperated; it certainly would not serve as a viable model for society today. Nevertheless, women and nonmale subjects could find creative ways to turn the tables in their favor by exploiting the breaking points in the patriarchal Sino-Vietnamese gendered system. Such is the focus of chapter 3.

THREE

WOMEN CROSS-DRESSING AS MEN

The Persistence of a Classical Trope since 1920

IN THE EARLY TWENTIETH CENTURY, Vietnamese modernist reformers depicted the nineteenth century and its legacy as a backward, feudal period in need of reform. Many of the problems of the Confucian era were captured most prominently through the professed principles and cultural production of the Self-Reliant Literary Group, which explicitly opposed Confucianism and sought to seek out everything that is "new, young, life-affirming, with a fighting spirit and a belief in progress."[1] Like their counterparts in the New Culture movement in China (1915–1919), Vietnamese modern reformers of the 1920s and 1930s demonstrated a categorical faith in science and modernity.[2] Conceiving of themselves and their peers as radical departures from historical precedent, they denounced the pernicious effects of so-called Confucian traditional mores.

Scholars of Vietnam have since captured this opposition to Confucianism in their reconstruction of the intellectual and cultural history of Vietnam's early twentieth century. In depicting the conceptual changes in Vietnamese thought during this period, for example, Marr, in his seminal work *Vietnamese Tradition on Trial, 1920–1945*, demonstrates that Vietnamese modernist reformers posed a challenge to "Vietnamese tradition" on multiple fronts, including the questioning of Confucian gendered oppression.[3] Likewise, more recent scholarship of the period has highlighted the departure from this "tradition," including, but not limited to, fields such as urban design, fashion, literature, and journalism as the bases for various political projects.[4] This body of scholarship remains valuable in capturing the profound sense of change on the part of a segment of the younger Vietnamese intelligentsia, whose influence on Vietnamese culture this book addresses in the next chapter.

In this chapter, I complicate the cultural reception of nineteenth-century Confucianism in Vietnam during the interwar period. Although it is true that modern ideas entering Vietnam during this time led to significant cultural changes, it does not follow that nineteenth-century Confucian ideas were entirely superseded, if they ever were, in the early twentieth century. Nor does it follow that Confucian ideas took the form that modernist reformers have presented them to be. As this chapter suggests, the extent to and manner in which "traditional" Confucian ideas appeared in Vietnam's early twentieth century needs to be reconsidered. In particular, focusing on the period from 1920 to 1945, I demonstrate the persistence of a heretofore underexamined classical trope of gender and sexual transgression. I use the term "classical" because the trope hails from at least the nineteenth century, when the Nguyễn dynasty absorbed earlier premodern Sino-Vietnamese cultural production. Specifically, the term "classical" refers to the explosion of narratives in verse composed since the eighteenth century in the *nôm* script, the demotic characters created from Han graphs and used for local phonetic or semantic value.[5] In the early twentieth century, many of these tales were translated into the modern romanized Vietnamese vernacular. Through these modern translations, we can observe stories of women who transgress gender and sexual norms in part by cross-dressing as men or performing "masculinity" to participate in the androcentric world of politics and letters. This classical trope furnished far more fluid gendered and sexual possibilities in the Vietnamese symbolic cultural sphere than the current scholarship has acknowledged.

In recovering this archive, the chapter illustrates three key points about the character of gender in the tales translated into the early twentieth century in Vietnam. First, within the strictures of Confucian society and culture, women were not entirely helpless and could turn the tables on the system in exercising some agency by appropriating the symbols and accoutrements of the masculine gender. Indeed, the evidence reveals that in some cases, such gendered appropriations were entirely acceptable and even encouraged by early twentieth-century Vietnamese commentators, as when they bolstered other prevailing societal values, such as Confucian virtue or patriotic nationalism. Second, precisely in their performance of masculinity, the female characters bring into high relief the degree to which gender in premodern Sino-Vietnamese documents appears as an artifact, not a natural phenomenon understood within the model of the biological sciences. If the biological paradigm defines "gender" as an attribute grounded on physiological difference, then the model of gender as artifact would suggest that it is more akin to an exquisite skill or artistic practice. Third, as the evidence will also show, many of these gender-crossing practices and performances were not necessarily linked to sexuality, understood in the sense of choosing a sexual object. That is, the fact that a woman who cross-dresses as a man or performs masculinity in no way implies anything about her erotic sexual preference, particularly for another woman. Such homoerotic implications existed in some cases, but within the terms of the cultural documents, it was not a logical necessity. In this regard, like the prior chapter on the variety of male genders, the cases of women cross-dressing as men evince cultural forms of gendered and sexual organization that depart from the nineteenth-century sexological model: gender transgression need not signify sexual or erotic transgression.

Now, while the reasons for these gendered performances are complex and varied, just as they are various, certainly one reason underlies them all: women's exclusion from the public sphere. This exclusion meant that, as we have seen, men could assume feminine personae in literary works; as we will see in this chapter, women must cross-dress as men if they wish to enter the androcentric world of politics and letters. For this reason, in no way is the chapter suggesting that the classical tales here were politically progressive or even proto-feminist. Rather, counterintuitively, the chapter insists that, from the modern translation of these classical texts, the so-called traditional Confucian paradigm held a more capacious vision of gender and sexual norms than the current scholarship has acknowledged.

This chapter draws on two kinds of sources. The first are early twentieth-century translations of nineteenth-century tales of women who cross-dressed as men. Some did so to enter into battle, serving as warriors; others did so as a part of the literary genre of the female knight-errant who, skilled in martial arts, dressed in male garb; still others disguised as men to participate in the world of commerce or to undertake the imperial civil service examinations and from there serve in various high royal positions. Regardless of the particular situation, these stories, which were translated into the modern Vietnamese vernacular in the early twentieth century, formed what this chapter calls the persistence of the classical trope of gender transgression. By "translation," I refer not simply to a process of fidelity from one text to another or from an "authentic" original to copy. Rather, "translation" implies an epistemic negotiation and potential resignification of the production of meaning and, by extension, a site of cultural knowledge production.[6] Because there are multiple translations of the classical tales as there are extant versions of the nineteenth-century source texts, the purpose here is less to engage in philological analysis—the search for cultural and textual "authenticity," which can be warranted in some contexts—than to reconstruct the early twentieth-century Vietnamese reception of this other history of gender variance, a history that links the Sino-Vietnamese classical past with the modern period. So, the chapter is less interested in the historical verisimilitude of these translations to their so-called authentic originals than in the Vietnamese interpretation and reception of the classical tales.

The second set of sources are modern analogies to the classical past—that is, stories, both fictional and biographical, of modern women who invoked classical heroines in their progressive claims for women's emancipation. If women of an earlier era could undertake much of what a man could, albeit in transvestite garb, so the argument goes, then why should modern Vietnamese women be denied access to the world of politics and letters? The classical tradition that I reconstruct, then, is simultaneously historical and imagined: "historical" insofar as a palpable corpus of extant documents existed narrating tales of gender transgression, and "imagined" insofar as their historical meaning is reappropriated for various modern social, cultural, and political ends. In the early twentieth century, Vietnamese "tradition"—depending on what it was and how one understood it—was simultaneously venerated and denounced. Thus, drawing on cultural and literary texts that display gender and sexual transgression, the chapter calls into question some of the prior stark divisions in the current scholarship: between the nineteenth and early twentieth century, between tradition and the modern, divisions that Vietnamese modernist reformers invented and that some scholars today have perpetuated. In so doing, I suggest a reconsideration not only of the contours of Vietnamese "tradition"—what counts as tradition and by and for whom?—but also the relation of "tradition" to the modern period.

Finally, because so little scholarship has meaningfully addressed the existence of gender and sexual transgression in the Vietnamese versions of these texts, the activity of highlighting them—recovering them from the proverbial dustbin of history—is a critical first step in debating the phenomenon's cultural significance. The chapter first sketches in broad strokes the context of the public debates on women's place in early twentieth-century Vietnamese society. Then, it turns to a delineation of the aforementioned sources. Ultimately, the chapter joins the previous ones in recovering the lively presence of "queer" subjects—of gender and sexual variance—in the Vietnamese cultural archive.

THE HISTORICAL CONTEXT: THE QUESTION OF WOMEN IN VIETNAMESE SOCIETY

In the early twentieth century, the Vietnamese intelligentsia debated the status and place of women in the context of an effort to strengthen the nation and seek a viable solution to the question of national independence from French colonialism. Some suggested that collaboration with the French would be the best path toward self-determination, while others insisted on revolt and revolution.[7] As a prior generation of scholar officials had failed to effectively resist the French, a new generation emerged, born in the nineteenth century but who lived to witness the early twentieth century.[8] In their search for a plausible way forward and in their promotion of national survival, some among this group advanced the idea that Vietnamese women could and should play a crucial role in the new Vietnamese nation to come.

For women to contribute to the Vietnamese nation, some Vietnamese intellectuals proposed extending education to women and girls. Whatever might be the best path forward toward national independence, according to these intellectuals, it was no longer feasible to relegate Vietnamese women to traditional precepts that kept them unschooled and illiterate. In a 1917 essay published in the journal *Southern Wind* (*Nam Phong*), for example, Phạm Quỳnh famously criticized the mentality of the Vietnamese "forefathers" (*các cụ ta*) toward women and girls as unacceptably antiquated for the times. Traditional

Vietnamese society, he explained, was unduly influenced by Confucianism, according to which women were relegated to the subordinate role, adhering to the Confucian notion of the "three submissions" (*tam tong*): as a daughter, she would defer to her father; as a wife, to the husband; as a widow, to the eldest son. In such submissive roles, so the cultural logic went, it made little practical sense for Vietnamese women to receive an education, and certainly not at the level that men could attain.

In such a worldview, moreover, men and women were divided according to the principle of "yin-yang" (*âm-dương*). Since women, representing *yin*, symbolized lack and meekness, it would be impossible for them to compensate for their innate deficit through education in the same way as men, who represented *yang*, symbolizing fullness and strength. On the basis of that cultural logic, Quỳnh explained, traditional Vietnamese society considered it utterly "useless" (*vô ích*) to try to educate women. Admittedly, Vietnamese girls were taught by their mothers, but they were taught the moral codes of conduct, consistent with Confucian precepts. "Never," he continued, "were women and girls allowed to expand their intellect [*trí thức*] as men."[9] Yet in Europe and elsewhere in the modern "civilized" world, the idea of women's "equality" (*bình-đẳng*) was increasingly the norm.[10] If Vietnamese society were ever to catch up with Europe and the rest of the world, this entrenched traditional worldview had to change. For this reason, Phạm Quỳnh in the same essay proposed an educational program for women, adjusted to each social class, with the aim of fostering "self-rule and self-protection" (*tự-chủ tự-trị*).[11]

Phạm Quỳnh's proposal sparked boisterous debate among Vietnamese intellectuals. Both in *Southern Wind* and elsewhere, intellectuals of different ideological persuasions entered the fray, proffering their views on the question of women in Vietnamese society. Traditionalists condemned anything that undermined what they perceived as Confucian precepts. The well-known literatus Nguyễn Bá Học published pieces criticizing Phạm Quỳnh for proposing modern schooling for Vietnamese women and defended arranged marriages.[12] Others suggested, conversely, that Confucian precepts in Vietnam were not always strictly observed and that women should, therefore, be allowed to partake in activities afforded to men.[13] Notably, the scholar literatus and revolutionary Phan Bội Châu (1867–1940) contributed, in his own way, to the debate by publishing a work in 1927 in which he suggested that Vietnamese women could serve as wives to the Vietnamese nation. In a quotation made famous today by the contemporary scholar and filmmaker Trịnh T. Minh-hà in her critical film *Surname Viet, Given Name Nam*, Phan suggested that when Vietnamese women are asked, "Do you have a husband yet?" they respond, "Yes, his surname is Viet and his given name Nam."[14] In offering this advice, he implied that Vietnamese women were committed partners in the national struggle against colonialism.

Despite the objections by some male Vietnamese intellectuals, an increasing number of young Vietnamese women and girls were being educated. In 1907, the short-lived educational movement Đông Kinh Nghĩa Thục (東京義塾), which provided public lectures on history, culture, and politics, was already willing to open its doors to young Vietnamese women.[15] Girls were also attending primary schools to be taught *quốc ngữ*, the modern romanized national script, in the growing number of Franco-Vietnamese schools, whose growth the French encouraged, in part, to compete with the existing indigenous educational system and to produce an adequate future supply of translators and interpreters serving the French colonial bureaucracy.[16] By 1930, the number of girls being schooled reached 40,752, approximately 10 percent of the total number of pupils receiving primary school education.[17]

In the context of these vociferous debates on women's education in Vietnamese society, a wide range of didactic books was published on the market. This period witnessed the explosive growth of morality tracts, textbooks, and manuals addressed to young women. Many of these publications were a response by some traditionalists to fears of increasing female impropriety and meant as didactic instruments to inculcate moral values. For example, the textbook *Reading Lessons in Feminine Moral Conduct* (1918), as the title itself implies, sought to educate young women and girls on proper behavior and decorum.[18] Likewise, the short-lived journal *Women's Bell* (*Nữ Giới Chung*) published in 1918 and edited by Sương Nguyệt Ánh, the daughter of the renowned nineteenth-century poet Nguyễn Đình Chiểu, focused on the proper role of women and girls in the Vietnamese family, consistent with the editor's own traditionalist worldview.[19] In the realm of literature, Vietnamese male authors engaged in the so-called battle of the novels. In response to literary works that depicted Vietnamese heroines speaking their minds and asserting themselves, the author Nguyễn Công Hoan produced "counternovels" that portrayed female protagonists who understood their place in the complex web of the Vietnamese Confucian family system.[20]

The purpose of this chapter is not to rehearse the accounts of the Vietnamese preoccupation with the question of women, which has already been provided elsewhere. The chapter instead shines a light on what the scholarship to date has hitherto overlooked and hence occluded in its historical accounts of "tradition": namely, the existence of gender-transgressive figures in the archive. Indeed, from our contemporary perspective, one can even call them *queer* figures. Specifically, as the evidence shows, the figure of the woman who transgresses gender norms—either by cross-dressing or by performing masculine roles—was a conspicuous presence in many of these "traditional" didactic documents. Some of the documents were early twentieth-century translations of premodern East Asian myths of larger-than-life heroines, which David Marr has coined as the genre of "female hagiography," biographical accounts of women who had contributed to overthrowing prior dynasties but who could also serve as models for the contemporary moment.[21] As we will see, however, current historical accounts of this period seem to have overlooked the topos of gender transgression, or excised it entirely, even when it figures prominently in or is even central to the story. Other didactic documents inculcating moral virtue that involve gender transgression include, but are not limited to, the genre of martial arts fiction, reform theater dramas, and scholar-beauty romances; the relevant features of each genre are discussed in due course. By examining these diverse documents deriving from a variety of genres, the chapter recovers the "queer" dimension of the Vietnamese cultural archive and situates it as a central feature of these didactic documents whose ostensible purpose is to transmit Vietnamese "tradition."

LEGENDARY HEROINES OF THE CLASSICAL PAST: EARLY TWENTIETH-CENTURY TRANSLATIONS

A set of narratives that form part of what I consider the persistence of the classical trope of gender transgression are stories of women who disguised themselves as men. Some of the stories are translations into the modern vernacular of tales deriving from nineteenth-century Vietnamese *nôm* texts, some of which are themselves adaptations of, or influenced by, Chinese legends. Still others are direct translations of premodern Chinese sources, some of which are known and others unknown. I have organized these documents thematically into two main groups. The first group concerns women who cross-dress as men in the context of war or commerce. These are stories of women who donned male garb to fight in battle or to participate in cultural or political activities typically reserved for men, such as serving as the emperor's wartime adviser or engaging in the world of commerce. The second group of documents centers on stories of women who cross-dress as men to undertake the imperial civil service examinations and, in some instances, serve in high royal positions. Regardless of the specific genre or circumstance, all the documents reveal the persistence of the classical trope of gender transgression in early twentieth-century Vietnam.

War and Commerce: Cross-Dressing Martial Heroes and Merchants

In the Confucian worldview, a clear gendered division existed between the feminine private space of the "inner" (*nei*, 內) chambers and the masculine public space of the "outer" (*wai*, 外) sphere. This division need not literally refer to actual physical locations but represents a relational dichotomy that governed Confucian gender constructions. Women who crossed this private and public division had to cross-dress as men, lest they violate this fundamental world order.[22] The fact that women engaging in warfare had to cross-dress as men also implied the allocation of gender expectation that "encoded physical courage as a male rather than a female attribute."[23] In this sense, to the extent that war is an extension of the "outer" sphere of politics and a public display of courage, any woman who engaged in battle could not do so as female: she had, instead, to cross-dress in male garb. Several documents illustrate this gendered norm.

In the story *The Female General Luu* (*Lưu Nữ Tướng*, 將劉女), a translation of an anonymous nineteenth-century *nôm* tale written in verse, the heroine, Mộng Lan, vows to avenge her father. A corrupt mandarin official had unjustly framed her father, who would eventually succumb to an illness, exacerbated in part by the ensuing political scandal. In response to this injustice, Mộng Lan—endowed with a "lady's body and a hero's ambition" (*thân thiếu nữ, chí anh hùng*)—is determined to clear the family name.[24] She cross-dresses as a male general, "putting on pants, transforming into a male" (*thoa-quần đổi dạng nam-nhi*), to lead an army in a successful uprising against the mandarin.[25] In the course of her journey, the heroine encounters a male scholar named Tư Mã, who later becomes her soulmate. After successfully completing her mission, the heroine returns to a normal life: she sheds her male military garb, reverts to her former female self, and becomes one of two of Tư Mã's wives.[26]

At least two key issues about this document merit further elaboration. First, the idea of female warriors would not have been something strange to the Vietnamese. In the early twentieth century, tales of the famed Trung sisters who fought against Chinese armies circa 40 BCE circulated. For example, both the scholar-literatus Phan Bội Châu and the young intellectual Nguyễn An Ninh invoked these heroines as allegories for various contemporary political ends.[27] Phan Bội Châu even invoked the practice of women donning male garb. In a 1907 letter summoning his compatriots to rise up and resist French colonialism, he cited Vietnam's long history of women warriors, including the story of Bùi Thị Xuân, a female general who led the Tây Sơn army against the Nguyễn lords in the late eighteenth century. He explains: "Heroes in head scarves can slay those with whiskers and eyebrows; wearers of hairpins and dresses are not ashamed to wear armor."[28] Regardless of how these female warriors were appropriated, it is clear that they would have been part of the common cultural repertoire among a literate Vietnamese audience. Hence, a similar nineteenth-century tale of a female general Luu fighting in battle would not have been anything unusual for the Vietnamese.

Second, with respect to the act of cross-dressing, the document suggests that it was acceptable in certain contexts. In the preface to the 1922 version, Phạm Văn Phương explains that the purpose of his translation of *The Female General Luu* is twofold: first, it celebrates the birth of the modern vernacular, the romanized national script; second, it shines a light on a female character who is a paragon of Confucian virtue. He explains: "I believe this story exhibits sufficiently the virtues of integrity, piousness, decorum, and righteousness [*trung, hiếu, tiết, nghĩa*] consistent with moral principles. The heroic character of the young woman, her courage, her chastity are all qualities worthy of respect, capable of serving as mirrors for all the female students [*các cô nữ học-sinh ta*] of today."[29] The virtues that he cites are clearly Confucian: piousness, decorum, and righteousness. The purpose of the tale's translation, then, appears to be didactic—to educate the growing number of young women being schooled in the modern Franco-Vietnamese educational system and being taught the modern vernacular.

In the early twentieth century, as already noted, traditional scholars pro-mulgated Confucian precepts, stories, and textbooks in response to the growing idea of women's education. The republication of *The Female General Luu* and other gender-transgressive tales appears to be part and parcel of this Confucian traditionalist response.

A similar narrative in which a female cross-dresses as a man to fight in battle recurs in another story, this time, in the Chinese legend of Hoa Mộc Lan (*Huā MùLán*; 花木蘭)—or Mulan, in English. Long before it became known in US literary and popular culture, especially through the work of Maxine Hong Kingston,[30] the story appeared in a seven-volume Vietnamese work published in 1928 titled *Mulan Joins the Army* [*Mộc Lan tòng quân*]. The work, a translation from an unspecified Chinese source, opens with the folk "ballad of Mulan," which was initially incorporated into an anthology sometime during the Song period (960–1276 CE) but originated as far back as the fifth or sixth centuries in northern China.[31] In the preface of the Vietnamese version, the translator encapsulates the legend to his audience: "Who is Mộc Lan? She is a girl whose surname is Chu, fourteen years old, and who dressed as a male [*cải nam trang*] to replace her father in battle for twelve years."[32] By going to battle in her father's stead, the translator explains, Mulan has "fulfilled her filial duty" (*nghĩa vụ con thảo*).[33]

The prior Vietnamese rendition of the Mulan story is a Confucianized version. The Vietnamese translator's yoking of the figure of Mulan with "filial duty" suggests a departure from the legend's narrative origins. The legend of Mulan most likely originated from a northern non-Chinese state, that is, a non-Han Chinese culture that championed valor, martial skill, and acumen in mili-tary affairs. The figure of women warriors riding on horseback would have been antithetical to the Confucian ideals of the gentle and graceful lady. It was only much later, beginning in the Tang dynasty (618–907 CE), that the Mulan tale began to be modified and appropriated to Confucian ends. So, while the prior synopsis in the Vietnamese preface would at first seem unadorned and matter-of-fact, there are many premodern versions of the Mulan story.

Moreover, not all versions endow Mulan with the surname Chu. In Feng Lan's delineation of four premodern variations of the story, only one attaches the surname Chu to Mulan: an anonymous work published sometime around 1732 or after titled "The Legendary Story of a Girl Who Is Loyal, Filial, Heroic, and

Chaste." In this version, Mulan is portrayed as a thoroughly Han Chinese woman with the recognizable surname that is the equivalent of the Vietnamese Chu.[34]

The ending of this Chinese version is also similar, though not identical, to the Vietnamese one. In the Chinese version, Mulan is confronted with an irresolvable dilemma. While Mulan is at home tending to her parents' tombs, the emperor summons her to the royal palace so she can serve the kingdom. Mulan's refusal to return to the capital leads to a scandal, causing the emperor to make repeated summons. Mulan seems caught in an impossible situation: if she obeys the emperor, thereby fulfilling her loyalty to the throne, she will nevertheless violate her filial duty. Torn between the two, Mulan commits suicide.

In the Vietnamese version, Mulan is similarly confronted with the same dilemma, but there is no tragic ending. The emperor summons her to serve the kingdom, she refuses, he makes repeated summons, and she refuses again. Whereas Mulan commits suicide in the Chinese version, in the Vietnamese version the emperor forgives her. Impressed by her loyalty to the kingdom and filial devotion to her parents, the emperor frees her from any obligation to serve the royal palace, thereby allowing her to fulfill her filial vows. Finally, rather than tragically commit suicide, Mulan opens a thriving women's martial arts school. In his concluding remarks, the Vietnamese translator acknowledges that he took the liberty to freely expand and contract segments as he saw fit: "I did not translate word for word . . . at times there were ten things that I contracted into one, and one that I expanded into ten."[35] The Vietnamese version, then, is not intended to be a replica of the Chinese "original," which, in any event, is likely a historical permutation of the Mulan legend.

In both *The Female General Luu* and *Mulan Joins the Army*, the Vietnamese translators and publishers of these stories reveal the terms and conditions under which women could transgress gender norms. The stories suggest three such conditions. First, as we have seen, they justify the act of cross-dressing in the name of higher Confucian virtues, such as piousness and righteousness. Women who cross-dress as men do so to exemplify these higher virtues, and so the act of gender transgression becomes not only permissible but also extolled. Second, the act of gender transgression is temporary. Neither female General Luu nor Mulan cross-dress as men indefinitely. As soon as their mission is completed, they relinquish their male military uniforms. Third, the heroine ultimately reverts to her former female self. Once her mission is completed, the female General Luu even marries a man. In the case of the Mulan story, while there are many versions of the tale as there are endings, most conclude with the heroine returning to her former life.[36]

The prior conditions highlight, then, both the cultural limits and the possibilities of women's symbolic position in a "traditional" Sino-Vietnamese society. On the one hand, the gender transgression of the woman warrior is not an unbridled license to transgress. She does not cross-dress as a man in a cultural vacuum or beyond recognizable societal norms. On the other hand, as the prior stories also imply, some women could subvert, even transcend, their gendered roles given the right conditions. The Confucian "traditionalists" who were promulgating these premodern stories in the Vietnamese print public sphere in no way stigmatized the gender difference that these women warriors displayed. Under the right circumstances, then, the act of cross-dressing was an acceptable form of gender pluralism in Vietnam's early twentieth century.[37]

If these texts furnish cases of women cross-dressing as male warriors, the topos of gender transgression also appears in another story but in a different context. This time, the act of gender transgression takes place in the androcentric world of commerce. In *A Filial Female Dressed as a Male* (*Hiếu Nữ Nam Trang*), a four-part short story serialized in *The Civilizing Daily* newspaper (*Khai Hóa Nhật Báo*, 開化日報), the elderly widowed merchant Mr. Huang (*Vương ông*), faces a dilemma. He has two daughters, the eldest has already married and left the home, and the younger one, Ả-thông, is still a minor and under his care. He needs to go on the road to conduct business but does not want the potential trouble that could arise were his daughter to accompany him, not only because the journey could be unsafe but also because, apparently, it would be unseemly for a girl to appear in public. Yet if he were to stay home, he would not be able to bring in enough income to feed the family. To resolve the dilemma, the daughter one day proposes to the father the following:

> Beloved father, I have thought of a solution that will allow me to accompany you. The father then asked, What solution? She replied: I have decided to cross-dress [*cải trang*]. In the olden days, maid Mulan [*Hoa-mộc-lan*] replaced her father in battle, and nobody was able to tell the difference. That was a life and death situation and she was still so determined, whereas my situation is simply accompanying you while you sell goods, which is hardly dangerous by comparison, and so what's the fear.[38]

The father agrees to the proposal, and the daughter cross-dresses as a boy. Over time, with the help of the clever and industrious daughter, the family business thrives such that the merchant decides to hire a male helper named Lã-ưng. The business continues to flourish, and the elderly merchant wishes to marry off her daughter to Lã-ưng, except that the latter still does not know that the cross-dressing daughter is a woman. The merchant eventually dies, leaving the business to his daughter and male helper. The cross-dressing heroine informs her elder sister of the news of their father's death. At this meeting, the elder sister questions her younger sister about her relationship with the male helper. The elder sister suspects they are "husband and wife." Upset by the insinuation of her lack of chastity, the cross-dressing heroine declares: "If I am not still truly a virgin [*trinh*], may the demons [*quỉ thần*] condemn me!" The elder sister remains incredulous, and word gets out about the argument. Eventually, the male helper Lã-ưng hears of the argument and realizes that his business partner has been a woman all along. He decides to ask for her hand in marriage, praising her as a truly "virtuous woman" (*liệt-nữ*). She accepts, they bear two sons, and the story ends.

This story derives, in fact, from Feng Menglong's *Stories Old and New* (*Kim cổ kỳ quan*, 今古奇觀 怕), a fiction collection from the late Ming dynasty. The fundamental elements of the plot are virtually identical to the story of the heroine Huang Shancong (黃善聰) in Feng Menglong's four tales of "true women who are in men's disguise" narrated in his collection.[39] In that story, the opening lines reveal a widowed merchant by the name of Huang—as in the Vietnamese version—who sells incense and other miscellaneous items. The name of the younger daughter—Shancong (善聰)—is similar to that of the heroine in the Vietnamese version (Ả thông, 聰). While the romanized phonetic spelling of each name is slightly different, they share, in fact, the same Sinitic character. The story then narrates the merchant's dilemma regarding bringing his young daughter with him on the business trip. The merchant resolves his dilemma by deciding to dress his daughter up as a boy ("That's it! Since I'll have no company on my journey, why don't I dress her up as a boy and take her with me?").[40] Whereas in the Vietnamese version it is the daughter who thinks of this idea, in Feng Menglong's version it is the merchant who does. Several years later, Mr. Huang falls ill and dies, leaving Shancong an orphan. The daughter later meets a young man, another merchant, by the name of Li Ying—the same name as that of the male helper—Lã-ừng—in the Vietnamese version. The two consider themselves "brothers" and share the same living quarters. Their shared business flourishes such that Shancong has enough funds to transport her father's coffin back to their hometown for a proper burial. Upon her return to her village, Shancong meets her elder sister. Like the Vietnamese version, both have an argument over the question of Shancong's chastity. One day, the young sister's male business partner, Li Ying, appears at their doorstep. When the young man discovers Shancong's true gender, he asks for her hand in marriage. Despite moments of doubt (and other issues that will not detain us here), the younger sister ultimately consents, and the two marry. As we can see, the fundamental plot structure of Feng Menglong's story of the heroine Huang Shancong virtually mirrors the Vietnamese version.

The Vietnamese version of the tale of Huang Shancong, like the original, demonstrates that the practice of women cross-dressing as men in no way poses a problem when it is subordinated to a higher moral cause, in this case, the Confucian virtue of filial piety. *A Filial Female Dressed as a Male (Hiếu Nữ Nam Trang)* departs from prior stories in that no war or battle is involved. Instead, the narrative focuses on a merchant family and a talented young daughter who supports her father and his business. Despite this difference, the story bears a remarkable "family resemblance" to the stories of the cross-dressing martial heroes: both involve young women who disguise themselves as men to participate in an androcentric space—war or commerce—in the name of having a higher value to their families and society. In each case, the heroines are daughters piously fighting or serving on behalf of their fathers. Indeed, scholars have suggested that during the Ming period, the heroine Huang Shancong and her name were recorded in the *Official History of the Ming Dynasty* as the "second Mulan."[41] She is the "second Mulan" not because she possesses martial skills, but because, like her legendary predecessor, she represents a paragon of the Confucian virtue of filial piety. While Feng Menglong's version of the Huang Shancong story does not explicitly compare her to Mulan, the Vietnamese version of the story does: it was the younger daughter who noted the sacrifices of Mulan in proposing to cross-dress as a boy to accompany her father: "I have decided to cross-dress [cải trang]. In the olden days, maid Mulan [Hoa-mộc-lan] replaced her father in battle, and nobody was able to tell the difference."[42] Both Mulan and Huang Shancong demonstrate their filial devotion, Mulan by taking her father's place in battle, Shancong by lending him a helping hand on the road. When her father dies, Shancong eventually manages to transport his coffin home for a proper burial, as does Mulan in some versions of the tale. Both Mulan and Huang Shancong, in short, are the embodiments of the "virtuous women." Through such embodiments, women in the world of these and other like narratives can cross-dress as men as long as they do so in the name of higher values, in this case, that of Confucian filial piety.

Talented and Beautiful: Cross-Dressing Scholars and Royal Officials

Another group of documents describes stories of women who cross-dress as men to sit and pass the imperial examinations and, in some cases, serve in official royal positions. Although many such stories surfaced in the archive, this chapter focuses primarily on two such tales that exemplify this genre and whose publication appeared particularly pronounced in the Vietnamese press.

In *Female Baccalaureate Graduate (Nữ Tú Tài)*, an early twentieth-century translation of an anonymous nineteenth-century text written in verse, the heroine, Phi Nga, dons male garb before leaving her hometown to attend a boarding school to prepare for the imperial examinations. She assumes the male name Tuấn Khanh. In the course of her journey, she befriends two male classmates, Tử Trung and Soạn Chi. One day, the heroine, disguised as a male student, challenges her two other male classmates to a contest: whoever can locate the arrow that she shoots will be introduced to the heroine's sister for hand in marriage. The "sister" in question is none other than the female version of the heroine herself. Tử Trung is able to find the arrow, and so should be the one to ask for Phi Nga's hand in marriage. But no sooner does he find the arrow than he learns that he has to urgently return to his hometown for family reasons. So he hands the arrow to the other friend, Soạn Chi. Meanwhile, the heroine learns that her family has been wrongly framed for a crime that she must help solve to clear the family name. On her way home, a second female character, Cảnh, harbors amorous affections for the heroine dressed in male garb. The story ultimately concludes with Tử Trung visiting the heroine in her hometown. When Tử Trung discovers that "he" is, in fact, a "she," the two decide to marry. The amorous advances of the other two characters, Soạn Chi and Cảnh, toward the heroine are resolved when the two become an amorous couple. With the main conflicts resolved, the story promptly ends.

The story of a woman cross-dressing as a man to pass the imperial examinations was not something entirely foreign in Vietnamese cultural history. Such a practice recalls the case of Nguyễn Thị Duệ, a woman who dressed as a man to pass the imperial examination during the sixteenth-century Mạc dynasty in Vietnam. She is purportedly the first Vietnamese woman, albeit disguised as a man, to have done so. She was subsequently invited to teach in the imperial palace under the reign of the Lê dynasty (1428–1789).[43] Today, in addition to a road and shrine dedicated to her in her birthplace of Hải Dương, some contemporary Vietnamese scholars reconstructing the history of these examinations have also paid some attention to her life and singular achievement.[44] It is unclear whether the story of Nguyễn Thị Duệ was known to the Vietnamese public in the early twentieth century, but the story of *Female Baccalaureate Graduate* (*Nữ Tú Tài*) circulated frequently in the Vietnamese press.

Female Baccalaureate Graduate was translated into the Vietnamese modern vernacular in the early twentieth century numerous times. Its translation into *quốc ngữ* appeared as early as 1911, and it was republished by other Vietnamese presses in 1914, 1923, 1927, and 1930.[45] With respect to the plot, these modern vernacular translations appear relatively consistent from year to year. A theatrical version was also apparently performed live in Hà Nội. While there is no known extant record of the dramatic script and its adaptation for the stage, one newspaper advertised that the tale would be performed on the evening of June 4, 1929.[46] The fact that it was republished many times in the span of two decades and dramatized on stage suggests, minimally, a public interest in the story.

From these extant documents we can reasonably infer that *Female Baccalaureate Graduate* is, in fact, a Vietnamese rendition of the renowned folktale of Liang Shanbo and Zhu Yingtai (Lương Sơn Bá và Chúc Anh Đài, 梁山伯祝英臺), the Chinese version of Romeo and Juliet. In this folktale, a young woman name Zhu Yingtai leaves home to attend school in male disguise. During her few years of study, she shares a room with her male schoolmate Liang Shanbo, who remains unaware she is a woman. When Zhu's parents arrange for her to be married to another man, Liang Shanbo discovers too late that she is a woman and ultimately dies from grief. When Zhu mourns at his grave, the tomb opens up, and she jumps into it, uniting with her beloved in death.

In his study of this folktale, Altenburger explains that there are many historical permutations of the story. The prior account is the earliest version. In a subsequent version, prevalent during the Song dynasty (960–1279), the two lovers ultimately transform into butterflies, a symbol of mandarin scholars, and fly away.[47] While different permutations were influenced by different literary trends and historical conditions, Altenburger explains that there is nevertheless a common five-part narrative structure to most versions: First, the heroine disguises herself as a male during some period of study away from home and befriends another scholar. Second, the two male scholars share the same room, but the other is not aware of the heroine's sex. Third, the heroine leaves school early, and the male friend promises to visit her soon at her home. Fourth, the male friend visits the heroine belatedly and discovers that she is actually a woman. His marriage proposal is rejected because another man has already proposed to her. The male friend dies (typically from heartache). Fifth, the heroine visits the male friend's tomb. Upon her wailing, the tomb opens up, and she disappears into it.[48] In *Female Baccalaureate Graduate*, the first four of those five parts of the folktale's narrative structure are approximately satisfied. The conclusion of the Vietnamese version deviates from the Chinese one in rendering a happy ending.

Despite that different conclusion, another reason that *Female Baccalaureate Graduate* most likely represents a Vietnamese variation of the folktale of Liang Shanbo and Zhu Yingtai is that the story is based on a Chinese source containing virtually the same narrative. The Vietnamese text itself indicates that the original story is based on Feng Menglong's *Stories Old and New*. The opening lines of *Female Baccalaureate Graduate* state: "As seen in the book *Stories Old and New* [*Kim cổ kỳ quan*] / The Văn family had a Female Baccalaureate Graduate [*nữ-tú-tài*] / . . . who excelled at riding horses and shooting bows / whose body was disguised as a hero [*giả anh-hùng*]."[49] While Vietnamese critics certainly acknowledge the general source on which *Female Baccalaureate Graduate* is based, they do not link the Vietnamese version to the specific folktale of Liang Shanbo and Zhu Yingtai (*Lương Sơn Bá và Chúc Anh Đài*).[50] Yet an examination of the source text makes clear that the two tales are actually one and the same. In *Stories Old and New*, Feng Menglong devotes a chapter to narrating four different stories that, according to him, involve "true women who are in men's disguise."[51] Of the four stories, one is the folktale of Liang Shanbo and Zhu Yingtai. The other is the Mulan legend, and another is that of Huang Shancong, a Vietnamese version of which we have already discussed. The fourth is the story of Huang Chonggu (黃崇嘏), a woman who is appointed to an official position while disguised as a male scholar on the basis of her finely crafted poems. Each of the four stories is distinct, and only one involves a romance between two scholars who meet during their studies away from home, namely Liang Shanbo and Zhu Yingtai. In the Vietnamese version, the story's ending and characters' names are different. But as already noted, there are multiple historical permutations of the folktale. Therefore, if *Female Baccalaureate Graduate* was based on Feng Menglong's collection, it must be a Vietnamese interpretation of the folktale of Liang Shanbo and Zhu Yingtai.

The Vietnamese translation of the Chinese folktale of Liang Shanbo and Zhu Yingtai is significant in that it raises the question of cultural reception and interpretation. Vietnamese critics, admittedly, have left precious little substantial commentary on the meaning of *Female Baccalaureate Graduate*. The literary critic Nguyễn Đình Hòa groups it with other eighteenth-century verse narratives, such as the now-classic *The Tale of Kiều*, in their use of Chinese stories to exalt the "role of women and the praising of love within the decisive struggle to protect and defend the couple's personal happiness."[52] Other critics merely acknowledge *Female Baccalaureate Graduate*'s origins in Feng Menglong's anthology and note that a version was translated into *nôm*, the Vietnamese demotic script, in the nineteenth century and then rendered into modern Vietnamese by the first decades of the twentieth century.[53] Despite the dearth of critical commentary on this work, we can still make some reasonable inferences about the story's meaning. The storyline of this Chinese romance is not in itself unfamiliar to a contemporary Vietnamese audience. The story has been popularized through Vietnamese "reformed opera" (*cải lương*) both in Vietnam and in the diaspora, and it is often known as the story of Lương Sơn Bá and Chúc Anh Đài, the Vietnamese names for Liang Shanbo and Zhu Yingtai.[54] Yet the title of this story—or at least one version of it—in the early twentieth century was *Nữ Tú Tài*. The difference in the story's title suggests that the name "Female Baccalaureate Graduate" itself served a contingent and didactic purpose: the juxtaposition of the word "female" and "baccalaureate" emphasizes an element of wonder that a woman, albeit cross-dressed as a man, at the time could succeed in achieving such a high level of education. The significance of *Female Baccalaureate Graduate*, therefore, centers not on the thematic question of male friendship, romantic love, or filial piety—which, as Altenburger notes, have been all valid central themes in the story's varied historical permutations—but on the emphasis on female talent and beauty.[55]

This interpretation of *Female Baccalaureate Graduate* is historically consistent with the version of the Chinese folktale that prevailed since the mid-seventeenth century and onward in China. Although the folktale itself predated the seventeenth century, the story underwent different historical modifications, evolving and adapting to new emerging literary genres. One such literary genre was the scholar-beauty (*caizi jiaren*, 才子佳人) romance of the early to middle Qing period (ca. 1650–1750). Scholar-beauty romances were relatively short fictional works, often anonymously written, that depicted comedies of errors and romances between scholars and beautiful ladies. A key feature of the scholar-beauty romance is the depiction of women characters who are "smart, capable, and chaste" and "equal to or better than their male counterparts in terms of literary talent."[56] To demonstrate their rival talents, however, the woman character in the story must cross-dress as a man to participate in the androcentric world of letters and politics. Through the adventures of this cross-dressing character, scholar-beauty stories celebrated the values of chastity, chivalry, virtue, and wit.[57]

In Vietnam, scholar-beauty stories written in *nôm* were popularized in the eighteenth and nineteenth centuries, and some were then translated into the Vietnamese modern vernacular in the early twentieth century.[58] *Female Baccalaureate Graduate* most likely belongs to this genre in virtue of its cross-dressing heroine, its thematic focus on her superior talent and beauty, and—unlike the tragic versions of the Chinese folktale—its happy ending. Of course, the reason for *Female Baccalaureate Graduate*'s circulation in Vietnam's early twentieth century was probably not its genre per se. Rather, the story contained thematic elements that most likely resonated with Vietnamese society. The story's focus on female talent would have been relevant to a Vietnamese public that was vociferously debating the question of women's literacy and education.

Another prominent story involving female talent and education that circulated in Vietnam's early twentieth century is the tale of Mạnh Lệ Quân (Meng Lijun). In this tale, Mạnh Lệ Quân, the daughter of a garrison leader, is arranged to marry the handsome son of another military family, Hoàng Phủ Thiếu Hoa (Huang-fu Shao-hua). In the course of the wedding arrangements, things go awry and she is forced to marry another official's son, Lưu Khuê Bích

(Liu Kui-bi), who is known as a rake. So Mạnh Lệ Quân forces her maidservant, Tô Ánh Tuyết (Su Yìng-xue), to marry him in her stead. Mạnh then dresses up as a young man and escapes. Taking the name Lệ Minh Đường (Li qun-yu), Mạnh sits for the imperial civil service exams and becomes a top graduate. Mạnh is later engaged to a young woman and discovers on the wedding night that the bride is none other than the former maidservant, Tô Ánh Tuyết. The two decide to continue the charade in the hope that Mạnh will later be reunited with Hoàng Phủ Thiếu Hoa. In a significant episode, after Mạnh Lệ Quân cures the emperor's mother of a life-threatening disease and serves as the emperor's adviser, she and her gender identity become an object of suspicion. Intent on discovering her "true" gender identity, the emperor invites Mạnh Lệ Quân to a drinking party, where he hopes to remove her shoes to expose her bound feet, a tell-tale sign of her womanhood. The story concludes when her so-called true gender is revealed, as she reverts back to her female self and reunites with Hoàng Phủ Thiếu Hoa, the man to whom she was initially supposed to be engaged.

This story derives from the Chinese legend of Mèng Lìjūn (孟麗君), the heroine of a seventeenth-century Qing dynasty tale written by Chen Duan-sheng in her work Love Reincarnate (Tái Sanh Duyên, 再生緣). The tale belongs to the genre of tanci ("plucking lyrics") of the eighteenth and nineteenth centuries as a part of the culture of literate women in the lower Yangzi region.[59] Written in a series of seven- and ten-character lines of verse intermingled with brief prose paragraphs, the tanci genre continued many scholar-beauty themes concerning talented women who cross-dressed as men, except that the stories were composed by women and for literate women audiences. The Vietnamese name Mạnh Lệ Quân is a rendition of the Chinese Mèng Lìjūn, which means "Beautiful Gentleman."[60] In response to the male-centered narratives of Confucian society, tanci narratives often depicted female characters, cross-dressed as men, engaging in adventurous pursuits that they would otherwise not experience. By engaging in forms of fantasy—imagining alternative roles that women could assume—many of the works in the genre also enacted forms of social critique. While scholars differ widely on the specific character of the critique, some insist that the act of cross-dressing was a form of self-fashioning.[61] Others claim that it exemplifies feminine forms of writing.[62] Still others suggest that these works embody female utopias.[63]

Translated into modern Vietnamese in the early twentieth century, the tale of Mạnh Lệ Quân had a conspicuous presence in the popular press and cultural imagination. The tale was published more frequently than any other gender-transgressive literary work examined thus far, with the first extant copy appearing in 1923 and recurring in various versions over the following decade.[64] A surviving but incomplete prose version was published in 1929, and a complete fifteen-volume novel version was published in 1930.[65] The reform theater movement also popularized the story in its various theatrical renditions in 1927, 1928, 1929, 1933.[66] The tale was reportedly dramatized on stage in Hà Nội on Sunday evening, October 3, 1928, and again several weeks later, according to advertisements in the *Hà Thành Midday Newspaper*.[67]

Indeed, so well known was the Mạnh Lệ Quân tale that it appears in one of the poems by Xuân Diệu, a renowned figure of the New Poetry movement. In the poem "Nhị Hồ" (Two Lakes, or Two-Chord Fiddle] in the anthology *Poésies* (1938), Xuân Diệu alludes to the Mạnh Lệ Quân heroine and the play's distinctive music. The poem's title is difficult to translate because of the double entendre. *Nhị Hồ* literally means "two lakes," but it can also refer to the classical Vietnamese two-chord fiddle, also known as the Chinese *huqin* instrument. These details are relevant insofar as the poem is densely packed with nature imagery, musical metaphors, and allusions to premodern East Asian culture, including the mythic heroine in question. In the poem, Xuân Diệu writes:

> The grass leaves are peaceful; the night, deserted
> Suddenly arises a musical chord
> The fiddle captures the feeling of solitude,
> Without tears, but with sadness
> The melody turns to the piece of *Mạnh Lệ Quân*
> Collecting from afar since time immemorial.[68]

The fact that Xuân Diệu openly wrote about the figure of Mạnh Lệ Quân in his acclaimed anthology suggests that the figure must have been widely known to his implied readers. The fact that Mạnh Lệ Quân is associated with a distinct melody further suggests that the story was common cultural knowledge among literate Vietnamese audiences of the 1920s and 1930s.

A central theme of the Mạnh Lệ Quân tale that preoccupied Vietnamese translators and playwrights of the time was precisely the gendered motif of cross-dressing. One indication of this cultural fixation can be partly gleaned from the fact that the *Hà Thành Midday Newspaper* juxtaposed its advertisement of the drama next to that of *The Rowdy Hero*, a story involving gender transgression examined in the previous chapter.[69] In several theater renditions of the Mạnh Lệ Quân story, playwrights focused on scenes principally involving cross-dressing. In one published version, the drama zooms in on the first part of the tale, when the heroine prepares for her escape from the home to partake in the imperial examinations. The heroine asks the servant, Vinh Lan, to purchase a scholar's wardrobe for her and to find a larger pair of shoes, presumably to mask any perception of the heroine having bound feet, a cultural sign of the female gender.[70] The front cover displays the scene in which the heroine requests a larger pair of shoes (fig. 3.1). Once she has them, the heroine is depicted going on a journey with her servant (fig. 3.2.) In another published version, palace officials are shown questioning the heroine's true gender (fig. 3.3). Still, another version emphasizes the episode in which palace officials scheme to remove the heroine's shoes so as to verify her true gender. The queen concocts a plan whereby she will ask the heroine to draw, coincidentally, a picture of Quan Âm Thị Kính (also known as Kuan-yin or Avalokiteśvara), the female Boddhisatva who cross-dressed as a monk while living in a monastery (fig. 3.4). After the heroine finishes the drawing, the queen will ostensibly "reward" her with some wine. The queen's true motive, however, is to have Mạnh Lệ Quân become inebriated so that palace officials can remove her shoes. The scheme proceeds as planned, and it is discovered that the heroine, who has been the emperor's "male" minister, in fact, possesses petite feet. The book's front cover displays a photograph of this latter shoe-removal scene (fig. 3.5).

The cultural fixation on shoes and bound feet highlights the traces of an alternative gender regime. If one definition of "gender" is the cultural and historical organization of masculinity and femininity, then the practice of footbinding is one form that such organization takes, much the same way that wearing high heels today may be associated with femininity. Although scholars have interpreted this phenomenon in different ways—as an eroticized fetish, symbol of the leisure class's taste, sign of the invisibility of female labor, or simply a "feudal" practice—almost all agree that the practice was a form of female gender differentiation.[71] In her study of the history of foot-binding in China, Dorothy Ko links the practice to the cultural processes of inculcating

Giá : 0$60.

TUỒNG HÁT CẢI-LƯƠNG

MẠNH-LỆ-QUÂN

GIẢ TRAI

DEPOT LEGAL
INDOCHINE

NGƯỜI ĐẶT : TRƯƠNG-QUANG-TIỀN No

Bổn tuồng nầy, có 15 cái hình chụp, in trong giấy láng, tuyệt đẹp.
MỖI CUỐN ĐỀU CÓ KÝ TÊN NGƯỜI ĐẶT.

Mạnh-lệ-Quân trao bạc và nói với con Vinh-Lan :
Nầy, mầy hãy bảo mua cho được đôi giày lớn hơn cỡ giày nầy.

SAIGON
IMPRIMERIE DE L'UNION
1927

FIGURE 3.1. Cover page of the drama titled *Mạnh Lệ Quân Pretends to Be Male*. The heroine asks the servant to go purchase her a pair of shoes. Bibliothèque Nationale de France.

FIGURE 3.2. Mạnh Lệ Quân dressed in male clothing while the servant carries the baggage. Bibliothèque Nationale de France.

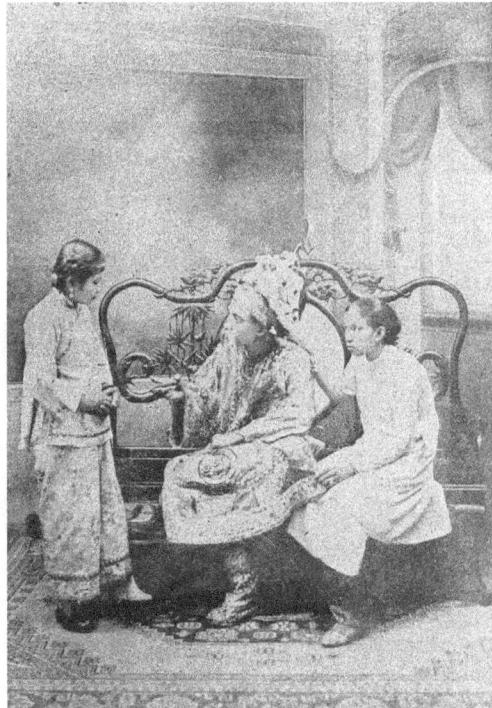

FIGURE 3.3. The royal palace questions whether the heroine, disguised as a general, is male or female. Bibliothèque Nationale de France.

FIGURE 3.4. The heroine, disguised as Lệ Minh Đường, is asked to draw a picture of Guan-yin, the Bodhisattva of Mercy who cross-dressed as a monk. Bibliothèque Nationale de France.

FIGURE 3.5. Cover page of the drama *Mạnh Lệ Quân's Shoes Are Removed*. The caption states: "While Lệ Minh Đường is inebriated as if dead the two palace helpers remove the shoes." Bibliothèque Nationale de France.

female identity. As the practice was inextricably linked to rituals of domesticity and women's handiwork in shoemaking, foot-binding became a "focal" point of female identity.[72] By focusing on the feet as a marker of femininity, then, the Mạnh Lệ Quân tale and its circulation in the early twentieth-century Vietnamese press demonstrate the cultural persistence of this alternative form of gendered organization.

Given the Vietnamese interest in Mạnh Lệ Quân's gender identity in the theatrical works discussed here, it behooves us to ask how some Vietnamese writers understood the tale. Is the story an affirmation or denunciation of this gendered system? I suggest that, even as the stories ratify the Confucian system, they simultaneously open up possibilities for their Vietnamese audiences to imagine otherwise.

Like many cross-dressing tales examined thus far, Mạnh Lệ Quân's story was praised by Vietnamese male critics in the framework of Confucian values. In a preface published in 1924, the male critic Dương Bá Trạc explains the sources of the story's literary "excellence": "There is another excellent quality to the play. That excellence [cái hay] is captured in the words that the translator has displayed on the book's cover: 'Loyalty, Filial Piety, Altruism, Uprightness.' When we speak of these four words in our society today, even those of us with beards must feel embarrassed and ashamed, much less those in our society who have never received a moral education [giáo dục] and who have never had to bear social responsibility."[73] In that passage, gender crossing in no way renders the heroine deviant or pathological. On the contrary, far from being considered abnormal, Mạnh Lệ Quân is a paragon of Confucian virtue. Mạnh Lệ Quân's gender crossing is an issue to the extent that it reveals, by juxtaposition, men's inadequacies. That a woman was able to pass the imperial exams merely brings into relief the degree to which men—"those with beards"—must strive even more to approximate Confucian virtue. The critic later explains: "Whether male or female, to be human is to require these four virtues."[74] He continues, "One cannot be human in the absence of these four virtues: even if one were, one would not know how one has devolved and transformed into some other species [giống], certainly not the human one."[75] This reception of this tale by the critic is representative. Gender difference for male critics is neither the crux of the problem nor their primary focus. Rather, their focus is squarely on the story's moral message of disseminating traditional Confucian virtues.[76]

The Vietnamese reception of Mạnh Lệ Quân raises a fundamental irony concerning women's position in a Confucian society. On the one hand, Confucian ethics constrained the scope of women's professional possibilities. On the other hand, women in such a society could gain greater freedom if they succeeded in their acts of cross-dressing as men. Counterintuitively, such cross-dressing was most prevalent during eras when Confucian social ethics were strongest. To male critics, the idea of a woman cross-dressing as a man was innocuous because it in no way challenged the prevailing androcentric social order. As one scholar notes, female impersonation was strongest during the Ming and Qing dynasties but scarce during the Yuan dynasty.[77] This is not surprising in a society that constrained women's options in the public sphere. As Judith Zeitlin has suggested, although premodern Chinese narratives may exhibit characters who transgress gender boundaries, they nevertheless do so in the name of some of the highest Confucian ideals—filial piety, integrity, loyalty, honor, and so forth. The result is that the gender transgression in no way subverts the prevailing social order but, instead, ratifies it.[78]

Despite this qualifying context, I would like to suggest another possibility on the part of the Vietnamese audience's interpretation of the gender-transgressive acts we have examined so far. Rather than buttressing conservative orthodoxy, these texts instead serve to inspire and radically imagine society otherwise. The basis for this claim comes from two kinds of evidence: the nature of the stories themselves and their reception and reappropriation by a younger generation of women. I discuss each point in turn.

First, it is significant that Confucian orthodoxy appears to us through the medium of literature and drama. As such, the stories we are considering are not necessarily mimetic reflections of empirical reality. Rather, as literary texts, engaged with the imagination, it is more plausible to consider them evidence of the realm of the possible—of desire, fantasy, and aspiration, of that which could be. This point is bolstered by the fact that the Mạnh Lệ Quân story belongs to the *tanci* genre, written by and for literate women of the royal palace. In this regard, even as the tales promulgated Confucian social norms, they also served to inspire their female audiences of possibilities beyond the constraints that society had imposed on them.

One such inspired possibility is women's agency. As these stories suggest, women in Confucian society are not entirely helpless and can turn the tables on the patriarchal system. In the stories *Female Baccalaureate Graduate* and the tale of Mạnh Lệ Quân, the heroines demonstrate active agency in determining their lives. Phi Nga, the heroine in *Female Baccalaureate Graduate*, sets up a bow-and-arrow competition among her two male classmates to help decide on her future husband. When Mạnh Lệ Quân learns that she will have to marry a rake, she schemes a way out of the situation by cross-dressing as a man and having her female servant take her place in the marriage. Furthermore, both heroines exhibit the audacity to leave their homes and families to undertake and pass the imperial examinations. Consistent with the scholar-beauty and *tanci* genres, then, both stories portray female protagonists who sparkle with wit and acumen that rival, or exceed, that of their male counterparts.

It is not a stretch of the imagination to posit that some Vietnamese women audiences saw in these stories, not the affirmation of conservative orthodoxy, but the potential breaking points of their society, leading them from there to reimagine it radically anew. Indeed, evidence suggests exactly such a scenario: in the early twentieth century, some women writers in the Vietnamese press did draw precisely on these classical tales, reappropriating them to serve other political ends.

MODERN ANALOGIES TO THE CLASSICAL PAST

The final group of documents evincing the persistence of the classical motif of gender transgression derives from stories, both fictional and biographical, of modern women who pushed the perceived limits of societal gender norms and, in the process, appealed to classical heroines to justify their respective causes. Of the heroines discussed thus far, the two that most frequently recur in these modern narratives are the figures of Mạnh Lệ Quân and Hoa Mộc Lan (Huā MùLán, 花木蘭).

Both classical heroines were invoked in stories published by the journal *New Women's News* (*Phụ Nữ Tân Văn*). In a three-part series, the journal reported the case of a boisterous British colonel by the name of Barker who was legally married to a Mrs. Elfreda Haward. As a result of her uncommonly large body and masculine behavior, none of the soldiers under Barker's command realized that he was actually the woman Valerie Smith. "He" was discovered to be a "she" only when arrested upon failing to appear at a court summons. Although a large audience reportedly attended the hearing, the Vietnamese press neither acknowledged nor displayed feelings of shock or horror over the gender-crossing and homoerotic overtones of the women's relationship.[79] This attitude is consistent with the English print media of the time, which, according to Laura Doan, "overlooked the link between (masculine) dress and (homo)sexuality."[80]

Despite its potential reception as a far-fetched European scandal, the anonymous writer of the news story displays her artful skill in linking it to a prior tradition. The writer begins by praising the Chinese legend of Mạnh Lệ Quân, the heroine who disguised herself as a man to sit for the imperial exams. That the title of the article is "The Rebirth of Mạnh Lệ Quân" implies that Barker is the reincarnation of this classical heroine. In the third article of the series, the author writes, "This story is exactly the same as that of Mạnh Lệ Quân long ago who disguised herself as a man to be the king's prime minister and who married Lưu Yến Ngọc as her wife."[81] By effectively substituting one character for another, the article sutures the temporal and cultural distance that spans the two women's worlds. This rhetorical effect is made clear by the author's use of "our sisters": "If only women were allowed equality of education and social standing as men are, then just as our sisters in times past were able to reach the first-rank doctorate in the feudal Court exams, so our sisters today can also become court barristers."[82] The psychic identification with characters of the past, sometimes enacted by scholars and social movements, produces a shared sense of historical burden and continuity, even as the identification elides manifold layers of difference. This is a strategy that the gender historian Joan W. Scott has coined "fantasy echo."[83] The result is a European story of female gender crossing that is not only less distant and foreign but also a historical repetition of a classical canon of knowledge that literate audiences shared in Vietnam's early twentieth century.

The topos of female gender crossing recurs in another piece in the *New Women's News* in the same year. This time the event took place in neighboring China, where a young woman named Vương Khuê, disguised as a man, rose to the high rank of deputy army commander.[84] She joined the army after her parents had died, and she had no living relatives. This article also begins by appealing to a premodern legend: the Chinese heroine Mộc Lan, who, for twelve years, disguised herself as a man to replace her dead father in the army. Likewise, Vương Khuê also rose through the army ranks because of her talent. When she was discovered, according to the article, the general in charge was in no way upset or angry but rather impressed by the young woman's brilliance. Treating her with "respect and dignity," he decided to keep her in the army with her rank.

Another document that appeals to a classical heroine in justifying the women's modern emancipation movement is the memoir of the Chinese woman Trịnh Dục Tú (Zhèng Yùxiù, 鄭毓秀, 1891–1959). As the first female lawyer and judge in Chinese history, Tú wrote a memoir in 1925 that was translated into Vietnamese in three volumes. In the memoir, she describes growing up with a sense of disidentification with the patriarchal social and cultural norms of Chinese society. Although society may have classified her as "female," she exhibited all the predispositions that Chinese society would characterize as belonging to a male, specifically her thirst for learning, her high professional ambitions, and her dreams of traveling the world. So when she reached the age for foot-binding, she refused it.[85] Her so-called masculine predispositions led others to label her a "freakish girl" (*quái nữ*) with an excessive appetite for freedom.[86] Her mother even called her a boy: "You are no longer a girl anymore! . . . you're more comparable to the boys."[87] Despite the pronouncements of her gender, Trịnh Dục Tú explained that her mother raised her with high hopes that she would someday accomplish great things. Her mother recounted to her tales of "female knight errants" (*vị nữ hào kiệt*) who loaned their talents to the "Chinese nation" (*nước Trung Hoa*). One such memorable tale was the story of Mulan. The protagonist explains:

> I still recall that one afternoon when mother held me in her arms and told me about a heroine who lent her female body to save the nation from the wretched clutches of war.
>
> Who is this heroine? A long time ago, there was a family that bore only a daughter and named her Mu Lan [*Mậu Lan*].[88]

In the prior passage, Trịnh narrates her formative years when her mother inculcated in her grand ambitions by recounting the tale of Mulan. In this rendition, the fundamental elements of the tale are all there. The female warrior dresses in male garb and goes to battle in her father's stead. The key difference appears to be the nationalistic framing of this premodern narrative. Trịnh Dục Tú, like Mulan, wishes to depart from the patriarchal gendered conventions of Chinese culture. But if different versions of the tale have invoked different justifications for Mulan's cross-dressing, the reason this time appears to be in the name of the nation. Trịnh aspires to the grand ambitions that Chinese culture considers a male preserve but does so only to increase the "glory" (*vinh quang*) of the Chinese nation. Despite the nationalistic framing or perhaps because of it, the memoir invokes the classical figure of Mulan, in part, to justify the protagonist's gender transgression. The implication of the comparison is that if this hallowed figure in Chinese history was able to break with patriarchal norms, why should Trịnh Dục Tú, then, not also be able to do so?

Another document that invokes a classical heroine in appealing for change in women's place in society is a Vietnamese novel titled *Nguyễn Tuyết Hoa* (fig. 3.6). In five volumes, the novel recounts the life of the eponymous heroine who travels to Japan to learn about the textiles industry. To do so, however, she disguises herself as a man because it would presumably be socially unacceptable for a woman to travel by herself. Along the way, she learns the Japanese language and martial arts. While disguised as a man, the heroine receives compliments from fellow travelers of how "handsome" he looks, suggesting the success of her disguise. Upon her return to Vietnam, she establishes an all-female workers factory and a women's cultural association that trains its members in martial arts. When her father arranges for her hand in marriage to a man, she decides against bearing children because it would hamper her ability to manage the business, and so she arranges for her husband to marry a second wife to fulfill the reproductive role. In short, the novel depicts a picture of a successful Vietnamese woman who defies the gendered norms of her time.

The analogy to a classical heroine appears in the novel's preface. The author, Trương Hoàn, discusses the role of literature in society. "Good" literature helps to edify readers, much the same way as "healthy" foods help nourish the body, "mind" (*tâm*), and "spirit" (*tin thần*).[89] The author then introduces the novel in question and its eponymous heroine, Nguyễn Tuyết Hoa, who embodies the virtues that Vietnamese readers should emulate. Comparing the protagonist to the classical heroine Mạnh Lệ Quân, the author explains: "Take Nguyễn Tuyết Hoa and compare her to Mạnh Lệ Quân of long ago. Lệ Quân was able to become a high-level official; Tuyết Hoa, a rich and successful person. Both maidens must have been geniuses of unusual talent to reach the level that they did. This novel depicts a pious family that makes a living that is the desire of many women. This is a novel worth meditating on, one that is not simply a means of enter-

FIGURE 3.6. Cover page of the first volume. An artist's sketch of the heroine Nguyễn Tuyết Hoa. Bibliothèque Nationale de France.

tainment."[90] The ostensible purpose of the novel, then, is didactic. It aims to teach its implied female readers—a burgeoning group in the Franco-Vietnamese schools—the virtues of Nguyễn Tuyết Hoa and Mạnh Lệ Quân. Both heroines defy gender stereotypes in reaching positions of high esteem in their respective societies: Lệ Quân becomes a mandarin official, and Tuyết Hoa, the female boss of a textile factory. Both heroines exhibit martial skills: the former serves as the emperor's military adviser, and the latter teaches martial arts to members of her women's association. At the same time, both are engaged as pious second wives: Mạnh Lệ Quân was initially married to a woman, but later, both become wives to the same man, whereas Nguyễn Tuyết Hoa serves as the elder wife to her husband. In its advocacy for the expansion of women's roles in Vietnamese society, the novel deploys the earlier figure of Mạnh Lệ Quân in its justification. In short, the novel suggests that Nguyễn Tuyết Hoa is the modern incarnation of the classical figure of Mạnh Lệ Quân.

CONCLUSION

As this chapter has demonstrated, the reception of nineteenth-century Confucian culture in Vietnam's early twentieth century needs to be reconsidered. Vietnamese modernist reformers of the 1920s and 1930s have depicted the period as a backward, feudal era of gender oppression. As a result, relying on the depictions by modernist reformers, cultural historians of the period have captured this strand of Confucian gender oppression in their scholarship. Despite this portrayal, the chapter has recovered an alternative interpretive reception of Confucian "tradition." In particular, the chapter has reconstructed the persistence of a heretofore underexamined group of classical narratives involving gender and sexual transgression.

In these narratives, women protagonists transgress gender and sexual norms by cross-dressing as men or performing "masculinity" to participate in the androcentric world of politics and letters, what I refer to as the classical trope of gender transgression. In the early twentieth century, many of these nineteenth-century tales were translated into the modern Vietnamese vernacular, thereby furnishing far more fluid gendered and sexual possibilities in the Vietnamese symbolic cultural sphere than the current scholarship has acknowledged. The chapter has surveyed a wide range of narratives from women warriors, filial daughters engaged in commerce, to talented and beautiful female scholars who passed the imperial examination, eventually, to serve in high royal positions. Drawing on these tales, some Vietnamese publishers adopted and reappropriated them for various political ends. Some saw in these Confucian classical tales inspiration in support of the modern women's emancipation movement.

Nevertheless, the fact that these gender-transgressive stories were modern translations of nineteenth-century classical tales suggests that they most likely circulated among, and were known primarily by, elite Vietnamese society, those still acquainted with the previously thriving but steadily declining Sino-Vietnamese Confucian culture. If this chapter has focused primarily on the reception and meaning of this earlier cultural "tradition" in Vietnam's early twentieth century, in the next chapter, we turn our attention to the other side of the same coin: modernity. We will focus on the general print public sphere and the younger generation of French-educated Vietnamese, some of whom had little to no interest in this earlier East Asian cultural past, a direct consequence of the French colonial state's effacement of the Confucian imperial exams. Was the rhetoric of gender transgression confined to a narrow Confucian elite, or did it extend to the general popular culture? If it did extend to the popular culture, what is the character of such rhetoric? Was it a rhetoric of stigmatization and pathologization? These are some of the problems that the next chapter investigates in more depth.

FOUR

GENDER PLASTICITY
New Bodies and Genders in
the Public Imagination

SCHOLARS TEND TO NARRATE COLONIAL Vietnamese modernity by underscoring a transition from patriarchal tradition to the rise of the women's liberation movement. Whereas women in the nineteenth century were subordinate to a Confucian patriarchal regime, serving as either imperial concubines or objects of exchange in arranged marriages, the early 1930s are considered the decisive historical markers of gender emancipation and the advancement of the ideals of the "New Woman."[1] David Marr writes, for example, that the "women question" became a focal point around which other societal issues revolved. Women saw themselves, Marr writes, as a "social group with particular interests, grievances, and demands."[2] Shawn McHale likewise suggests that between 1918 and 1930, a "sea change" took place in Vietnamese society's perception of the place of women. Women's groups, McHale writes, eventually "adopted a more activist stance and engaged in spirited debates over women's liberation."[3] In short, scholars mark this period as the inaugural moment when women achieved a collective consciousness in Vietnam.

In this chapter, I illuminate a new and previously overlooked narrative that decenters rather than contradicts the prevailing history. In writing the history of a "social group" and its liberationist politics, most current scholars take for granted that certain gender categories had already been congealed, presuming a lack of historical disagreements over what served as the binding glue to collective consciousness. In the early 1930s, I argue, Vietnamese popular culture conceived of the gendered body as far more plastic and open to different modalities of becoming. This outlook, in part, emerges from the rise of a more open-minded younger generation. In a world in which modern scientific innovation challenged convention, this generation experienced a profound crisis of knowledge about the natural world—a crisis that, as we will see, also subverted fundamental truths concerning the gendered and sexual body.[4]

This chapter joins the work of both queer scholars and historians who interrogate the premises and power-making effects of those who presume a heteronormative ideology. As I explained in the introduction and elsewhere, by "heteronormativity," queer scholars refer to how cultures and institutions naturalize dimorphism: the principle of identity that produces a binary, stable, and coherent alignment of anatomical sex, gender, desire, and psyche. So powerful is this ideological fiction that it leads historians to naturalize and reproduce it at the expense of past diverse forms of sexual and gendered subjects. This has led queer scholars to recomplicate past histories that had previously been effaced by heteronormative interpretations.[5] This kind of interrogation parallels recent critiques voiced by the Vietnam and Southeast Asian historians Nhung Tuyết Trần and Anthony Reid. In "The Construction of Vietnamese Historical Identities," they conclude their survey of current scholarship with the following insight: "Most essays in this book are marked by an interest in crossing borders and exploring ambiguities. They seek to document voices that have been ignored or marginalized, whether those of women, subalterns, or cosmopolitan misfits." They continue, "Their interpretive frameworks leave more open ends, windows and adjoining corridors than previous work."[6] As part of a study examining the norms and normative limits of twentieth-century Vietnamese cultural life, this chapter investigates the formation of variant genders and sexualities that flourished during the period that scholars have long considered the genesis of the Vietnamese women's emancipation movement (1930–1940). In so doing, I aim to disrupt the conventional emplotment that collapses the history of modern gender emancipation into that of heterosexual dimorphism.

This chapter has two main sections. The first explores Vietnam in the middle of the 1920s, a period that witnessed the rise of "radicalism" propagated by urban youth. This cultural and political context is essential to seeing both disjuncture and continuity from earlier Sino-Vietnamese forms of gendered and sexual expression. It helps us appreciate the profound novelty of the new bodily forms and sexual subjectivities that exploded in the public discourse of the 1930s in the wake of this movement. Together, these sections reveal that the normative meaning of gender and sexuality in this period was far more dynamic and expansive than contemporary scholarship has acknowledged.

THE RISE OF URBAN YOUTH, 1926–1930

The year 1926 represents a pivotal moment in the history of Vietnamese anticolonialism. It marks a decisive transition between two generations. Even though the French had already occupied Vietnam for more than sixty-five years, the older generation clung to the East Asian classical tradition and struggled to overcome the challenges brought about by modernity. The complex, at times burdensome, Confucian bureaucracy to which the nineteenth-century Nguyễn dynasty emperors helped build lacked the agility to respond to Western military might, technological savvy, and sheer determination to seize colonial land. Generations of mandarin scholars could not step outside their cultural cosmology to understand the West's imperialist worldview.[7] By the mid-1920s, a younger generation emerged of students, teachers, journalists, and interpreters, among others. The historian Huệ Tâm Hồ Tài has since attached to this new generation the term "radicalism." They were the product of the uneven growth of the colonial education system that officially closed all the traditional academies that trained candidates for the now-defunct imperial Confucian exams by 1919.[8] It is no coincidence that by 1925, after the colonial state's loosening of the freedoms of the press and expression, publishers released translations of works by Western thinkers and writers such as Kant, Hegel, Marx, Bergson, Spinoza, and Nietzsche.[9] Indeed, by the middle of the 1920s, students were leaving for France in droves, in search of an education they could not find at home.[10] These students are noteworthy because their return in the early 1930s coincides with a period of philosophical upheaval when society witnessed a wider variety of sexual subjectivities than historians and scholars have previously acknowledged.

This younger generation embodied and laid claim to a profound shift in values. Of the famous figures in this cohort, including Trần Huy Liệu, Phan Văn Hùm, Tạ Thu Thâu, Đào Duy Anh, perhaps the one who best exemplified this paradigm shift was Nguyễn An Ninh. A lawyer educated in France who spent his formative years in Paris, Ninh returned to his country an iconoclast and staunch defender of individual autonomy. Having founded the satirical journal *La Cloche Fêlée*, he became something of a colonial gadfly: his persistent questioning of authority led to his arrest in March 1926. Huệ Tâm Hồ Tài has argued that, rather than in the Communist Party, the "origins" of the Vietnamese revolution ought to be located in this generation with its eclectic melding of anarchism and a quest for individual freedom. She writes, "Political radicalism and cultural iconoclasm fused together" when urban youth "challenge[d] the authority of their parents and teachers in a wave of strikes that gave them their first taste of control over their lives." She continues, "Most of those who took part in the protests of 1926 were born after the turn of the century . . . they were the products of Sarraut's [the Indochinese Governor General's] educational reforms."[11] Whether manifested in their demands to break loose from the shackles of arranged marriages, their insistence on romantic love, or their fight for women's emancipation, these urban youth exhibited a clear rupture with the older generation of scholar-officials (fig. 4.1). Given the rise of a younger genera-

FIGURE 4.1. Cover page of the journal *Phụ Nữ Tân Văn* (*New Women's News*). Bibliothèque Nationale de France.

tion and the spread of cultural iconoclasm in the context of the state's loosening of the freedoms of the press and expression, it is no stretch of the imagination to claim that the early 1930s witnessed a dramatic questioning of traditional sex/gender regimes and the emergence of new gendered and sexual subjectivities.

NEW BODIES AND GENDERS UNDER
FRENCH COLONIALISM

The relentless penetration of modern life by technological and scientific advances led the Vietnamese to examine the fundamentals of their society. Unlike Europe and the United States, where economic and cultural development generally grew at a steady pace, other regions, including Southeast Asia, encountered the onslaught of modernity with a profound sense of disorientation. In his analysis of the double consciousness of the colonized intelligentsia, Pheng Cheah explains that their social situation endows them with the "gift/curse" to perceive much earlier the technological forces that "destabilize and change human consciousness."[12] Likewise, explaining the response of Vietnamese colonial poets and writers, Neil Jamieson likens it to the "emotional experiences of going from Rousseau to Camus in a single lifetime."[13] In short, the early 1930s was marked by epistemic upheaval—it was a world in perpetual motion.[14]

Vital to this upheaval was the question of gendered and sexual norms. Looking back at the end of the decade in 1938, in a New Year's edition of *These Days* (*Ngày Nay*), Phan Khôi published the revealing article "The History of Short Hair: Annam since 1906."[15] As someone who had been born in the prior century but lived to witness the twentieth, Khôi offered rare insights into the transformation of Vietnam to a modern French colony. Before 1906, according to Khôi, Vietnamese men allowed their hair to grow long—just like the "women of today." So powerful was this new cultural norm of short hair for men that boys tried to keep their hair short indefinitely. But this was not always so. Khôi cites the 1908 court case in the central imperial region against a group of entrepreneurs. Unemployed but resourceful, these individuals were the proto-barbers of today's Vietnam. After they began cutting men's hair, however, the imperial court charged them with violating the public decency law (*luật bất ưng vi trọng*) and imprisoned them for eighteen months. According to Khôi, the French colonials called this case the "révolte de cheveux tondus" (the revolt of short hair).[16] Khôi's article helps dramatize both the changing character of gender identity and its eventual crystallization. Although scholars have already documented some of these changes, the current literature presumes gender as stable within a heterosexual matrix and uniformly aligns sex, gender, practice, and desire.[17] What has been less examined—and what I underscore—is the perception of sexual uncertainty in this decade.

The Blurring of Genders: Short Hair, Painted Nails, and Lipstick

In the early 1930s, the practice of trimming one's hair was fashionable for both men and women. Though hardly a surprise for us today, back then the Vietnamese had mixed feelings about the trend. Everywhere around them they saw new genders and bodies, and the unisex hairstyle was but one fad among others that flourished, no doubt, due to the mass of students who returned from their studies in Europe. In the 1920s and 1930s, according to Laura Doan, Europe exhibited unprecedented confusion over gender and sexual identity, because fashion-conscious women of all sexual persuasions appeared to "cross-dress" by donning boyish or mannish attire and by cutting their hair short (fig. 4.2).[18] In

Mốt mới

Đàn ông bắt trước đàn-bà dùng khăn san

Un...

deux

Un...

deux !

FIGURE 4.2. Cartoon of a new fashion: "Men wear shawls as women do." *Phong Hóa* (Mores), no. 25, December 9, 1932.

1934, Phan Văn Hùm said he had noticed the dramatic changes in men and women's comportment only within the past five or six years.[19] Observing the dizzying transformation she saw around her, one female writer opposed the new hairstyle because it would make Vietnamese women look too "Western."[20] Another asked about the historical origins of the bizarre fad.[21] Yet another remarked that, despite how strange women now looked, people would eventually get accustomed to the new trend.[22] Still another editorial came from a male writer who praised the idea. He reasoned that despite the androgynous effect—women looking "just like men"—it was probably a good thing: because the majority of the population is poor, trimming one's hair is both economical and practical in safeguarding against disease.[23] Still another writer predicted, "Women's hair will in the end look like men's, but we have not yet reached that point because some men today still prefer keeping their hair long."[24]

Hairstyle represented only one type of bodily dilemma in the midst of cultural upheaval. Applying cosmetics was another. The public hotly debated painting one's nails and applying lipstick and other kinds of facial cosmetics because they, like the practice of hair trimming, contributed to the blurring of the genders. In addition to its potential for cheap labor and raw resources, Indochina also provided the French cosmetic industry with new markets. Commenting on the effect of this industry, one writer observed, "As for male youths of this country: they brush their lips, apply lipstick and cosmetic powder *like girls*, wear the 'Charleston' pants, fashionable Paris shirts, sporting swanky clothes."[25] This blurring of the genders, which seemed to resemble something of the figure of the cross-dressing dandy, would become the butt of a joke in a scene in Vũ Trọng Phụng's novel *Dumb Luck* (1936).[26] After waking up one morning, Mr. Civilization combs his hair and makes his face. The narrator states, "He painted his fingernails with bright-red nail polish. Then he applied pancake to his cheeks and covered them with a layer of powder. With his black hair curling down the nape of his long neck, his bulging eyes and Adam's apple, and his milky white face, he looked like a feminine man of lipstick and powder."[27] Although this scene is probably a satirical attack on what "civilization" has become and reflects Vũ Trọng Phụng's cynical disapproval, the episode nevertheless captures the dramatic changes in gender norms seen in prior editorials.[28]

For some critics, the idea of women's emancipation was scandalous enough, promoted by a narrow cohort of women who were pushing the envelope too far. Vietnamese society, they reasoned, was simply not prepared for such wide-reaching changes. Some male readers, like the literatus Nguyễn Bá Học warned that, if women were to assume male activities, they would lose their sense of "traditional" propriety.[29] Another writer conceded that although women should probably shed their "shy and diffident" demeanor, they could avoid "losing their woman tendencies that would otherwise make them appear like men."[30] Thạch Lan displays a similar anxiety in his article entitled "European Women," part of a collection of missives he sent home recounting his adventures in Paris. Besides noting the sexual liberation that characterized European women, for which the Vietnamese counterparts were supposedly ill-prepared, Thạch Lan also cites the following dangers:

> I believe that although [European women] have more freedom than their An-namite counterparts, what will be the consequences of such freedom? Yes, in a few years, in ten or one hundred more years, women here in terms of their liberty will be on par with men, that is, women will be able to play and work like their male counterparts, just like men, except with one difference: they will still have menstruation, still give birth, and will still be weaker! Those aspects will never change! . . . [some censored lines] . . . *Women who turn into men* . . . [some censored lines] . . . like so—because it is impossible to alter one's body entirely, one's biology—otherwise, the family will be exterminated, and society will face an enormous crisis.[31]

Thạch Lan's letter suggests that unusual changes in sexual norms were taking place in Europe, changes in which women could turn into men. These changes, Thạch Lan warns, might lead to the end of the bourgeois nuclear family. His disbelief in the extent of the human body's plasticity forced him to resort to biological determinism, no matter how tenuous biology might have been as a foundation on which to ground gender.[32] Thạch Lan's apprehensions provide some measure of the extent of the new bodies and genders that exploded in the public discourse.

In the early 1930s, Vietnamese readers received spectacular news from Europe, the United States, and elsewhere about the diverse forms of sexuality and gender. These included women who vaguely looked like men, women who became men, half men, half women, men and women who desired only those of their own sex, and finally, men and women who underwent sex changes. Despite the outcry by some male writers, they could not stop the influx in the colony of these spectacular stories.

The Bearded Women Phenomenon

A core group of sources from the period display a preoccupation with what I call the "bearded women" phenomenon. Presenting a picture of a woman, usually European, who had grown a beard, the article would then attempt to explain away the phenomenon or ponder the unknown horizons of the human species. Today this image may strike some Vietnamese readers as an unpleasant icon that is discordant with the bourgeois idea of the "New Woman" who is imagined as modern, beautiful, smooth, and fashion conscious. It might contradict the preferred embodiment of Vietnam as a civilized nation on the world stage.[33] Yet if much of the inspiration for the New Woman came from Europe, it seems that this other less "respectable" history has been conveniently obstructed. Consider, for example, a passage from the following article: "When I was in Paris, I witnessed firsthand many women with long black beards. If they hadn't worn women's clothing, I would have thought they were men. I took this as a strange phenomenon and upon my return I consulted some medicine men [thầy thuốc] but some said this or that and others were ambiguous; still others simply admitted to not knowing why."[34] As the title of this article suggests—"A Question of Science"—the tone is less abject disgust or moral condemnation than it is measured curiosity. The rest of the article elaborates on the author's efforts to resolve this puzzling phenomenon. Drawing on another Chinese article addressing the same quandary, the author concludes with a scientific explanation: "So it is that a man's mustache like women's menstruation each follows the law of nature according to which excess blood is secreted. According to this theory, if women had poor blood, ceased menstruation below, that is, the blood were to flow upward, the result is that women will grow beards. There is nothing unusual about the phenomenon."[35] This fearless and cerebral exercise of explaining away the bearded women phenomenon resonated in a world in which superstition and myth were gradually banished by the powers of human reason. Imbued with passionate curiosity and wonder, such powers displayed the optimistic belief in the rational faculties to explain away seemingly unusual natural phenomena.[36]

It is no wonder, then, that some of these characteristics are also found in the bevy of other bearded women articles featured in the *Science Journal*. Curious about the origins of this unusual figure, one article traced it throughout European cultural history, beginning with the Greeks and Romans, followed by the Germans, and then on to the reign of Charles II, who favored three male soldiers, one of whom was a woman dressed as a man. Finally, the article mentions the story of Holland's Queen Marguerite, who grew a beard to display her "royalty."[37] Another article casually featured the story of a "beard contest" in France in which women were reportedly also contestants.[38] Still another marveled at the strangeness of this world in which some men exhibited large breasts and women, beards.[39] Yet another showed a picture of "her," a bearded woman, on its front page.[40]

Of course, some readers in the 1930s did feel aversion for this spectacle of bearded women. Consider the opening paragraph in the *New Women's News'* three-part series "Strange Women in the World":[41] "In this life, among our sisters, there are those naturally born with the strangest of organic forms that nobody can possibly imagine. Whether they are Siamese twins, those born without arms, legs, or those denuded with only a bodily trunk, yet are able to still survive; whether they are overly fat and four times the standard size of a person; or whether they grow beards etc. strange, strange, odd, odd . . . it seems impossible to list them all."[42] This passage produces a certain kind of "queerness" that renders certain subjects not only as nonnormative but also as challenging the limits of what's culturally possible. Like other "crippled" women, the "bearded" ones belong to those rare and deformed creatures that baffle the mind.[43] In another article published two years later, a writer speculates that this ubiquitous figure in France is probably afflicted with "diabetes," hence diminishing her "natural" beauty.[44] Yet despite these queer-producing effects, these articles display counternarratives. The passage, for instance, begins by invoking members of a larger community: "In this life, among our sisters." In the next paragraph of the same article, the reporter notes that some consider these strange women another species of humanity: "There is a Western writer who has circled the globe documenting all sorts of strange bodily forms and has categorized them as the 'fifth race' ('cinquième race')"[45] Although it is unclear who exactly this Western writer is—no name is provided—this taxonomic practice is part of the Enlightenment project to organize and master the natural world and, by so doing, produce all kinds of hierarchies. In this article, however, those subjects who are ostensibly queered are simultaneously marveled as the unknown horizons of humanity: "strange, strange, odd, odd . . . it seems impossible to list them all."[46] These figures signify not so much the limits of the possible as the limits of the *knowable*. In the diabetes article, the writer concludes, "Doctors [*bác-sĩ*] have tried to find the cause for why women grow beards, but since time immemorial they have left behind a big question mark."[47] In describing the historical milieu of this period, Marr comments: "Whatever their political persuasion, Vietnamese intellectuals of the 1920s and 1930s were fascinated with news from overseas. Stories ranged from the bizarre (the existence of bearded women in Europe), to the gravest problems of war and peace."[48] Far from being a straightforward process of queer marginalization, these articles on bearded women also display a general attitude of wonder and curiosity—an attitude that beholds and questions the Other, even when "it" may, at first, baffle or defy comprehension.

L'écriture féminine? *Writing Female Masculinity*

Another group of articles debated the relationship between writing and the status of women. In 1932, the female writer Nguyễn Thị Kiêm proposed a strategy for women to lay claim to a literary world traditionally dominated by men. Kiêm points to the long history of "womanization" (*nữ hóa*) by male authors. She cites the case of Đông Hồ, whose best works depict a wife sobbing and lamenting, and Tản Đà, whose poetry assumes the voice of a female lover.[49] The author concludes that these gender-crossing practices are "good" for literary culture insofar as they enrich the multiple perspectives available. By the same token, if they were to aspire to write like men, women would have to "masculinize" themselves. In her proposal, Kiêm explains, "One recent revolution worth paying attention to within literary feminine circles is female masculinization (*la masculinisation*), that is, the phenomenon whereby women transform themselves into a man."[50]

But what might such a transformation entail? How would one go about doing so? Would it also take the form of cross-gender identification? The tone of the article is serious, not ironic. During this period, the literate readership would have been aware of European female authors who wrote under masculine pen names, including George Sand or George Eliot.[51] For Kiêm, the practice of female masculinization would require that women "sacrifice" (*hy sanh*), indeed abandon, their specific "Self" (*bổn ngã*) if they wanted to replace it with one that was characterized by "scientificity, philosophical tendency, objectivity."[52]

The author's proposal, then, reversed the cultural logic. By appropriating precisely men's rhetorical strategy, this female writer asserted that women, too, could be a man's equal. Implicit in such a conception is an affirmation of the so-called masculine intellect as opposed to the feminine body. Such an aspiration, though, reaches its limit: "However much they wish to masculinize themselves," Kiêm concludes, "women cannot do so completely due to their character [*cái bản sắc*]."[53] The term *bản sắc*, literally translated as "character," also implies something immanent or fundamental to one's identity. As a result, these "characters," Kiêm suggests, pose an obstacle to this gender-crossing practice insofar as they represent insuperable dimensions of female identity.

Kiêm's proposition was challenged by Phan Văn Hùm, a Trotskyite philosopher who had been educated in France. Hùm was a frequent contributor to the *New Women's News*, which featured many articles written by European thinkers.[54] In his response "The 'Masculinization' Literature," Hùm attributes whatever stylistic changes or lack thereof in women's writing not to some essential identity but to women's changing position in relation to society's material and historical circumstances. After a brief history of women's oppression, Hùm reasons that because women could engage more actively with men in the public sphere, they would "conduct themselves more like men and, hence, write more like men . . . indeed, exactly like men." Hùm concludes: "For this reason, women's writing that appears 'stronger' is not due to the masculinization phenomenon so much as the liberation of society."[55] The article does not make clear exactly how gendered conduct in the public sphere might correspond to writing practice, but it is apparent that, for Hùm, the gendered practice of writing ought to be located less in an immutable identity than in the changing historical conditions of society. This claim parallels Hùm's general effort to launch what Judith Henchy describes an "offensive against linguistic mystification," the interest in opposing the claims of "mystical fads" with "materialist theories."[56]

Pushing Hùm's reasoning further, would the moment of "liberation" imply that all of society be masculinized? Or does society reach a point at which the gender distinctions are eradicated altogether? Because Phan Văn Hùm later supported the abolition of the traditional nuclear family, this question is not unwarranted. He reasoned that people can survive without this social unit, which was a hindrance to social progress in part because it encouraged group self-interest: "Society does not need the family unit, and that it is the dialectical negation to society's progress" (*Vâng, tôi quả quyết rằng: xã hội không cần có gia đình và gia đình là cái biển chứng trở ngăn sự tiến bộ của xã hội*).[57] Hence, the idea of overcoming, in a Hegelian sense, the distinctions of the sexes seems to be one implication of Hùm's argument. Whatever the case, the views of Nguyễn Thị Kiêm and Phan Văn Hùm belong to a larger cultural contestation over the social roles and meanings of gender in the 1930s.

Gender Crossings in the Literary Imagination

Literary works published during this period also thematized the practice of gender crossing. Certain short stories, for example, casually exhibited characters who dressed up as the opposite gender. In the serialized detective thriller "To Die Twice" (*Chết Hai Lần*), one of the male characters is disguised as a woman to carry out various spy missions. The narrator states: "This young woman is, in fact, the beggar at the club. She is a man dressed up as either a woman or some other form, an investigator for the party."[58] The protagonist's absence throughout the covert operation leads many to consider him either missing or dead. His "second" death, the real one, takes place when his undercover identity is revealed. In the serialized novella "The Heroes of Tiêu Sơn" (Tiêu Sơn Tráng Sĩ),[59] Khái Hưng likewise provides an episode in which women dress up as men in the historical backdrop of the Tây Sơn wars. In their perilous mission across the countryside, one of the women is disguised as a monk and the other as a prince. In describing these characters, Khái Hưng captures the androgynous blending of masculine and feminine traits: "Although his countenance fell slightly short of that of the monk, the prince was still very handsome, with glistening phoenix eyes, semicircular eyebrows, with two pinkish white cheeks and with lips that curved into a charming smile. That is nothing unusual because the monk and the prince were none other than young women dressed in men's clothes."[60] The story takes place in the late eighteenth and early nineteenth centuries, and it is unclear whether the novella accurately reflects the sexual norms of that era. Nevertheless, one can reasonably claim that the ambiguity of the 1930s sexual discourse permitted—if not encouraged—Khái Hưng to include quite casually these gender-crossing characters.

The topos of gender crossing plays an even larger role in his piece *Butterfly Soul Dreaming of an Immortal* (*Hồn Bướm Mơ Tiên*) (fig. 4.3). As already recounted in this book's introduction, the story centers on the gender identity of

FIGURE 4.3. Cartoon of a scene from the novella *Butterfly Soul Dreaming of an Immortal*. At the Buddhist temple, the hero Ngọc speaks to Lan, a young woman who cross-dresses as a monk. *Phong Hóa* (Mores), December 2, 1932.

the protagonist Lan, a woman dressed as a monk at the Long Giáng temple, and her encounter with Ngọc, a young man from Hà Nội. Struck by Lan's "handsome" features, especially the fair skin and sweet voice, Ngọc is suspicious that Lan may in fact be a woman and so makes sexual overtures to force disclosure of her identity.

Although it is beyond the scope of this chapter to survey the story's critical reception, I wish to point out that the character of Lan embodies the fantasy that Nguyễn Thị Kiêm considered impossible. One could say that the practice of "gender crossing," as Kiêm understood it, is doubly realized. Khái Hưng, a male writer, writes about the experience of a woman who, in turn, impersonates a man. By changing her clothes and behavior, Lan transgresses the supposedly immutable limits of gender identity and consummates a public fantasy. The critic Vũ Ngọc Phan mentions that mostly young women made up Khái Hưng's readership.[61]

In their assimilation of the dominant cultural logic and desire for so-called male attributes, Kiêm and the heroine Lan, one could argue, remain unwittingly conservative in affirming the masculine pole of the gender dyad and, in so doing, reproduce the societal hierarchy of power. This conclusion, however, need not follow. Indeed, it derives from a slightly static notion of gender identity that presupposes power's immobility. Rather than dismiss these documents as evidence of mere assimilation, they could be interpreted in more dynamic ways. Kiêm and her desire to write like a "man," after all, may derive less from her envy to be one than from recognition of the power conferred on masculine gender. Or, alternatively, the desire to assume the opposite gender—a kind of transgender operation—can also be seen as liberating. Examining cultural debates concerning transsexuals, Judith Butler writes that the operation is not "necessarily to stay within the binary frame of gender, but to engage transformation itself as the meaning of gender." Echoing Simone de Beauvoir, Butler continues, "If one is not born a woman but rather becomes one, then becoming is the vehicle for gender itself."[62] In the case of Kiêm and the heroine Lan, becoming a man is the transformative occasion for gender itself. Regardless of which interpretation one seeks to defend, my point is to illustrate the remarkable preoccupation with gender plasticity. Perhaps because definitions of gender identity during this time were, more or less, undergoing contestation, there was a space for the play and semblance of gender and sexual constitution.

Half-Male, Half-Female and Other Gender Ambiguities

Another preoccupation in the Vietnamese popular press was with the figure of the hermaphrodite or androgyne. Like the articles on bearded women, these sources not only reflect an open-minded and curious attitude but also leap toward other kinds of abstract visions of society, most notably the ideals of social justice.

From the late 1920s through the mid-1930s, the androgyne figure was appropriated for various political ends, including, but not limited to, the women's emancipation movement. Speculating on humankind's androgynous origins, for example, one article reprinted a translated excerpt of Anatole France's *Histoire comique*. The writer states in the preface, "According to today's scientists, the ancestors of humankind were apes. Yet, in the narrative republished below, our origins can be traced to the *Androgynes*." In a footnote, the author explains, "Perhaps because the Androgyne is comprised of half-man and half-woman, the French call their wives *ma moité* because men come from the other half of the

Androgyne."[63] As with any myth, this one can be interpreted in a number of ways. In the cultural context of the times, the author was probably implying that, because men and women derive from the same androgyne figure, they ought to be granted the same kinds of political rights.

Other writers also propagated this theory because it provided a convenient rhetorical idiom for opposing certain patriarchal ideologies that reduced women's life purpose to reproduction. In another article, for instance, the author begins by acknowledging this patriarchal reproductive paradigm. In another theory, the writer states that women are not derivative of the "race of men," but belong along with men to another one—the "androgynous race." The ancestors of another male race created sexual difference by destroying that prior androgynous race. The writer explains, "One line of theory believes that women are not men's reproductive machines; long ago women came from the same race [as men] and that is why men's and women's bodies were previously not as different as they are today."[64] If the "origins" of people's bodies are the same, so the logic goes, the social inequality that "civilized men" have created for women is, therefore, contrary to this prelapsarian "Nature."

But if some writers were reaching to the past to justify the gender emancipation movement, others reached toward the future to achieve the same goals. The public had already been exposed to the androgyne figure in a number of venues: in an investigation about a "hermaphroditic" Buddhist nun; a special news series about the world's "strange" women; reports about hermaphroditic sea organisms; another piece on Russian experiments with autogenic eggs; an article on the existence of hermaphrodites in Vietnam's diverse animal world; frequent news coverage in the *Science Journal* (fig. 4.4); and, finally, a two-part series on the scientific classification of different human hermaphrodites.[65] As a result, some speculated whether advances in science and technology would someday turn everyone into androgynes.[66] That piece was a response to the findings by two German scientists, E. Wolff and A. Ginglinger, who, according to the Vietnamese article, found a mechanism to induce artificially the production of hermaphrodites. The article concludes, "Someday all of humanity will be able to transform into half-male and half-female." Imagining a world in which humankind would have no other worries except eating and working, the writer continues, "The latter species will have been liberated from the precariousness of Nature."[67]

FIGURE 4.4. Cover page of an edition of *Science Journal* (*Khoa Học Tạp Chí*). *Khoa Học Tạp Chí*, no. 2, July 16, 1931. Bibliothèque Nationale de France.

Although it is unclear how precisely the androgyne achieves this "liberation" and contributes to this utopia, the figure may embody a future in which society's gender distinctions and inequalities will have been eradicated. This interpretation is bolstered by the publication of the short story "A Philosophical Science Novel: Tomorrow." Serialized in fourteen parts, the story depicts the adventures of a protagonist by the name of Văn-Minh (Civilization), who finds himself suddenly in a futuristic Vietnam, in the year 2936, when the distinctions between the sexes are blurred. The narrator observes, "The reason [the protagonist] could not distinguish right away their gender is that they resembled men." He continues, "Minh suddenly encountered a group of people who were at once male and female . . . he realized that the women he saw previously . . . were her-maphrodites."[68] Throughout the story, Minh finds himself sexually attracted to one of the hermaphroditic figures, Thanh Hương. The latter, in turn, observes: "Long ago, society's belief in the two sexes, male and female, was mistaken in presuming that women were completely women, men completely men . . . the truth is otherwise. There are some women who are very women-like and there are those who aren't at all." S/he concludes, "Perhaps someday we shall produce people who are neither 'men nor women'" (*Có lẽ, một ngày kia chung tôi sẽ có thể tạo nên những người 'không nam mà không nữ'*).[69] The implications of this utopia are far reaching: not only are homo- and bisexual desires culturally viable options; they are also social markers to be transcended in order to abolish alto-gether the distinctions of the sexes and their accompanying inequalities.

Indeed, this latter idea departs in some ways from its European coun-terparts. In her study of the New Woman on the Continent, Carroll Smith-Rosenberg writes that this group reappropriated the sexual rhetoric of the medical establishment only to use that rhetoric against it. She explains, "This rhetoric represented New Women as social and sexual hermaphrodites, as an 'intermediate sex' that existed between and thus outside of the biological and social order." Smith-Rosenberg continues, "Investing male images with feminist meanings, they sought to use male myths to repudiate male power—to turn the male world upside down."[70] The inversion of the hierarchy is a strategy some Vietnamese may have adopted. But as the previous story suggests, others also envisioned perhaps an even more radical utopia. In that utopia, the hierarchy is neither simply inverted, producing effectively another hierarchy, nor conceived as "sex-blind," changing the ocular field but retaining sexual difference; rather, the differentiation of the sexes is abolished altogether—it is a "sex-less" society.[71]

Moreover, as the story indicates, the utopia has neither formal marriage nor the nuclear family. Rather, affective relationships are freely entered at will. Upon discovering this news, Minh cries, "What! You guys don't have families?" (*Sao! Các anh không có gia đình?*), to which the hermaphrodite Thanh Hương responds, "This society has also eliminated another custom of the previous cen-tury. When a woman wishes to live with her lover, the two simply take an oath with each other." Thanh Hương continues, "The two love each other and do not need formal vows."[72] Hence, in some ways, this story presents not only a radi-cal interrogation of gender emancipation but also a reconfiguration of society's fundamental kinship structures. This is not unlike Phan Văn Hùm's idea of the abolition of the nuclear family. In all cases, these androgyne documents lend further weight to the argument that a deep sense of sexual ambivalence was in the air.

Sex Changes and the Frontiers of Reproductive Science

Further evidence of sexual ambivalence comes from sources that thematize the question of animal and human sex changes. In Europe and elsewhere, the emerging field of endocrinology developed a new model that focused on gonadal secretions, chemicals emanating from the reproductive organs, as keys to sex determination.[73] Scientific experiments that manipulated the sex hormones abounded, and news of such experiments reached Vietnam. One of the earliest articles on this subject published in 1931 titled "Changing One Sexual Organ for Another" reported on the results of experiments by scientists, including Hunter, Berthold, Pézard, Morris, and Steinach. One outcome of these experiments, according to the Vietnamese article, is the identification of the functional role of the sex glands. When researchers inserted a "bag of eggs" into some castrated chickens, they were able to reproduce once again. More significantly, when Steinach placed the "bag of eggs" into a castrated cock, the latter suddenly started forming "female" characteristics—its "breasts enlarged and when it approached other cocks, it was sexually aroused" (*mà con đực nầy tự nhiên biến ra có tánh chất con cái; vú nó lớn ra, mà tới gần con đực khác, xem ra cũng động tình*).[74] To make this experiment more vivid to readers, at the center of the article is a picture of two chickens with the caption: "The two chickens before the reader are both grown cocks, each about 2 years of age. At first glance, the one on the left is, without a doubt, a hen. But strangely that is not the case. Previously it was a cock, just like the one on the right, except that scientists were able to insert a bag of eggs in it, and then it transformed its colors and feathers, and became a hen, just as it appears before the reader."[75] One has to wonder about the ease with which normative judgments are passed off as unadulterated, "scientific" fact in performing these kinds of experiments, or the degree to which the writer has projected his or her own anthropomorphic anxieties onto the vagaries of the animal world, much the same way as, according to some scholars, contemporary reproductive science has created a heterosexual "romance" between the egg and sperm.[76] At any rate, despite the male-to-female sex opera-

tion on the animals in question, the overall response of this writer parallels that
of the bearded women and androgyne documents in her curious wonder about
science's unknown potential. Consider the way the author opens by asking,
"Today people now have a way of exchanging the . . . reproductive organs of one
species for another; able to make the elderly look young; perhaps one day people
will be able to find the elixir of life?" In the conclusion, the writer acknowledges
the disbelief of some readers: "Many people today may be skeptical, but not the
Euro-American scientists and the heights of their imagination."[77] Of course,
we now know that since Francis Bacon's seventeenth-century publication of
the *Novum Organum*, science's ability to master nature's role in the twentieth
century has led to far more ominous outcomes.[78] In the context of this passage
and its cultural milieu, however, the writer demonstrates an unusual receptivity
toward science's infinite potential to plumb the depths of the unknown and
reach the heights of the imagination—including, but not limited to, the search
for immortality. Once again, optimism and curiosity remain at the forefront.

Consider another piece on the strange case of a Chinese man who was reportedly capable of giving birth. Like the prior article, this one exhibits the
same attitude of openness to news of unusual events in the natural world. A
twenty-three-year-old young man by the name of Lin-A-li in the region of Yuen-
Tso-wei in the Guangdong province of southwestern China gave birth to a baby
boy.[79] As the article acknowledges, many locals in the province were, at first,
skeptical. Some readers today, in fact, may dismiss this story as impossible. The
"laws" of nature cannot be changed. But as Thomas Laqueur has demonstrated,
in the human sciences, unlike mathematics, so-called nature and laws are pro-
cessed through a historical and cultural grid often unbeknownst to the agent
of interpretation.[80] Or, alternatively, the lulling effects of an increasingly standardized society can foreclose the imaginings of other subcultural lives and biological variation. In our present time, this kind of story is not as far-fetched if
assuming that the "man" in question is transgendered.[81] In Vietnam during this
period, the journal *These Days* also published a cartoon of a pregnant man. The
caption reads: "Oh! Who Says Men Cannot Give Birth!"[82] Regarding the article
in question, my point is that this unusual news item caught the imagination of a
Vietnamese reporter. The anonymous writer states: "What a strange news story,
something that has been unheard of; since time immemorial, reproduction has
been a function that Nature has left to the female species. Yet, today we have

the story of a man who can give birth. How very odd!"[83] Once again, the writer may find the story "unusual," "odd," or even spectacular, but the writer in no way employs a pathologizing or criminalizing rhetoric. Whatever kind of queer effect the text may produce, unintentional or not, is tempered by a moment of humility and awe in a cultural milieu in which scientific innovation challenged conventional truths and, in so doing, brought about a crisis of knowledge and norms.

A cluster of other articles captures this same attitude of humility. One news item reported on the story of "Henriette Acces," who transformed into a man.[84] Another speculated on science's ability someday to allow people to undergo this process at will.[85] Yet another attempted to account for the makeup of human gender through Pézard's chicken sex-swapping experiments.[86] Later, another continued the discussion of these experiments and made mention of Dr. Magnus Hirschfeld's taxonomy of human sexuality.[87] Another narrated the adventures of Maryse Choisy, who disguised herself as a man to investigate an all-male Greek island.[88] One discussed the effects of hormones used to manipulate the sex determination of chickens, and another provided a front-page picture followed by an in-depth report of a Ms. "Zdeneck Konbek," who transformed into a man.[89] One article reported on the case of a German father who raised his daughter as a boy, his boy as a daughter, and each behaved according to the gender norms in which he and she were raised, respectively.[90] Yet another reported on an Italian family of boys who transformed into girls.[91] This list provides a mere sample of news items that unsettled fixed ideas about sex and gender.

Indeed, as late as 1937, despite the bevy of articles already published on this subject, the editors of *These Days* republished and translated a French article from the Parisian magazine *Lu et vu* concerning, once again, the possibility of sex-change operations in chickens. The article then asked whether this change was possible in human beings and concluded that sex operations were the frontier of reproductive science.[92] These documents serve to reinforce the palpable belief in the plasticity of gender, the body, and the latter's unknown possibilities.

CONCLUSION

In this chapter I have argued that in the 1930s the cultural discourse in Vietnam imagined the gendered and sexual body to be far more dynamic than has been supposed. This was a period that witnessed the emergence of a younger cohort of intellectuals. This younger generation signified a rupture with the prior generation in their relative amnesia about the East Asian cultural past, a direct consequence of the French's deliberate effacement of the Confucian imperial exams and replacement by a Franco-Annamite educational system. At the same time, this new system facilitated the younger generation's proficiency in the French language and access to European ideas. The Vietnamese exposure to these ideas contributed to an expansion of the normative limits of the gendered and sexual body.

Whereas scholars have tended to locate this period as the genesis of the modern Vietnamese women's liberation movement, they give short shrift to the historical articulation of the textured meaning of gender itself. As a result, they have plotted a narrative that collapses the history of gender emancipation to that of heterosexual dimorphism, submerging in the process other histories that reveal a far more complex meaning of gender. From stories about changes in bodily dress, such as the donning of lipsticks and trimming of hair; reports of women who possessed beards and women who attempted to undertake "masculine" writing; cases of cross-dressing in literary works and hermaphrodites who embodied a transcendence of sexual dimorphism; to accounts of sex changes and the unknown frontiers of reproductive science, these documents all lend interpretive weight to the claim that Vietnamese culture imagined the gendered and sexual body to be open to different modalities of becoming.

CONCLUSION

THIS STUDY HAS RECUPERATED THE history of variant genders and sexualities in Vietnam's early twentieth century (1920–1945) to argue that queerness was central to this dynamic period. Rather than delegitimize and stigmatize these diverse subjects, the period embraced a capacious conception of sex, gender, and desire that presupposed the dynamic plasticity of the human body. In reconstructing this history, *Queer Vietnam* problematizes any universal claim to a heteronormative version of the Vietnamese cultural past and insists that any understanding of the question of variant genders and sexualities in contemporary Vietnam would be incomplete without acknowledgment of this other gender history.

Even though Vietnam studies scholars have made substantial headway in reconstructing the cultural history of the interwar period, the queer dimensions of this period have been forgotten or overlooked and, hence, effectively erased from the historical record until now. The bulk of the scholarship has focused on themes related to Vietnam's transition from Sino-Vietnamese tradition to French colonial modernity and the social, literary, or political consequences of that tectonic shift. To the extent that gender is the focus, the current scholarship has collapsed the history of gender into that of heteronormative dimorphism. In so doing, current histories of the period have been founded on the exclusion of the "queer," subjects who depart from this gendered and sexual regime.

The study has shown that understanding the subject beyond a heteronormative notion of sex/gender allows us to account for subjects that we might otherwise overlook if we were to merely assume the sexed and gendered body within a contemporary heteronormative frame. Whether we look at sources that advocate a return to Confucian "tradition" or insist on the embrace of the "modern," queer subjects populate both sides of the putative temporal divide. In challenging contemporary scholarship's heteronormative assumptions, *Queer Vietnam* brings back alternative forms of gendered and sexual personhood into the analysis.

As already demonstrated, the first chapter provides the historical context to argue that Vietnam's interwar period evinced a cultural pluralism, whereby Sino-Vietnamese, Southeast Asian, and Western scientific paradigms coexisted and, at times intersected and competed with each other, but where the Western model had not yet achieved cultural hegemony. To demonstrate this claim, chapter 1 looked at, respectively, the realms of tradition, language, and practice. In the realm of tradition, Sino-Vietnamese and Southeast Asian conceptions of sex, gender, and desire continued to exert a powerful influence on Vietnamese culture. In the realm of language, today's Vietnamese term for "sex" and/or "gender" (*giới tính*) did not exist in this period. Instead, Vietnamese writers employed a wide variety of different vocabularies to designate the varied sedimented meanings of "sex" that the modern term has absorbed, condensed, and reduced. Finally, in the realm of practice, the chapter looked at the case of male sodomy to show that its meaning was linked less to a coherent homosexual identity, a key conceit of the modern sexological paradigm, than to the period's increasing cultural pluralism. Taken together, chapter 1 establishes the cultural and historical mise-en-scène.

Accordingly, chapters 2 and 3 illustrated an instance of the gender pluralism that characterized Vietnam's interwar period. Chapter 2 reconstructed the plural forms of genders, desires, relations, and practices of, by, and between men that are not tantamount to a homosexual identity. Analysis included the masculine figure of the eunuch mandarin, the feminine man who desired women, female impersonation by male poets, and the discourse of male friendship. The chapter concluded with a case study of a scandal that exploded in the print public sphere involving a man who cross-dressed as a nun. Besides showing the limits of gender transgression, the case drives home the persistent separation between gender crossing and male homosexual identity. Chapter 3 looked at early twentieth-century translations of premodern stories of women who cross-dressed as men or who performed masculinity, what the study has called the persistence of the classical trope of gender transgression. This trope reveals that women in premodern Vietnam and East Asia could, in certain instances, turn the tables on the patriarchal system by exploiting its breaking points. In so doing, they succeeded in enjoying, however provisionally, the benefits conferred on the masculine gender. In the early twentieth century, some Vietnamese drew on this classical gender-crossing trope to justify their claims to support the modern women's emancipation movement.

Chapter 4 reconstructs the new bodies and genders that exploded in the Vietnamese print public sphere of the time and, by extension, the cultural imagination. Occasioned, in part, by the return of a younger generation of Vietnamese youth educated abroad in France as well as political shifts transpiring in Europe and elsewhere, these new bodies and genders exceeded a heteronormative frame, pointing to novel, even utopian, forms of kinship arrangements and societal relationality.

The recovery of this archive opens up new critical conversations for the study of both Vietnam and queer Asia. With respect to Vietnam, the study's findings complicate some of the fundamental critical terms that scholars routinely rely on in their investigation of the Vietnamese past, namely "sex" and/or "gender." The fact that the contemporary term for "sex/gender" was not yet in use in this earlier period of Vietnam's history reveals the extent of its historical alterity. In bringing that alterity into stark relief, *Queer Vietnam* shines a light on the simultaneous strangeness of the contemporary heteronormative regime itself. This is a regime that is historically singular but has assumed the status of timelessness and universality.

In light of this historical insight, one is compelled to ask, What other narratives, subjectivities, and lifeworlds have, in effect, been suppressed or rendered invisible? Far from being comprehensive, this study has raised ideas, questions, and historical puzzles that serve as only the beginning of the ongoing and complex work of excavating Vietnam's "queer" past.

With respect to the vibrant corpus of scholarship on queer Asia, the study's findings depart from some of the current conclusions about the Asian region. Current scholarship on gender and sexuality has shown that the paradigm of nineteenth-century European sexual science, which contributed to the heteronormative regime that persists to this day, circulated the globe to penetrate parts of East Asia, particularly Meiji Japan and Republican China. Despite sexology's powerful influence in these areas, the same does not hold for Vietnam during the interwar period. While the discourse of sexology was certainly already underway, it had not yet achieved cultural hegemony. The study's findings, therefore, serve as the basis for the comparative study of queer Asia, demonstrating the uneven circulation of sexology's modernizing impulses in one corner of the Asian region in the early twentieth century.

Finally, *Queer Vietnam* has practical implications. Although it does not offer specific prescriptions, the study's findings can inform activism. In the late twentieth century and early twenty-first, several developments suggest that a thoughtful reflection on Vietnam's past may prove useful. One crucial development in Vietnam is the myth of a certain state-sponsored version of nationalist "tradition." According to this myth, before the arrival of the global LGBT movement, countries like Vietnam were strait-laced heterosexual countries in which gender and sexually variant subjects were imports from the West.

In the case of Vietnam, this myth surfaced amid the vociferous debates concerning the formal recognition of same-sex marriage. In a media appearance, Vietnam's Justice Ministry announced in 2012 that the state would consider legalizing same-sex marriage. A ministry spokesman gave an overview of the growing acceptance of same-sex marriages across the globe. Without outright declaring support for same-sex marriage, the spokesman implied that Vietnam ought to emulate other nation-states, in what appears to be a growing international norm.

In the wake of the announcement, nongovernmental organizations, civil society groups, and activists began to mobilize campaigns in support of the proposed measure. Vietnam held its first gay pride parade in Hà Nội and Ho Chi Minh City. An award-winning photo exhibit the "Pink Way" showcased the everyday lives of Vietnamese gays and lesbians. Flash mobs formed with young Vietnamese proudly displaying sticker slogans, such as "I love LGBT."

After approximately two years of debate, Vietnam ultimately decided against legalizing same-sex marriage. The reason for the decision was to preserve Vietnam's "fine cultural traditions." In fact, the revised Law on Marriage and the Family of 2014 opens with an explicit declaration of this assertion. Article 2, "Fundamental Principles of the Marriage and Family Regime," indicates that one of the key principles of marriage is to "perpetuate and promote the Viet-namese nation's fine cultural traditions and ethics on marriage and family."[1]

This declaration had been absent in all other family and marriage laws since their institution in 1959.[2] From a certain perspective, then, the state may have used the possibility of legalizing same-sex marriage to achieve some other po-litical end, such as the entry into the UN Human Rights Council, which it achieved, without having intended to grant such rights in the first place. Con-trary to displaying a moment of international liberal progressivism, the Viet-namese state flexed its muscle to inscribe into the nation's solemn laws the norms of heterosexuality.

Certain well-known concepts circulating within queer scholarship—such as homonationalism—cannot fully explain the Vietnamese case. According to the homonationalism thesis, some nation-states exploit gay and lesbian sub-jects as political instruments for racist and xenophobic ends. More specifically, homonationalism is a biopolitical regime that folds proper gays and lesbian sub-jects into the nationalist discourse at the expense of racialized others. The idea of homonationalism has caught traction long after and beyond the moment of its theorization. Yet while important in explaining a phenomenon that devel-oped in the West in the aftermath of the US War on Terror, the idea of homon-ationalism cannot be taken for granted as a theory with universal explanatory power. This is even more so in the case of Vietnam, which, after much public debate, decided not to legalize same-sex marriage and appears to have moved in the opposite direction, forming what we might call heteronationalism.

Yet the Vietnamese government's refusal to recognize same-sex marriage to preserve Vietnam's "fine cultural traditions" lacks historical grounding. If one understands "tradition" in the conventional sense of a long-established custom, then the historical singularity of the contemporary heteronormative paradigm reveals the lie in any such claim of enduring cultural continuity. It is not just that same-sex marriage, itself a modern practice, might not have belonged to the Vietnamese cultural past—nor did "heterosexuality" and its accompanying norms. The dominant form of kinship in Sino-Vietnamese tradition was based on a radically different paradigm: arranged marriages, polygamy, emperors, and concubines are certainly not what the present government has in mind. Like-wise, women who cross-dress as men or who perform masculinity are likely to be equally, if not even more, scandalous. The recuperation of the history of variant genders and sexualities in Vietnam can loosen the epistemological stranglehold of certain heteronormative versions of nationalistic "tradition." It can furnish a critical perspective on the current moment by providing grounded empirical responses to what has otherwise been an argumentative deadlock. Ultimately, in reconstructing a time when "queerness" was an integral element of Vietnamese culture, *Queer Vietnam* invites its readers to imagine what Vietnam once was and could become.

NOTES

Introduction

1. Khái Hưng, "Hồn Bướm Mơ Tiên" [Butterfly Soul Dreaming of an Immortal], *Phong Hóa* [*Mores*] (Hà Nội), November 4, 1932, 12. Henceforth, all translations unless otherwise noted are mine. The original quotation: "Quái lạ! Sao ở vùng nhà quê lại có người đẹp trai đến thế, nước da trắng mát, tiếng nói dịu dàng, trong trẻo như tiếng con gái."

2. Khái Hưng, "Hồn Bướm Mơ Tiên" [Butterfly Soul Dreaming of an Immortal], *Phong Hóa* [*Mores*] (Hà Nội), January 6, 1933, 3.

3. For more on the *Mores* journal, the Self-Reliant Literary Group, and its modernizing project, see Martina T. Nguyễn, *On Our Own Strength: The Self-Reliant Literary Group and Cosmopolitan Nationalism in Late Colonial Vietnam* (Honolulu: University of Hawai'i, 2021), 1–14.

4. On stylistic innovations, see Hà Minh Đức, preface to *Tổng Tập Văn Học Việt Nam* [*General Collection of Vietnamese Literature*], ed. Hà Minh Đức (Hà Nội: Nhà Xuất Bản Khoa Học Xã Hội, 2000), 12–13; Nhất Linh, preface to *Tổng Tập Văn Học Việt Nam* [*General Collection of Vietnamese Literature*], ed. Hà Minh Đức (1933; Hà Nội: Nhà Xuất Bản Khoa Học Xã Hội, 2000), 23. On its antecedents, the scholar Phan Cự Đệ has proffered three classical sources from which Khái Hưng may have adapted his thematic storyline, one of which is the premodern tale of the Bodhisattva of Mercy. Phan Cự Đệ, "Tự Lực Văn Đoàn" [The Self-Reliant Literary Group], in *Tự Lực Văn Đoàn: Trào Lưu—Tác Giả* [*The Self-Reliant Literary Group: Movement and Authors*], ed. Hà Minh Đức (Huế: Nhà Xuất Bản Giáo Dục, 2007), 470.

5. This synopsis is based on the late nineteenth-century versions written in *nôm*, the Vietnamese demotic script, on which early twentieth-century translations are based. According to Nguyễn Đình Hòa, the scene in which the heroine cross-dresses as a monk also appears in eighteenth-century verse. The figure of the female Boddhisatva of Mercy can be traced back even earlier, as the story had been popularized since the sixteenth century in theatrical

performances. See Maurice Durand, "Truyện Quan Âm Thị Kính (觀音氏敬)" [The Story of Kuan Yin], in *Thế Giới Của Truyện Nôm* [*The Universe of Nom Stories*], ed. Olivier Tessier (Ho Chi Minh City: Nhà Xuất Bản Tổng Hợp Thành Phố Hồ Chí Minh, 2022), 212–22; Nguyễn Đinh Hòa, *Vietnamese Literature: A Brief Survey* (San Diego, CA: San Diego State University, 1994), 97–99; George E. Dutton, Jayne S. Werner, and John K. Whitmore, eds., *The Child-Giving Guanyin (Sixteenth-Seventeenth Century)*, Sources of Vietnamese Tradition (New York: Columbia University Press, 2012), 180–86. For the Chinese versions, see Chün-fang Yü, *Kuan-yin: The Chinese Transformation of Avalokiteśvara* (New York: Columbia University Press, 2001), 293–94.

6. For more on the tale's early twentieth-century translation into the modern vernacular, see "Quan Âm Thị Kính," in *Tổng Tập Văn Học Việt Nam* [*General Collection of Vietnamese Literature*], ed. Lê Văn Quán (Hà Nội: Nhà Xuất Bản Khoa Học Xã Hội, 1993), 425–27.

7. Of course, the stories differ in significant ways. The identities and actions of the temple visitors are different. Whereas the Buddhist tale was written in verse, Khái Hưng wrote in novelistic form. Finally, the eighteenth-century popular narrative emphasizes the triumph of moral righteousness. According to the critic Nguyễn Đinh Hòa, Thị Kính's "true" gender ultimately serves to reveal her innocence. In contrast, according to the critic Vũ Ngọc Phan, Hưng's novella demonstrates the impossibility of romantic love. See Hòa, *Vietnamese Literature: A Brief Survey*, 99; Vũ Ngọc Phan, "Khái Hưng," in *Nhà Văn Hiện Đại: Phê Bình Văn Học* [*Contemporary Writers: Literary Criticism*] (1940; Sài Gòn: Nhà Xuất Bản Thăng Long, 1959), 828–29.

8. See, e.g., Vern L. Bullough and Bonnie Bullough, *Cross Dressing, Sex, and Gender* (Philadelphia: University of Pennsylvania, 1993), viii.

9. On the economic conditions, see Pierre Brocheux and Daniel Hémery, *Indochina: An Ambiguous Colonization, 1858–1954* (Berkeley: University of California, 2009), 116–180. On the emergence of science, see C. Michele Thompson, "Indochina," in *The Cambridge History of Science: Modern Science in National, Transnational, and Global Context*, ed. Hugh Richard Slotten, Ronald L. Numbers, and David N. Livingstone (Cambridge: Cambridge University Press, 2020), 593–608. On the overall colonial context, see David G. Marr, *Vietnamese Tradition on Trial, 1925–1945* (Berkeley: University of California, 1981).

10. The burgeoning scholarship on "queer Asia" is too vast to cite comprehensively here. Notable works include Howard Chiang, *After Eunuchs: Science, Medicine, and the Transformation of Sex in Modern China* (New York: Columbia University Press, 2018); Audrey Yue, "Queer Singapore: A Critical Introduction," in *Queer Singapore: Illiberal Citienzship and Mediated Cultures*, ed. Audrey Yue and June Zubillaga-Pow (Hong Kong: Hong Kong University Press, 2012); Evelyn Blackwood and Mark Johnson, "Queer Asian Subjects: Transgressive Sexualities and Heteronormative Meanings," *Asian Studies Review* 36, no. 4 (2012). On narrowing acceptable practices, see Tamara Loos, "Transnational Histories of Sexualities in Asia," *American Historical Review* 114, no. 5 (2009).

11. One task of critical historiography is to trace the lines of normative continuity—the social norms that appear seamlessly smooth and straight, much like a thick electrical power cord densely packed together—to its chronological and epistemological limit point. At this limit point, the electrical cord reveals its frayed ends. The ends that were once flattened, straightened, normalized can then appear as distinct elements in their sheer plurality. Like-

wise, at this limit point, the social structures that insist on heteronormative ways of being rupture, thereby relinquishing other subjects of history, other ways in which those of the past have lived. In such a history, we observe subjects for whom the categories of sex, gender, desire, and sexuality are not aligned according to heterosexual norms but dislocated in rather strange, indeed, "queer," ways. The value in reconstructing such a history is to illuminate for us other ways of being and becoming and, ultimately, to recognize the contingency of how we organize gender and sexuality. On the task of critical historiography, see Michel Foucault, "Nietzsche, Genealogy and History," in *Aesthetics, Method, and Epistemology*, ed. James D. Faubion, *Essential Works of Foucault, 1954–1984* (New York: New Press, 1998), 369–91; Joan W. Scott, "After History?," in *Schools of Thought: Twenty-Five Years of Interpretive Social Science*, ed. Joan W. Scott and Debra Keates (Princeton, NJ: Princeton University Press 2001), 98–99.

12. Georges Bataille, *Eroticism: Death and Sensuality*, trans. Mary Dalwood (1957; San Francisco: City Light Books, 1986), 68.

13. Bataille develops his notion of the general economy, which, unlike utilitarian models, is characterized by an expenditure without return, a "play of energy that no end limits." See Georges Bataille, *The Accursed Share: An Essay on General Economy*, trans. Robert Hurley, 3 vols. (New York: Zone Books, 1991), 1:9–77, at 1:23.

14. Regarding biological sex, scholars have questioned the extent to which sex, understood as the raw matter of nature, may already be acted on by culture, and hence sex may already be a form of gender. The issue is not that there is no nature but that "nature" may, in fact, admit more than the binary sexes that certain cultural ideologies demand. For a presentation of the problem, see David Halperin, "Sex/Sexuality/Sexual Classification," in *Critical Terms for the Study of Gender*, ed. Catharine R. Stimpson and Gilbert Herdt (Chicago: University of Chicago Press, 2014), 449–86. On the subtitle and its reflections, in this respect, the term "queer" also shares an intimate kinship with the burgeoning field of transgender studies, according to which a critique of heteronormativity need not be reduced to same-sex object choice as the sole or fundamental axis of difference. See Susan Stryker, "(De)subjugated Knowledges: An Introduction to Transgender Studies," in *The Transgender Studies Reader*, ed. Susan Stryker and Stephen Whittle (London: New York, 2006), 7.

15. This is one viable approach that Howard Chiang astutely proposes in the study of "transgender China." See Howard Chiang, "Imagining Transgender China," in *Transgender China*, ed. Howard Chiang (New York: Palgrave Macmillan, 2012), 3–19.

16. Christopher Goscha, *Vietnam: A New History* (New York: Basic Books, 2016), 41–44.

17. Goscha, *New History*, 49; Keith W. Taylor, *A History of the Vietnamese* (Cambridge: Cambridge University Press, 2013), 398; Li Tana, *Nguyễn Cochinchina: Southern Vietnam in the Seventeenth and Eighteenth Centuries* (Ithaca, NY: Cornell Southeast Asia Program Publications, 1998).

18. See, e.g., Goscha, *New History*, 32; Taylor, *A History of the Vietnamese*, 218–23; Tana, *Nguyễn Cochinchina: Southern Vietnam in the Seventeenth and Eighteenth Centuries*, 102–3; David Biggs, *Footprints of War: Militarized Landscapes in Vietnam* (Seattle: University of Washington Press, 2018), 23–26; William B. Noseworthy and Van Son Quang, "A View of Champā Sites in Phú Yên Province, Vietnam: Toward a Longue Durée of Socio-Religious Context," *Religion* 13, no. 7 (2022).

19. Alexander Woodside, *Vietnam and the Chinese Model: A Comparative Study of the Nguyễn and Ching Civil Government in the First Half of the Nineteenth Century* (Cambridge, MA: Harvard University Press, 1971), 13–14.

20. On the making of French Indochina, see Brocheux and Hémery, *Indochina*, 15–69; Goscha, *New History*, 73–93.

21. Defined as the space located below the state but above the city or village wherein individuals engage in symbolic exchange and contestation, the "public sphere" is a term coined by Jürgen Habermas in the context of Europe in the seventeenth and eighteenth centuries. Shawn McHale argues it can be applied, with modifications, to the years 1920–1945 in Vietnam. See Shawn McHale, *Print and Power: Confucianism, Communism and Buddhism in the Making of Modern Vietnam* (Honolulu: University of Hawai'i Press, 2004), 7.

22. McHale, *Print and Power*, 18.

23. McHale, 26.

24. For a study of the south's journalistic culture, see Philippe Peycam, *The Birth of Vietnamese Political Journalism: Sài Gòn, 1916–1930* (New York: Columbia University Press, 2012).

25. McHale, *Print and Power*, 8.

26. Peter Zinoman, ed., *Dumb Luck: A Novel by Vu Trong Phung* (Ann Arbor: University of Michigan Press, 2002), 4.

27. Hoài Thanh and Hoài Chân, "Một Thời-Đại Trong Thi Ca" [A Period of Poetry], in *Thi Nhân Việt-Nam* [*Vietnamese Poets*] (1942; Sài Gòn: Nhà Xuất Bản Hoa Tiến, 1968), 43.

28. Thanh and Chân, "Một Thời-Đại Trong Thi Ca," 11.

29. See Howard Chiang, "Deciphering Desire," in *After Eunuchs: Science, Medicine, and the Transformation of Sex in Modern China* (New York: Columbia University Press, 2018), 125–77; Gregory M. Pflugfelder, *Cartographies of Desire: Male-Male Sexuality in Japanese Discourse, 1600–1950* (Berkeley: University of California Press, 1999), 235–85. For sexology's global spread, see Veronika Fuechtner, Douglas E. Haynes, and Ryan M. Jones, "Introduction: Toward a Global History of Sexual Science: Movements, Networks, and Deployments," in *A Global History of Sexual Science, 1880–1960* (Oakland: University of California Press, 2018), 1–26; Paolo Ben, "Global Modernity and Sexual Science: The Case of Male Homosexuality and Female Prostitution, 1850–1950," in *A Global History of Sexual Science, 1880–1960*, ed. Veronika Fuechtner, Douglas E. Haynes, and Ryan M. Jones (Oakland: University of California Press, 2018); Chiang, *After Eunuchs*.

30. See my article: Richard Quang-Anh Tran, "An Epistemology of Gender: Historical Notes on the Homosexual Body in Contemporary Vietnam, 1986–2005," *Journal of Vietnamese Studies* 9, no. 2 (2014).

31. Pastreich observes that the success of the dissemination of Sinitic fiction in Vietnam depended, ironically, on the adoption of the romanized alphabet. Emanuel Pastreich, "The Reception of Chinese Literature in Vietnam," in *The Columbia History of Chinese Literature*, ed. Victor H. Mair (New York: Columbia University Press, 2001), 1102–3.

32. Cultures, it must be emphasized, are formed through translation. This is so even for nations today like China that propagate an image of homogeneity and monolingualism that are, in fact, consequences of modern nation building projects in translating diverse regional dialects into a standardized language. See Dagmar Schäfer, "Translation History, Knowl-

edge and Nation Building in China," in *The Routledge Handbook of Translation and Culture*, ed. Sue-Ann Harding and Ovidi Carbonell Cortés (London: Routledge, 2018), 134–53; Jeffrey Weng, "What Is Mandarin? The Social Project of Language Standardization in Early Republican China," *Journal of Asian Studies* 77, no. 3 (August 2018). For the notion that translation is a process of epistemic negotiation and innovation, see William J. Spurlin, "The Gender and Queer Politics of Translation: New Approaches," *Comparative Literature Studies* 51, no. 2 (2014).

33. The novel on which *The Tale of Kiều* is based is *Jin Yun Qiao zhuan* (金雲翹傳; The Story of Jin, Yun, and Qiao), by Qingxin cairen (青心才人). See Paola Zamperini, *Lost Bodies: Prostitution and Masculinity in Chinese Fiction*, Women and Gender in China Studies (Leiden: Brill Publishers, 2010), 13–14; Huỳnh Sanh Thông, introduction to *The Tale of Kiều: A Bilingual Edition* (New Haven, CT: Yale University Press, 1983), xx–xxi.

34. Peter Zinoman, "Vũ Trọng Phụng's *Dumb Luck* and the Nature of Vietnamese Modernism," in *Dumb Luck* (Ann Arbor: University of Michigan Press, 2002), 4.

35. See also my article on colonial Vietnamese urban reportages: Richard Quang-Anh Tran, "Sex in the City: The Descent from Human to Animal in Two Vietnamese Classics of Urban Reportage," *International Quarterly of Asian Studies* 50, nos. 3–4 (2020).

36. Mary Louise Roberts, *Civilization without Sexes: Reconstructing Gender in Postwar France, 1917–1927*, ed. Catharine R. Stimpson, Women in Culture and Society (Chicago: University of Chicago, 1994), 4. See also Carolyn J. Dean, *The Frail Social Body: Pornography, Homosexuality, and Other Fantasies in Interwar France* (Berkeley: University of California, 2000), 101–2.

37. See, for example, the book and related film by Andrea Weiss, *Paris Was a Woman: Portraits from the Left Bank* (San Francisco: Harper San Francisco, 1995). See also Shari Benstock's study of American and English expatriate women in Paris challenging patriarchal norms: *Women of the Left Bank: Paris, 1900–1940* (Austin: University of Texas Press, 1986).

38. See *Từ Điển Tiếng Việt* [Vietnamese Dictionary] (Hà Nội: Nhà Xuất Bản Văn Hóa Thông Tin, 2005), 874.

39. Michel Foucault, *History of Sexuality* (New York: Vintage Books, 1990), 1:101.

40. Marr, *Vietnamese Tradition on Trial, 1925–1945*, 2.

41. Martina Thục Nhi Nguyễn, "Wearing the Nation," in *On Our Own Strength: The Self-Reliant Literary Group and Cosmopolitan Nationalism in Late Colonial Vietnam* (Honolulu: University of Hawaiʻi), 79–114; Ben Tran, *Post-mandarin: Masculinity and Aesthetic Modernity in Colonial Vietnam* (New York: Fordham University Press, 2017), 4–5.

42. Ben Tran, "Queer Internationalism and Modern Vietnamese Aesthetics," in *Post-Mandarin: Masculinity and Aesthetic Modernity in Colonial Vietnam* (New York: Fordham University Press, 2017), 105–18.

43. Nguyễn Quốc Vinh, "Deviant Bodies and Dynamics of Displacement of Homoerotic Desire in Vietnamese Literature from and about the French Colonial Period (1858–1954)," 1997, http://www.talawas.org/talaDB/suche.php?res=1056&rb=0503&von=.

44. See, for example, the denunciation by the May Fourth intellectuals against an older, more "traditional" cohort of 1910 writers. Perry Link, *The Uses of Literature: Life in the Socialist Chinese Literary System* (Princeton, NJ: Princeton University Press, 2000), 177–78.

Chapter 1

1. Hữu Sào, "Bà Đồng" [Female Spirit Medium], *Khoa Học Tạp Chí* [*Science Journal*] 215 (June 1, 1939).

2. See C. Michele Thompson, "Indochina," in *The Cambridge History of Science: Modern Science in National, Transnational, and Global Context*, ed. Hugh Richard Slotten, Ronald L. Numbers, and David N. Livingstone (Cambridge: Cambridge University Press, 2020), 593–608.

3. Dror notes that the cult of Liễu Hạnh is allegedly to have originated sometime in the sixteenth century, but evidence of the pantheon came afterward in the late seventeenth and early eighteenth century. See Olga Dror, *Cult, Culture and Authority: Princess Lieu Hanh in Vietnamese History* (Honolulu: University of Hawai'i Press, 2007), 73–74. Nguyễn Văn Huyên noted circa 1945 that the cult was "widespread" with many women devotees. A colonial-era reportage also notes that popular religious pilgrimages, of which spirit medium rituals played a part, were frequented by "thousands of women" (*hàng nghìn người đàn bà*). Historical and anthropological studies repeatedly show that women are the chief demographic officiants and followers. See Nguyễn Văn Huyên, *The Ancient Civilization of Vietnam* (1945; Hà Nội: Thế Giới Publishers, 1995), 257; Nguyễn Văn Vĩnh, "Hương Sơn Hành Trình" [A Journey to Hương Sơn Temple], in *Hầu Thánh* [*Serving the Spirits*] (1914; Hà Nội: Nhà Xuất Bản Văn Hóa Thông Tin, 2002), 256–59; Thien Do, *Vietnamese Supernaturalism: Views from the Southern Region* (London: Routledge Curzon, 2003), 100; Claire Chauvet, "Changing Spirit Identities: Rethinking Four Palaces' Spirit Representation in Northern Vietnam," in *Engaging the Spirit World: Popular Beliefs and Practices in Modern Southeast Asia*, ed. Kirsten W. Endres and Andrea Lauser (New York: Berghahn Books, 2011), 87; Philip Taylor, *Goddess on the Rise: Pilgrimage and Popular Religion in Vietnam* (Honolulu: University of Hawai'i Press, 2004), viii.

4. Barbara Watson Andaya, *The Flaming Womb: Repositioning Women in Early Modern Southeast Asia* (Honolulu University of Hawai'i Press, 2006), 21–24.

5. On the French colonialists, see Barley Norton, *Song for the Spirits: Music and Mediums in Modern Vietnam* (Urbana: University of Illinois Press, 2009), 23–24. In the early twentieth century, the literatus Phan Kế Bính denounced spirit mediumship as "superstitious" (*mê tín*). See Phan Kế Bính, *Việt-Nam phong-tục* [*Vietnamese Customs*] (Sài Gòn: Nhà sách Khai Trí, 1973), 341–42. For more on the attitudes of the indigenous elite to popular religion, see Dror, *Cult, Culture and Authority*, 165–68; Oscar Salemink, "Spirit Worship and Possession in Vietnam and Beyond," in *Routledge Handbook of Religions in Asia*, ed. Brian S. Turner and Oscar Salemink (New York: Routledge, 2014), 232–33.

6. Scholars have problematized the reductive conception of modernity according to which it is contrasted to irrational "premodern" traditions. In this chapter, I retain the usage of "premodern traditions" not to perpetuate this dichotomy but to underscore, in fact, the persistence in modernity of beliefs and practices with long historical roots. For an overview of the problematization of Southeast Asian modernity and tradition, see Kirsten W. Endres and Andrea Lauser, "Multivocal Arenas of Modern Enchantment in Southeast Asia," in *Engaging the Spirit World: Popular Beliefs and Practices in Modern Southeast Asia*, ed. Kirsten W. Endres and Andrea Lauser (New York: Berghahn Books, 2012), 2–18.

7. Keith Taylor, "The Early Kingdoms," *Cambridge History of Southeast Asia* 1 (1999): 137–47.

8. Taylor, 148–53.

9. Alexander Woodside, "Early Ming Expansionism, 1406–1427," *Papers on China* 1 (1963).

10. See, e.g., Christopher Goscha, *Vietnam: A New History* (New York: Basic Books, 2016), 32; Keith W. Taylor, *A History of the Vietnamese* (Cambridge: Cambridge University Press, 2013), 218–23; Li Tana, *Nguyễn Cochinchina: Southern Vietnam in the Seventeenth and Eighteenth Centuries* (Ithaca, NY: Cornell University Press, 1998), 102–3; David Biggs, *Footprints of War: Militarized Landscapes in Vietnam* (Seattle: University of Washington Press, 2018), 23–26; William B. Noseworthy and Van Son Quang, "A View of Champā Sites in Phú Yên Province, Vietnam: Toward a Longue Durée of Socio-Religious Context," *Religion* 13, no. 7 (2022).

11. See the chapters "Foreign Merchants" and "Life in Đàng Trong: A New Way of Being Vietnamese" in Tana, *Nguyễn Cochinchina*, 59–77, 99–116.

12. See Alexander Woodside, *Vietnam and the Chinese Model: A Comparative Study of the Nguyễn and Ching Civil Government in the First Half of the Nineteenth Century* (Cambridge, MA: Harvard University Press, 1971), 2–4; George Dutton, *The Tây Sơn Uprising: Society and Rebellion in Eighteenth Century Vietnam* (Honolulu: University of Hawai'i, 2006).

13. David G. Marr, *Vietnamese Anticolonialism, 1880–1925* (Berkeley: University of California, 1971), 44–76; Alexander B. Woodside, *Vietnam and the Chinese Model: A Comparative Study of Vietnamese and Chinese Government in the First Half of the Nineteenth Century* (Cambridge, MA: Harvard University Press, 1971), 126–32.

14. Tana, *Nguyễn Cochinchina*, 68–71.

15. Woodside, *Comparative Study of the Nguyễn and Ching Civil Government*, 116–18; Charles Wheeler, "Interests, Institutions, and Identity: Strategic Adaptation and the Ethno-evolution of Minh Hương (Central Vietnam), 16th–19th Centuries," *Itinerario* 39, no. 1 (2015).

16. Charlotte Furth, *A Flourishing Yin: Gender in China's Medical History* (Berkeley: University of California Press 1999), 52.

17. Thomas Laqueur, "Destiny Is Anatomy," in *Making Sex: Body and Gender from the Greeks to Freud* (Cambridge, MA: Harvard University Press, 1990), 25–62.

18. Laqueur, "Discovery of the Sexes," in *Making Sex: Body and Gender from the Greeks to Freud* (Cambridge, MA: Harvard University Press), 149–92.

19. Furth, *A Flourishing Yin*, 55.

20. Furth, 52.

21. Furth, 53.

22. Christopher Goscha, *Vietnam or Indochina? Contesting Conceptions of Space in Vietnamese Nationalism, 1887–1954*, Nordic Institute of Asian Studies 28 (Copenhagen: Nordic Institute of Asian Studies, 1995).

23. The reason for "traditional" medicine's historical longevity far into the twentieth century is partly the rise of nationalism and the creation of "our medicine" (*thuốc ta*). See

Laurence Monnais, C. Michele Thompson, and Ayo Wahlberg, "Southern Medicine for Southern People," in *Southern Medicine for Southern People: Vietnamese Medicine in the Making*, ed. Laurence Monnais, C. Michele Thompson, and Ayo Wahlberg (Newcastle-upon-Tyne: Cambridge Scholars Publishing, 2012), 10–12.

24. Tiến Lương, *Nam-Nữ Phòng Trung Bí Mật Tân Y Thuật: Sách thuốc chữa những bệnh kín của đàn ông, đàn bà, con trai và con gái* 男女房中秘密新醫術 [*New Medicine for the Male and Female Chamber: A Medicine Book to Cure Private Diseases of Men and Women*], trans. Tô-Linh Thảo (Nam Định: Nhà In Mỹ Thắng [Mỹ Thắng Publishing House], 1933).

25. Hồng Chung Anh, *Nam Nữ Tu Tri: Guide Moral des Rapport Sexuels* [*Moral Guide to Sexual Relations*] (Hà Nội: Đông Tây [East West Publishers], 1932), 70.

26. Thomas W. Laqueur, *Solitary Sex: A Cultural History of Masturbation* (New York: Zone Books, 2003), 14–15.

27. Thomas Laqueur, "Why Masturbation Became a Problem," in *Solitary Sex: A Cultural History of Masturbation* (New York: Zone Books, 2003), 264–65.

28. Laurence Monnais-Rousselot, "In the Shadow of the Colonial Hospital: Developing Health Care in Indochina, 1860–1939," in *Viet Nam Exposé: French Scholarship on Twentieth-Century Vietnamese Society*, ed. Gisele Bousquet and Pierre Brocheux (Ann Arbor: University of Michigan Press, 2002), 140–86.

29. Monnais, Thompson, and Wahlberg, "Southern Medicine for Southern People," 8.

30. Sokhieng Au, *Mixed Medicines: Health and Culture in French Colonial Cambodia* (Chicago: University of Chicago Press, 2011), 118.

31. Lương, *Nam-Nữ Phòng Trung Bí Mật Tân Y Thuật*; Lê Văn Phấn, *Đông-Tây Y-Học và Nam Nữ Ái Tình (Médecine Occidentale et Sino-Annamite et de l'amour)* [*Western and Sino-Annamite Medicine and Love*] (Sài Gòn: Imprimerie Trần Trọng Cảnh, 1936), 1:2.

32. Phấn, *Đông-Tây Y-Học và Nam Nữ Ái Tình*, 1.

33. See Monnais, Thompson, and Wahlberg, "Southern Medicine for Southern People," 8–9. A similar phenomenon arguably occurred in the development of the French colonial asylum, whereby the growth of the institution depended on the increasing participation of local Vietnamese actors. See Claire E. Edington. *Beyond the Asylum: Mental Illness in French Colonial Vietnam* (Ithaca, NY: Cornell University Press, 2019), 122–23.

34. Liên Thị Trân, "Henriette Bui: The Narrative of Vietnam's First Woman Doctor," in *Viet Nam Exposé: French Scholarship on Twentieth-Century Vietnamese Society*, ed. Gisele Bousquet and Pierre Brocheux (Ann Arbor: University of Michigan, 2005), 296–97.

35. Trân, "Henriette Bui," 294.

36. Thùy Linh Nguyễn, *Childbirth, Maternity, and Medical Pluralism in French Colonial Vietnam, 1880–1945* (Rochester, NY: University of Rochester Press, 2016), 4.

37. The term "syncretic" is appropriate here, as it implies either potential mixing or co-existence, or both. For more on the terminology to imply religious, cultural, or linguistic mixing and the relevant usages, see Charles Stewart, "Creolization, Hybridity, Syncretism, Mixture," *Portuguese Studies* 27, no. 1 (2011): 48–55; Paul Christopher Johnson, "Syncretism and Hybridization," in *The Oxford Handbook of the Study of Religion*, ed. Michael Stausberg and Steven Engler (Oxford: Oxford University Press, 2016), 754–72.

38. George E. Dutton, Jayne S. Werner, and John K. Whitmore, eds., *The Child-Giving*

Guanyin (Sixteenth-Seventeenth Century), Sources of Vietnamese Tradition (New York: Columbia University Press, 2012), 180–86.

39. Tana, *Nguyễn Cochinchina,* 101–12.

40. Dror, *Cult, Culture and Authority,* 74.

41. Andaya, *Flaming Womb,* 83.

42. Nguyễn Thế Anh, "The Vietnamization of the Cham Diety Pô Nagar," *Asia Journal* 2, no. 1 (June 1995): 65.

43. Le Failler and Tessier describe Oger's project as imbued with a "resolutely ethnographic perspective." Philippe Le Failler and Olivier Tessier, preface to *Technique de Peuple Annamite* [*Mechanics and Crafts of the Annamites*], ed. Philippe Le Failler and Olivier Tessier (Hà Nội: Nhà Xuất Bản Thế Giới, 2009), 121.

44. For more details on the spirit medium rituals and costumes, see Maurice Durand, *Technique et panthéon des médiums viêtnamiens (đồng)* (Paris: École Française d'Extrême-Orient, 1959), 45:1–48; Ngô Đức Thịnh, *Lên Đồng: Hành Trình của Thần Linh và Thân Phận* [*Len Dong: Journeys of Spirits and Fates*] (Ho Chi Minh City: Nhà Xuất Bản Trẻ, 2007), 226–37.

45. The continued existence of this Vietnamese cult is partly (and ironically) due to French colonial administrators who saw themselves as protectors and promoters of Vietnamese popular culture. See Dror, *Cult, Culture and Authority,* 168–72.

46. See my article "Sex in the City: The Descent from Human to Animal in Two Vietnamese Classics of Urban Reportage," *International Quarterly of Asian Studies* 50, nos. 3–4 (March 27, 2020).

47. Lộng Chương, "Hầu Thánh: Tiểu Thuyết Phóng Sự [Serving the Spirits: Novelistic Reportage]," in *Hầu Thánh* [*Serving the Spirits*] (1942; Hà Nội: Nhà Xuất Bản Thông Tin, 2002).

48. Here is the line in support of this claim: "The practice of spirit mediumships has led her to a place where she has forgotten even her responsibility as a woman and especially as a mother" (*Đồng bóng đã đưa bà đến chỗ quên cả thiên chức của người đàn bà, và nhất là của người mẹ*). Chương, "Hầu Thánh," 53.

49. Chương, 125.

50. Here is the original passage describing Mr. Ký Sìn's condition: "Thằng Ký Sìn bây giờ lại nghiện thuốc phiện. Bao nhiêu tiền [. . .] nó phá kỳ hết [. . .] Nó bây giờ thân tàn . . ." Chương, 174.

51. Chương, 53.

52. Chương, 75.

53. The original quotation: "Chàng cho là người ta còn có thể tin nhầm được như thế, là vì óc còn tối tăm, trí còn ngu muội. Chàng mong một ngày kia, người ta có thể đem khoa học để giải thích những điều huyền hoặc, và giáo hóa lại lòng người." Chương, 23–24.

54. Barley Norton, "Mediumship, Modernity, and Cultural Identity," in *Songs for the Spirits: Music and Mediums in Modern Vietnam* (Urbana: University of Illinois Press, 2009), 26.

55. See Norton, 26; Kirsten W. Endres, "Spirited Modernities: Mediumship and Ritual Performativity in Late Socialist Vietnam," in *Modernity and Re-enchantment: Religion in Post-revolutionary Vietnam,* ed. Philip Taylor (Singapore: Institute of Southeast Asian

Studies Publishing, 2007), 203; Vinh, "Deviant Bodies and Dynamics of Displacement of Homoerotic Desire in Vietnamese Literature from and about the French Colonial Period (1858–1954)," 1997, http://www.talawas.org/talaDB/suche.php?res=1056&rb=0503&von=.

56. See Chương, "Hầu Thánh," 53–54.

57. Charlotte Furth, "Androgynous Males and Deficient Females: Biology and Gender Boundaries in Sixteenth- and Seventeenth-Century China," *Late Imperial China* 9, no. 2 (1988): 3.

58. This is the qualifying claim that Sang makes in response to arguments concerning premodern East Asia's tolerance of gender and sexual variances relative to the Christian West. See Tze-Ian D. Sang, "Revisiting Premodern Chinese Female-Female Relations," in *The Emerging Lesbian: Female Same-Sex Desire in Modern China* (Chicago: University of Chicago Press, 2003), 64.

59. Chương, "Hầu Thánh," 53.

60. Here is the original passage: "Này 'ông,' sao cứ hững hờ, để khách má hồng thương nhớ thế, có sang đây tiếp chuyện mợ nó không này!" Chương, 30–31.

61. See Chương, 66.

62. See Chương, 76.

63. See Chương, 81.

64. See Ngo Duc Thinh, "The Mother Goddess Religion: Its History, Pantheon, and Practices," in *Possessed by the Spirits: Mediumship in Contemporary Vietnamese Communities*, ed. Karen Fjelstad and Hien Thi Nguyễn (Ithaca, NY: Cornell Southeast Asia Program Publications, 2006), 22–25. See also Chauvet, "Changing Spirit Identities," 93–94.

65. Endres and Lauser, "Multivocal Arenas of Modern Enchantment in Southeast Asia," 10–11.

66. See Trọng Lang, "Đồng Bóng" [Spirit Mediums], *Phong Hóa* [*Mores*] 165 (December 6, 1935): 11.

67. Trọng Lang, "Đồng Bóng" [Spirit Mediums], *Phong Hóa* [*Mores*] 166 (December 13, 1935): 10.

68. Do, *Vietnamese Supernaturalism*, 99.

69. The language he uses is belittling. He states that Vietnamese female mediums have a way of dancing that is as "capricious" [*ỡng ẹo*] as that of European women. He concludes: "How wretched [*khốn nạn*] for the ignorant people who only believe in the fantastic [*huyễn hoặc*] and not the self-evident [*hiển nhiên*]." Bính, *Việt-Nam phong-tục*, 341–42.

70. Georges Bataille, *Eroticism: Death and Sensuality*, trans. Mary Dalwood (1957; San Francisco: City Light Books, 1986), 68; Dror, *Cult, Culture and Authority*.

71. See Dror, *Cult, Culture and Authority*, 80. On how Vietnamese states have domesticated popular cults and religions to their own political ends, see Taylor, *Goddess on the Rise*, 23–56.

72. As a result of space limitations, I do not analyze here the case of "young men" (*anh dàng ông*) who assume opposite gendered roles as "young female spirit mediums" (*cô đồng*). This practice is described in both Lộng Chương's and Trọng Lang's reportages. See Chương, "Hầu Thánh," 73–74; Lang, "Đồng Bóng [Spirit Mediums]," *Phong Hóa* [*Mores*] 166 (December 13, 1935): 10.

73. Shawn McHale, *Print and Power: Confucianism, Communism and Buddhism in the Making of Modern Vietnam* (Honolulu: University of Hawai'i Press, 2004), 147–50.

74. Michel Foucault, *History of Sexuality* (New York: Vintage Books, 1990), 1:154.

75. John Dupré, "Gender and the End of Biological Determinism," in *Why Gender?*, ed. Jude Browne (Cambridge: Cambridge University Press, 2021), 57–77.

76. See Peter Zinoman, "The Question of Communism," in *Vietnamese Colonial Republican: The Political Vision of Vũ Trọng Phụng* (Berkeley: University of California, 2014), 85.

77. Hoàng Thiếu Sơn, "Làm Đĩ: Cuốn Sách Có Trách Nhiệm Và Đầy Nhân Đạo [*To Be a Prostitute*: A Book with Responsibility and Humanity]," in *Làm Đĩ: Tiểu Thuyết* [*To Be a Prostitute: A Novel*] (Hà Nội: Nhà Xuất Bản Văn Học, 2005), 17.

78. Phụng writes: "In Vietnamese society incest is becoming widespread." ["Xã hội Việt Nam này, thật vậy đã bắt đầu loạn dâm"]. See Phụng, 39.

79. See Sơn, "Làm Đĩ: Cuốn Sách Có Trách Nhiệm Và Đầy Nhân Đạo [*To Be a Prostitute*: A Book with Responsibility and Humanity]," *Làm Đĩ*, 17.

80. As quoted and republished in Phụng, *Làm Đĩ* [To be a Prostitute] (1936; Hà Nội: Nhà Xuất Bản Văn Học, 2005), 277.

81. The original quotation: "Đặc điểm của cơ thể và của tâm lí làm cho hai phái nam và nữ hoặc giống đực và giống cái có chỗ khác biệt nhau." See *Từ Điển Tiếng Việt* [*Vietnamese Dictionary*] (Hà Nội: Nhà Xuất Bản Văn Hóa Thông Tin, 2005), 874.

82. P. J. Pigneaux and J. L. Taberd, *Dictionarium anamitico-latinum, primitus inceptum ab illustrissimo et reverendissimo P. J. Pigneaux. Dein absolutum et editum a J. L. Taberd* (Fredericnagori vulgo Serampore: ex typis J. Marshman, 1838); P. J. B. Trương-Vĩnh-Ký, *Petit dictionnaire Français-Annamite* (Sài Gòn: Imp. de la Mission, à Tân-Định, 1884); *Việt Nam Tự Điển/Hội Khai-Trí-Tiến-Đức Khởi* [Vietnamese Dictionary] (Hà Nội: Trung-Bắc Tân-Văn, 1931).

83. Trần Trọng Kim, *Việt Nam Văn Phạm* [Vietnamese Grammar] (Hà Nội: Lê Thăng Xuất Bản, 1940).

84. Đào Duy Anh, "Hán Việt Từ Điển" [Sino-Vietnamese Dictionary] (Sài Gòn: Trường Thi, 1932), 271.

85. George E. Dutton, "'Society' and Struggle in the Early Twentieth Century: The Vietnamese Neologistic Project and French Colonialism," *Modern Asian Studies* 49, no. 6 (November 2015).

86. Anh, "Hán Việt Từ Điển," 166.

87. The original quotation: "1. Say mê quá . . . 2. Say mê về sắc-dục." See "Những điều lợi hại của sự nam nữ giao tiếp tự do" [The Harm of Dealings between Men and Women], *Phụ nữ thời đàm* [Women, Current Events, Commentary] 1 (1931): 148.

88. Nguyễn Hữu-Tiến, "Nam-Âm Thi-Văn Khảo-Biện [Survey of Southern Sounds and Poetic Literature]," *Nam Phong* [*Southern Wind*] 3, no. 18 (December 1918): 353.

89. Leon Antonio Rocha, "Xing: The Discourse of Sex and Human Nature in Modern China," *Gender and History* 22, 3 (2010): 608.

90. The Grand Ricci Dictionary of the Chinese Language suggests a subtle difference in meaning between the characters 慾 and 欲. While their meanings appear to have overlapped at some point, the dictionary suggests that 慾 is more associated with sexual desire, whereas

欲 appears to mean only "want" in general. I wish to thank Catherine Churchman for first raising this point. See "Grand Dictionnaire Ricci de la Langue Chinoise 利氏漢法辭典 [Grand Ricci Dictionary of the Chinese Language]," in *Yü*, vol. 6 (Paris: Instituts Ricci, 2001).

91. Phạm Quỳnh, "Tự Vựng: Quốc Ngữ, Chữ Nho, Chữ Pháp" [Vocabulary: Vietnamese, Chinese, and French], *Nam Phong* [*Southern Wind*] 1, no. 5 (1917): xxxv.

92. I wish to thank Catherine Churchman for raising this point. See also *Bảng Tra Chữ Nôm* [Nôm Lookup Table]. (Hà Nội: Nhà Xuất Bản Khoa Học Xã Hội, 1976), 2:218.

93. Trương-Vĩnh-Ký, *Petit dictionnaire Français-Annamite*, 1070.

94. P.G.V, *Dictionnaire Franco-Tonkinois: Illustré (Từ điển tiếng Pháp—tiếng Bắc Kỳ. Có minh hoạ)* [*French-Tonkinese Dictionary*] (Hà Nội: F. H. Schneider, 1898), 347.

95. He writes: "To speak about the feminine or masculine gender of humans, one can use the following terms: man, woman, boy, girl. Place them after the noun. For example: human man, human woman, a youth boy, a youth girl, group male, group female, elder man, elder woman" (literal translation). Original quotation: "Nói về giống đực giống cái của loài người: Những tiếng dùng để trỏ giống đực giống cái của loài người, thì có những tiếng: đàn ông, đàn bà, trai, gái, nam, nữ. Những tiếng ấy đặt sau tiếng danh-tự: người đàn ông, người đàn bà, con trai, con gái, phái nam, phái nữ, cụ ông, cụ bà, bác trai, bác gái." See Trần Trọng Kim, *Việt Nam Văn Phạm* [*Vietnamese Grammar*] (Hà Nội: Lê Thăng Xuất Bản, 1940), 38–39.

96. Quan Bác Sĩ Devy, *Cho Khỏi Ốm Đau* [*To Prevent Illness*], trans. Đỗ Uông (Hà Nội: Imprimerie Nghiêm-Hàm, 1928), 6–7.

97. Dutton, "'Society' and Struggle in the Early Twentieth Century."

98. Anh, "Hán Việt Từ Điển," 630.

99. Rocha, "Discourse of Sex and Human Nature in Modern China," 609.

100. J. F. M. Génibrel, *Dictionnaire Annamite-Française: comprenant, 1 tous les caractères de la langue Annamite vulgaire, avec l'indication de leurs divers sens propres ou figurés, et justifiés par de nombreux exemples, 2 les caractères chinois nécessaires à l'étude des Tứ Thơ, ou quatre livres classiques chinois, 3 la flore et la faune de l'Indo-Chine* (Sài Gòn: Impr. de la mission à Tân Định, 1898), 688.

101. Định Phúc Bảo, "Mười khoản vệ-sanh cốt-yếu" [Ten Cardinal Items on Hygiene], *Y thoại tùng biên* 醫話叢編 [*Volume Collection of Medical Discourse*] 1 (1931): 33.

102. See Howard Chiang, "Deciphering Desire," in *After Eunuchs: Science, Medicine, and the Transformation of Sex in Modern China* (New York: Columbia University Press, 2018), 125–77.

103. See Gregory M. Pflugfelder, "Doctoring Love: Male-Male Sexuality in Medical Discourse from the Edo Period through the Early Twentieth Century," in *Cartographies of Desire: Male-Male Sexuality in Japanese Discourse, 1600–1950* (Berkeley: University of California Press, 1999), 235–85.

104. My translation from the French. J. F. M Génibrel, *Dictionnaire Annamite-Française*, 763–64.

105. Anh, "Hán Việt Từ Điển," 706.

106. Anh, 706.

107. Lê Hữu Mỹ, "Tính Dục Học (Éducation sexuelle): Thế nào là Ái Tình?" [Sexual

Education: What Is Love?]," *Y Học Tân Thanh: La nouvelle voix de la médecine* [*The New Voice of Medicine*] 5 (December 3, 1938): 57–58.

108. Hội Khai-Trí Tiến Đức Khởi Thảo [Moral Enlightenment Association], *Việt Nam Tự-Điển* 越南字典 [*Vietnamese Dictionary*] (Hà Nội: Imprimerie Trung-Bắc Tân-Văn [Central and Northern New Literature Publishing House], 1931), 525.

109. Hội Khai-Trí Tiến Đức Khởi Thảo, 525.

110. Nguyễn Can Mộng, *Nam học Hán văn khoá bản,* 南學漢文課本 [*Vietnamese Study of Chinese Characters Textbook*] (Hà Nội: Imprimeur Mặc Đình Tư, 1920), 19–20; Nguyễn Đạo Quán, *Khai tâm hán văn giáo khoa: Năm thứ nhất* [*Introduction to Chinese Character Textbook: First year*] (Hà Nội: Nghiêm Hàm, 1924), 128; Nguyễn Khắc Bỉnh, *Hán học nhập môn Tam tự văn* 漢學入門三字文 [*Three-Character Script for Introductory Sinology*] (Hà Nội: Hợp thành ấn quán 1928), 48; Nguyễn Trần Mô, "Nam-Hoa Tự-Điển 南華字典" (Hà Nội: Thư Hương Xuất Bản, 1943), 61.

111. Quách Cang, *Nam-Nữ Khả-Độc Loại-Dục Vệ-Sinh* [*The Sexual Education of Males Females*] (Sài Gòn: Imprimerie Chan-Thanh, 1939).

112. Cang, 53.

113. Cang, 302.

114. My translation from the French. Génibrel, *Dictionnaire Annamite-Française*, 761.

115. My translation from the Vietnamese and French. Quỳnh, "Tự Vựng," xvi.

116. Haiyan Lee, "The Cult of *Qing*," in *Revolution of the Heart: A Genealogy of Love in China, 1900–1950* (Stanford, CA: Stanford University Press, 2007), 34–35.

117. Thơ Ngọc Nguyễn and Phong Thanh Nguyễn, "Philosophical Transmission and Contestation: The Impact of Qing Confucianism in Southern Vietnam," *Asian Studies* 8 (2020): 91–95, https://doi.org/10.4312/as.2020.8.2.79-112.

118. Anh, "Hán Việt Từ Điển," 706.

119. Nguyễn Văn Khái, *Nam Nữ Hôn-Nhân Vệ Sinh* 生衛姻婚女男 [*Male Female Marriage Hygiene*] (Hải Phòng: Văn Minh Publishers, 1924), 53–54.

120. Tôn Văn Cân and Tử Quyền, *Thai-Sản Đương Tri* 知當產胎 [*Knowledge on Giving Birth*] (Sài Gòn: Viet & Fils Publishers).

121. Cân and Quyền, 10–13, esp. 6, 11, 12, 14, 19, 21, 24, and 25.

122. An-Nhân and Lê-Trúc, *Nam Nữ Bí-Mật Chỉ Nam* [*Male Female Secrets for Men*] (Hà Nội: Nhật Nam Thư Quán Publishers, 1932).

123. An-Nhân and Lê-Trúc, 10.

124. Cang, *Nam-Nữ Khả-Độc Loại-Dục Vệ-Sinh*, 57.

125. Tani Barlow, *The Question of Women in Chinese Feminism* (Durham, NC: Duke University Press, 2004), 37–63.

126. Barlow, 37.

127. Barlow, 49–55.

128. Văn Hương, "Gái Đời Nay: Lời một vị phu-nhân có nền nếp mắng răn con gái là bậc tân học" [Females These Days: Words of a Dignified Woman Scolding the New Women], *Phụ Nữ Tân Văn* [*New Women's News*] (September 12, 1929): 10. Martina Nguyễn has suggested other terms for "New Women," such as *phụ nữ mới* and *thị tân*, terms that once again in no way index the modern vocabulary of "sex." See Martina Thục Nhi Nguyễn, *On Our*

Own Strength: The Self-Reliant Literary Group and Cosmopolitan Nationalism in Late Colonial Vietnam (Honolulu: University of Hawai'i Press, 2021), 100–7. See also Vũ Công Định, "Cái 'mốt' mới của chị em tân-tiến" [The New Fashion of the New Women], *Đông Pháp* 報 東法 [*Eastern Way Newspaper*] (November 16, 1939): 1. The terms *tân phong nữ sĩ* and *gái tân phong* both derive from a novel by the southern novelist Hồ Biểu Chánh titled *Tân Phong Nữ Sĩ* [*New Styled Women*] (1937; Sài Gòn: Nhà Xuất Bản Văn Hóa Sài Gòn, 2006). See also Shawn McHale, "Printing and Power: Vietnamese Debates over Women's Place in Society, 1918–1934," in *Essays into Vietnamese Pasts*, ed. Keith W. Taylor and John K. Whitmore (Ithaca, NY: Southeast Asia Program, Cornell University, 1995), 186n46.

129. McHale, "Printing and Power," 186n46.

130. Quỳnh, "Tự Vựng," xxxix.

131. Chánh, *Tân Phong Nữ Sĩ* [*New Styled Women*], chap. 5, para. 12.

132. Deriving from the Vietnamese vernacular for female, the term *gái* in *nôm* script is 妎, the equivalent of the Chinese *nữ* (女). See Vũ Văn Kính and Khổng Đức, *Ngũ Thiên Tự: Trình Bày Việt-Hán-Nôm* [*Five Heavenly Scripts: Presentation of Vietnamese-Chinese-Nôm*] (Ho Chi Minh City: Nhà Xuất Bản Văn Hóa Thông Tin [Culture and Information Publishing House], 1998), 32.

133. Hương, "Gái Đời Nay," 10.

134. Mark D. Jordan, "Sodomy," in *Gay Histories and Cultures*, ed. George E. Haggerty, John Beynon, and Douglas Eisner (New York: Garland Books, 2000), 828–29; Patrick Vandermeersch, "Sodomites, Gays and Biblical Scholars: A Gathering Organized by Peter Damian?," in *Sodom's Sin: Genesis 18–19 and Its Interpretation*, ed. Eibert Tigchelaar (Boston: Brill 2004).

135. As quoted in Robert Mills, *Seeing Sodomy in the Middle Ages* (Chicago: University of Chicago Press, 2015), 22–23.

136. Michel Foucault, *History of Sexuality* (New York: Vintage, 1978), 1:43.

137. On Gia Long, see Woodside, *Comparative Study of the Nguyễn and Ching Civil Government*. On Chinese laws of the late Qing dynasty, see Vũ Thị Nga and Nguyễn Huy Anh, *Tập Bài Giảng: Lịch Sử Nhà Nước và Pháp Luật Việt Nam (Từ Nguồn Gốc Đến Giữa Thế Kỷ XX)* [*Lectures: History of the Vietnamese State and Law (From the Origins to the 20th Century)*] (Hà Nội: Nhà Xuất Bản Chính Trị Quốc Gia [National Politics Publishing House], 1996), 187; Trần Trọng Kim, *Việt Nam Sử Lược* [*Compendium of Vietnamese History*] (1920; Sài Gòn: Bộ Giáo Dục Trung Tâm Học Liệu Xuất Bản [The Ministry of Education Center's Publication House], 1971), 2:173. On fornication, see Paul-Louis-Félix Philastre, *Le Code Annamite* (Paris: Ernest Leroux Éditeur, 1876), 2:528.

138. Tài Văn Tạ, *The Vietnamese Tradition of Human Rights* (Berkeley: University of California Institute of East Asian Studies, 1989), 128.

139. Matthew H. Sommer, "The Penetrated Male in Late Imperial China: Judicial Constructions and Social Stigma," *Modern China* 23, no. 2 (1997): 147.

140. Sommer, 170.

141. Sommer, 146.

142. Sommer, 147.

143. French term in original. Anh, "Hán Việt Từ Điển," 417.

144. Pierre Brocheux and Daniel Hémery, *Indochina: An Ambiguous Colonization, 1858–1954* (Berkeley: University of California Press, 2009), 15–69.

145. Michael David Sibalis, "The Regulation of Male Homosexuality in Revolutionary and Napoleonic France, 1789–1815," in *Homosexuality in Modern France*, ed. Jeffrey Merrick and Bryant T. Ragan Jr. (New York: Oxford University Press, 1996), 80–101. See also Scott Eric Gunther, "Introduction: Republican Values and the Depenalization of Sodomy in France," in *The Elastic Closet: A History of Homosexuality in France, 1942–Present* (New York: Palgrave Macmillan, 2009), 1–24.

146. Vernon A. Rosario II, "Pointy Penises, Fashion Crimes, and Hysterical Mollies: The Pederasts' Inversions," in *Homosexuality in Modern France*, ed. Jeffrey Merrick and Bryant T. Ragan Jr. (Oxford: Oxford University Press, 1996), 149; Sibalis, "Regulation of Male Homosexuality in Revolutionary and Napoleonic France," 80–81.

147. Lear and Cantarella observe that pederasty, the asymmetrical relationship between an adult man in Ancient Greece and an adolescent boy, adhered to strict codes that formed part of the boy's cultivation in becoming a citizen exercising civil and political duties. On the historical meanings of pederasty, see Andrew Lear and Eva Cantarella, *Images of Ancient Greek Pederasty: Boys Were Their Gods* (New York: Routledge, 2008), 1–9. On the historical erosion of the distinction between male "sodomy" and "pederasty" since the eighteenth century in France, see Claude Courouve, *Vocabulaire de l'homosexualité masculine* (Paris: Payot, 1985), 169–79. See also Michael Rey, "Police and Sodomy in Eighteenth-Century Paris: From Sin to Disorder," in *The Pursuit of Sodomy: Male Homosexuality in Renaissance and Enlightenment Europe*, ed. Kent Gerard and Gert Hekma (New York: Harrington Press, 1989), 145.

148. Sibalis, "Regulation of Male Homosexuality in Revolutionary and Napoleonic France," 85. See also William Peniston, *Pederasts and Others: Urban Culture and Sexual Identity in Nineteenth-Century Paris* (New York: Harrington Press, 2004), 11–66.

149. Judith Surkis, *Sexing the Citizen: Morality and Masculinity in France, 1870–1920* (Ithaca, NY: Cornell University Press, 2006), 21-42.

150. Robert A. Nye, "Sex Difference and Male Homosexuality in French Medical Discourse," *Bulletin of the History of Medicine* 63, no. 1 (1989).

151. Some of the measures in force included the registration of female prostitutes, the monitoring of the spread of venereal diseases, and the quarantining of infected prostitutes at municipal dispensaries. Because prostitutes were prohibited from soliciting publicly on the streets, the authorities limited the activity to certain state-sanctioned brothels. See Isabelle Tracol-Huỳnh, "Prostitutes, Brothels and the Red Light District: The Management of Prostitution in the City of Hà Nội from the 1870s to the 1950s," in *Translation, History and the Arts: New Horizons in Asian Interdisciplinary Humanities Research*, ed. Ji Meng and Atsuko Ukai (Newcastle, UK: Cambridge Scholars Publishing, 2013), 176–93. See also Christina Firpo, *Black Market Business: Selling Sex in Northern Vietnam, 1920–1945*, Studies of the Weatherhead East Asian Institute (Ithaca, NY: Cornell University Press, 2020), chap. 2.

152. Alain Corbin, *Women for Hire: Prostitution and Sexuality in France after 1850*, trans. Alan Sheridan (Cambridge, MA: Harvard University Press, 1990); Isabelle Tracol-Huỳnh, "Between Stigmatisation and Regulation: Prostitution in Colonial Northern Vietnam," *Culture, Health & Sexuality* 12 (2010); Christina Firpo, "Sex and Song: Clandestine Pros-

titution in Tonkin's Ả Đào Music Houses, 1920s–1940s," *Journal of Vietnamese Studies* 11, no. 2 (2016).

153. Tracol-Huỳnh, "Between Stigmatisation and Regulation," 83.

154. In explaining her research focus on heterosexual female prostitution during the late French colonial period, Firpo has observed: "While homosexual and male forms of sex work certainly existed, historical documentation of them is scant aside from a few anecdotal cases." Firpo, *Black Market Business*, 14.

155. *Dossier relatif aux activités de la prostitution, les faits concernant au filles publiques années, 1916–1931* [Files on prostitution activities, the facts concerning the public girls, 1916–1931], D901.12 (Sài Gòn, 1916), National Archives II, Ho Chi Minh City.

156. French term in the original. Vũ Trọng Phụng, "Để Đáp Lời Báo Ngày Nay: Dâm Hay Là Không Dâm?" [To Respond to the Newspaper *These Days*: Sex or No Sex?], in *Tranh Luận Văn Nghệ Thế Kỷ XX* (*Literary and Artistic Debates in the Twentieth Century*), ed. Nguyễn Ngọc Thiện (1937; Hà Nội: Nhà Xuất Bản Lao Động, 2002), 1130.

157. Phụng, "Để Đáp Lời Báo *Ngày Nay* Dâm Hay là Không Dâm?," 1130.

158. French term in original. Anh, "Hán Việt Từ Điển," 417.

159. David G. Marr, *Vietnamese Tradition on Trial, 1925–1945* (Berkeley: University of California, 1981), 139–66; Ben Tran, *Postmandarin: Masculinity and Aesthetic Modernity in Colonial Vietnam* (New York: Fordham University Press, 2017), 1–20.

160. Peter Zinoman, ed., *Dumb Luck: A Novel by Vu Trong Phung* (Ann Arbor: University of Michigan Press, 2002), 119.

161. Benedict Anderson, *The Spectre of Comparison: Nationalism, Southeast asia and the World* (London: Verso Books, 1998), 2.

162. Parentheses in original. Trọng Lang, "Hà Nội Lầm Than (The Wretched of Hà Nội)," in *Phóng Sự Việt Nam* [*News Reportages of Vietnam*], ed. Phan Trọng Thưởng, Nguyễn Cừ, and Nguyễn Hữu Sơn (1938; Hà Nội: Nhà Xuất Bản Văn Học [Literature Publishing House], 2000), 214.

163. Lang, 216.

164. Ruth Ginio, *The French Army and Its African Soldiers: The Years of Decolonization* (Lincoln: University of Nebraska Press, 2017), 4–5.

165. The question of Asia-Africa relations has become of increasing scholarly interest. See, e.g., Philippe Peycam, "Exploring the Possibility of a South East Asia-Africa 'Axis of Knowledge'," *South East Asia Research* 27, no. 1 (2019).

166. French term in original. Anh, "Hán Việt Từ Điển," 306.

167. Harriet M. Phinney, "Objects of Affection: Vietnamese Discourses on Love and Emancipation," *positions: east asia cultures critique* 16, no. 2 (Fall 2008); Neil Jamieson, *Understanding Vietnam* (Berkeley: University of California Press, 1995), 108–58.

168. Vũ Trọng Phụng, "Thủ Đoạn" [Stratagems], in *Chống Nạn Lên Đường* [*The Prevention of Vice on One's Journey*], ed. Lai Nguyễn An (Hà Nội: Nhà Xuất Bản Hội Nhà Văn, 2000), 34.

169. For a discussion of Vũ Trọng Phụng's cynicism, see the introduction in Zinoman's *Dumb Luck*.

Chapter 2

1. Gert Hekma, "'A Female Soul in a Male Body': Sexual Inversion as Gender Inversion in Nineteenth-Century Sexology," in *Third Sexes, Third Gender: Beyond Sexual Dimorphism in Culture and History*, ed. Gilbert Herdt (New York: Zone, 1994), 219.

2. Michel Foucault, *History of Sexuality* (New York: Vintage Books, 1990), 1:43.

3. Randolf Trumbach, "Gender and the Homosexual Role in Modern Western Culture: The 18th and 19th Centuries Compared," in *Homosexuality, Which Homosexuality?*, ed. Dennis Altman et al. (Amsterdam: An Dekker/Schorer; London: GMP, 1989), 149–70.

4. Randolf Trumbach, "The Birth of the Queen: Sodomy and the Emergence of Gender Equality in Modern Culture, 1660–1750," in *Hidden from History: Reclaiming the Gay and Lesbian Past*, ed. Martin Duberman, Martha Vicinus, and George Chauncey Jr. (New York: Meridian, 1989), 129–40.

5. On the notion that the fop was effeminate but not homosexual, see Susan Staves, "A Few Kind Words for the Fop," *Studies in English Literature, 1500–1900* 22, no. 3 (1982): 413–28; Philip Carter, "Men about Town: Representations of Foppery and Masculinity in Early Eighteenth-Century Urban Society," in *Gender in Eighteenth-Century England*, ed. Hannah Barker and Elaine Chalus (London: Routledge, 2014), 31–57.

6. Tôn Thất Bình, *Đời Sống Cung Đình Triều Nguyễn* [*Life inside the Nguyễn Imperial Court*] (Thuận Hóa: Nhà Xuất Bản Thuận Hóa, 1993).

7. Michel Đức Chaigneau, *Souvenirs de Hué (Cochinchine)* [*Memories of Hué (Cochinchine)*] (Paris: L'Imprimerie Impériale, 1867).

8. The passage in French: "A ce moment, entrait sans bruit, la tête baissée, un personage dont l'ensemble me paraissait un squelette habillé; il ressemblait assez à une femme et était en costume d'homme, mais il n'était ni l'un ni l'autre: c'était le chef des eunuques, que le roi avait mandé pour me server d'introducteur prés de la reine. Ce pauvre homme offrait un des types de laideur [ugliness] les plus complets que j'aie vus: sa figure, petite et décharnée, ressemblait, par sa couleur et par ses rides, à une pomme de reinette oubliée dans un grenier depuis plusieurs mois; ses yeux étaient creux et sans expression, son nez plat, son menton pointu et orné d'une verrue garnie de quelque poils, seule barbe qu'il possédât; sa bouche rentrée indiquait que le malheureux n'avait plus de ces petits os si nécessaires à la mastication. Quant à sa voix, elle était tout à fait feminine et criarde. Il portait un large turban, qui rendait sa figure encore plus petite, une courte tunique bleue et un pantalon de soie blanche. Cet homme n'avait sans doute pas conscience de sa malheureuse situation, car, en quittant la salle, il marchait en se dandinant et en se donnant un certain air d'homme important." Chaigneau, *Souvenirs de Hué*, 113–14.

9. Frank Proschan, "Eunuch Mandarins, Soldats Mamzelles, Effeminate Boys, and Graceless Women: French Colonial Constructions of Vietnamese Genders," *GLQ: A Journal of Lesbian and Gay Studies* 8, no. 4 (2002): 436.

10. As quoted in Proschan, 447.

11. "Lê Văn Duyệt," in *Từ Điển Bách Khoa Việt Nam* [*The Encyclopedia of Vietnam*] (Hà Nội: Nhà Xuất Bản Từ Điển Bách Khoa [Encyclopedia Publishing House], 2002), 672.

12. Bình, *Đời Sống Cung Đình Triều Nguyễn*, 55.

13. Other Vietnam studies scholars, unsurprisingly, have called into question the veracity of Tôn Thất Bình's reconstruction of nineteenth-century Vietnamese eunuchs, especially

for his unreflective use of sources and, at times, lack of source citations in support of his historical claims. See Bradley Camp Davis, "Finding Eunuchs in Imperial Vietnam: Questions and Sources," *South East Asia Research* 30, no. 4 (2023): 426–33.

14. Bồ Tùng-Linh [Pu Songling], "Duyên Chàng Lại Cái [Fate of Female Contaminated Male]," in *Liêu-Trai Chí Dị (異誌齋聊) [Strange Tales from Liao Zhai]* (Sài Gòn: Nhà in Đức-Lưu-Phương [Đức-Lưu-Phương Publishing House], 1933), 80–91.

15. Italics in the original. Tùng-Linh, "Duyên Chàng Lại Cái," 80.

16. For more on this term in the context of Pu Songling's tales, see Judith T. Zeitlin, *Historian of the Strange: Pu Songling and the Chinese Classical Tale* (Stanford, CA: Stanford University Press, 1993), 253. On eunuchs in the late nineteenth and early twentieth century in China, see Howard Chiang, *After Eunuchs: Science, Medicine, and the Transformation of Sex in Modern China* (New York: Columbia University Press, 2018), chap. 1.

17. For an ethnographic study of this contemporary term, see Paul Horton, "Recognising Shadows: Masculinism, Resistance, and Recognition in Vietnam," *International Journal for Masculinity Studies* 14, no. 1 (2019).

18. Tùng-Linh, "Duyên Chàng Lại Cái," 85.

19. Tùng-Linh, 91.

20. Charlotte Furth, "Androgynous Males and Deficient Females: Biology and Gender Boundaries in Sixteenth- and Seventeenth-Century China," *Late Imperial China* 9, no. 2 (1988): 5.

21. Furth, 14.

22. Lê Văn Phát, *Lê Van Duyệt* (Sài Gòn: Imprimateur de L'Union Nguyễn Văn Của, 1924), 8.

23. Phát, 8. The original quotation: "Những người 'ẩn-cung-hình' giúp việc trong nội của vua phân ra làm ba hạng: (1°) Yêm-hoạn (閹患), tục kêu là bộ-nắp nghĩa là chỗ âm dương thì có một cái lỗ trên có nắp đậy; (2°) Tầm-hoạn (蠶患), (bởi chữ tầm mà ra) nghĩa là cái ngọc-hành nhỏ và hình trang như tầm vậy. Quan tả-quân ẩn cung hình như vậy; (3°) Cung hoạn (宮患) là người thường nhơn bị thiếu."

24. Phát, 9. The original quotation: "Mỗi khi đối dịch với Tây-sơn thì ngài được đắt thắng luôn luôn. Ra chôn chiến trường, ngài điều binh rất nên cang đảm; cả thảy đều khâm phục, ai ai cũng lấy đó làm gương để giục dạ [encourage] ba quân [the whole army]."

25. Ngô Tất Tố, *Gia-định tổng trấn Tả-quân Lê Văn -Duyệt [The Governor of Gia Định, Lê Văn Duyệt]* (Hà Nội: Nhà In Mai Linh, 1937). As we shall see later, "masculinity" need not emanate from the male sex, so the use of this term in no way excludes the notion of a masculine woman.

26. Tố, 13–15 (note number elided). The original quotation: "Xưa nay những đứng anh hùng hào kiệt chép ở trong sách, phần nhiều là hạng mình cao bảy thước, lưng rộng mười gang, diện mạo rất vỹ, Trái lại, Duyệt thì tầm người lùn nhỏ, mặt mũi không lấy gì làm khôi ngô. Vậy mà tinh nhanh, hăng tợn, có tài giỏi lái có sức khỏe. Tánh Duyệt rất ngang tàng, không ưa học văn, chỉ thích học võ [...] Sự thực thì Duyệt gặp Chúa Nguyễn chỉ vì cái tướng ẩn cung (1) mà trời đã phú cho Duyệt."

27. Tố, 127.

28. Regarding works about the Nguyễn dynasty written by modernizing literati, Marr

notes that "books into the early 1920s continued to canonize Gia Long and his commanders, especially Le Van Duyet and Vo Tanh." Marr, *Vietnamese Tradition on Trial*, 268.

29. Gary Taylor, "Contest of Reproductions: The Rise of the Penis, the Fall of the Scrotum," in *Castration: An Abbreviated History of Western Manhood* (London: Routledge, 2000), 85–110.

30. See Peter Zinoman, "The Crisis of Vietnamese Sexuality," in *Vietnamese Colonial Republican: The Political Vision of Vũ Trọng Phụng* (Berkeley: University of California Press, 2014), 139–40.

31. Chương Dân, "Tình Hình sanh hoạt của bọn Hoạn Quan sau khi nền quân chủ bị úp đổ" [The Circumstances of Palace Eunuchs after the Demise of the Monarch]," *Phụ Nữ Tân Văn [New Women's News]* 91 (July 16, 1931): 9. The original quotation: "Loài người chia ra hai tánh (*sexe*), là nam và nữ. Vậy mà thỉnh-thoảng lại có thứ phi nam phi nữ nữa mới lạ cho . . . Giống người phi nam phi nữ ấy, theo chế độ mấy nước phương Đông ta ngày trước, chuyên sung vào việc hầu-hạ chốn cung vua, kêu là hoạn-quan hoặc thái giám."

32. Dân, 9. Archaic spelling in original quotation: "Có gì đi nữa, *họ cũng là một giống người với ta,* cái tình-cảnh đau-thương của họ, ta cũng nên biết qua mới phải."

33. The author Chương Dân acknowledges he took the information from a Chinese source: "Lấy tài liệu từ một điều tra trong báo Tàu."

34. See Howard Chiang, "Castration and the Feminized Male Sex," in *After Eunuchs: Science, Medicine, and the Transformation of Sex in Modern China* (New York: Columbia University Press, 2018), 193–98.

35. Dân, "Tình Hình sanh hoạt của bọn Hoạn Quan," 9.

36. For a profile of this literati generation, see David Marr, "A Generation of Lasts and Firsts," in *Vietnamese Anticolonialism, 1885–1925* (Berkeley: University of California, 1971), 77–97.

37. Nguyễn Chánh Sắt and Tự Bá-Nghiêm, *Hiệp Nghĩa Phong Nguyệt: Đệ Nhị Tài-Tử* 俠義風月第二才子 [*Righteous Heroes of Wind and Moon: The Second Talented Man*] (1931; Sài Gòn: Imprimerie Librairie J. Viet et Fils, 1931), 1:3.

38. See Isobe Yuko 磯部佑子 and Nguyễn Văn Hoài, trans., "Về đặc trưng truyền bá tiểu thuyết tài tử giai nhân Trung Quốc ở Đông Á—lấy Nhị độ mai, Hảo cầu truyện làm đối tượng khảo sát chính yếu [The Spread of Chinese Scholar-Beauty Romances in East Asia: The Case Study of Er Du Mei and Hao Qiu Zhuan]," *Tạp Chí Khoa Học Văn Hóa và Du lịch [Journal of the Science of Culture and Tourism]* 14 (2013).

39. Yuko and Hoài, trans., "Về đặc trưng truyền."

40. Daria Berg, "The Happy World of Scholar-Beauty Romances," in *The Columbia History of Chinese Literature*, ed. Victor H. Mair (New York: Columbia University Press, 2001), 666–69. See also Richard C. Hessney, "Beautiful, Talented, and Brave: Seventeenth-Century Chinese Scholar-Beauty Romances" (PhD diss., Columbia University, 1978); Zuyan Zhou, *Androgyny in Late Ming and Early Qing Literature* (Honolulu: University of Hawai'i Press, 2003), 95–126.

41. Keith McMahon, "The Chaste 'Beauty-Scholar' Romance and the Superiority of the Talented Woman," in *Misers, Shrews, and Polygamists: Sexuality and Male-Female Relations in Eighteenth-Century Chinese Fiction* (Durham, NC: Duke University Press, 1995), 99.

42. David M. Halperin, *How to Do the History of Homosexuality* (Chicago: University of Chicago Press, 2002), 110.

43. Martin W. Huang, *Negotiating Masculinities in Late Imperial China* (Honolulu: University of Hawai'i Press, 2006).

44. Huang, 138.

45. Vũ Đình Long, preface to *Anh Hùng Náo* [*The Rowdy Hero*] (Hà Nội: Kim-Đức-Giang Ấn-Quán, 1924), 4.

46. *Anh Hùng Náo* [*The Rowdy Hero*], trans. Vũ Đình Long (Hà Nội: Kim-Đức-Giang Ấn-Quán, 1924), vol. 1.

47. *Tục Anh Hùng Náo* 續英雄鬧 [*The Rowdy Hero Continued*], trans. Vũ Đình Long (Hà Nội: Thực Nghiệp, 1925), vol. 3; *Tục Anh Hùng Náo* 續英雄鬧 [*The Rowdy Hero Continued*], trans. Vũ Đình Long (Hà Nội: Thực Nghiệp 1925), vol. 4.

48. Kim Giang, trans., "Hào Kiệt Kết Duyên" [Two Heroes Join in Wedlock, Part 1 of 3]," *Khai Hóa Nhật Báo* 開化日報 [*Civilizing Daily*] (Hà Nội), September 20, 1924; Kim Giang, trans., "Hào Kiệt Kết Duyên" [Two Heroes Join in Wedlock, Part 2 of 3], *Khai Hóa Nhật Báo* 開化日報 [*Civilizing Daily*] (Hà Nội), October 4, 1924; Kim Giang, trans. "Hào Kiệt Kết Duyên" [Two Heroes Join in Wedlock, Part 3 of 3], *Khai Hóa Nhật Báo* 開化日報 [*Civilizing Daily*] (Hà Nội), October 6, 1924.

49. "Hát tại rạp Cầu-Muối Sài Gòn: Tuồng hát tối thứ bảy 9 Avril 1927" [Shows at the Cau Muoi Theater Sài Gòn: Dramas Performed Saturday Evening April 9, 1927]," *Đông Pháp thời báo* [*Đông Pháp Times Newspaper*] (Sài Gòn), April 11, 1927.

50. "Tối thứ ba 3 Décembre 1929: Anh Hùng Náo" [Wednesday Night December 3, 1929: The Rowdy Hero], *Hà Thành ngọ báo* [*Hà Thành Midday Newspaper*] (Hà Nội), December 3, 1929, 3.

51. Félix Mộng-Trân, *Tang-Đại Giả Gái* 桑代野姼 [*Tang-Dai Disguises as Female*] (Sài Gòn: Imprimerie Nguyễn Văn Viết, June 1925).

52. Nguyễn Phúc An, *Tuồng Hát Cải Lương: Khảo & Luận, 10 Năm Bốn Tuồng Để Yếu (1922-1931)* [Reform Theatre: Research and Writing, 10 Years of Reform Theatre, 1922–1931] (Thành Phố Hồ Chí Minh: Nhà Sách Tổng Hợp Thành Phố Hồ Chí Minh, 2022), 143.

53. See Thạch Lam, "Sự Nghiệp của Ông Vũ Đình Long" (The Career of Mr. Vũ Đình Long), *Phong Hóa (Mores)* 184 (April 24, 1936): 8.

54. *Anh Hùng Náo* [*The Rowdy Hero*], trans. Vũ Đình Long (Hà Nội: Kim Đức Giang Ấn-Quán, 1924), 5:284.

55. *Anh Hùng Náo*, 5:284.

56. *Anh Hùng Náo*, 5:284.

57. Thế Phụng, "Bài Phản Đối của ông Thế Phụng" [A Rebuttal by Mr. Thế Phụng], *Phụ Nữ Tân Văn* [*New Women's News*] 6 (1929): 13.

58. Phụng, 13.

59. Irigaray, for instance, claims that the history of Western philosophy is the history of the effacement of female sexuality. See Luce Irigaray, *Speculum of the Other Woman*, trans. Gillian C. Gill (Ithaca, NY: Cornell University Press, 1974). On "transvestite ventriloquism," see, e.g., Elizabeth D. Harvey, "The Voice of Gender," in *Ventriloquized Voices: Feminist Theory and English Renaissance Texts* (London: Routledge, 1992), 1.

60. See Jack Halberstam, *Female Masculinity* (Durham, NC: Duke University Press,

1998); Jean B. Noble, *Masculinities without Men? Female Masculinity in Twentieth Century Fictions* (Vancouver: University of British Columbia Press, 2003).

61. Paul Rouzer, *Articulated Ladies: Gender and the Male Community in Early Chinese Texts in Late Imperial China* (Cambridge, MA: Harvard University Press, 2001), 6.

62. Emanuel Pastreich, "The Reception of Chinese Literature in Vietnam," in *The Columbia History of Chinese Literature*, ed. Victor H. Mair (New York: Columbia University Press, 2001), 1099.

63. Huệ Tâm Hồ Tài, *Radicalism and the Origins of the Vietnamese Revolution* (Cambridge, MA: Harvard University Press, 1992), 29.

64. Thanh Tùng, ed., *Nguyễn Vỹ, Văn Học Từ Điển: Tiểu Sử Tác Giả* [Literary Dictionary: Biographies of Writers] (Sài Gòn: Nhà Xuất Bản Khai-Trí, 1973), 213.

65. Đ. C. Liệu, L. K. Kế, et al., *Từ Điển Việt-Anh* [Vietnamese-English Dictionary] (Ho Chí Minh: Nhà Xuất Bản Hồ Chí Minh, 2000), 759.

66. See Warner, *A Wild Deer amid Soaring Phoenixes* (Honolulu: University of Hawai'i Press 2003), 169n31; Anna M. Shields, *One Who Knows Me: Friendship and Literary Culture in Mid-Tang China.* (Cambridge, MA: Harvard University Asia Center, 2015), 47–48; Kenneth J. DeWoskin, *A Song for One or Two: Music and the Concept of Art in Early China*, Michigan Papers in Chinese Studies 42 (Ann Arbor: University of Michigan, 1982), 105.

67. Nguyễn Du, *The Tale of Kiều*, trans. Huỳnh Sanh Thông (New Haven, CT: Yale University Press, 1983), 21, *l.* 386. The original line: "Gió bắt mưa câm, / đã cam tệ với *tri-âm* bấy chầy."

68. Trần Văn Quế, *Côn Lôn Quần Đảo Trước Ngày 9-3-1945* [The Poulo Condore Archipelago before March 9, 1945] (Sài Gòn: Thanh Hương Tùng Thơ, 1961) 130.

69. "Tìm tri kỷ trong mục Sợi Tơ Hồng" [Finding a Soulmate in the Red Silk column], *Báo Loa* [*The Loudspeaker*] 91 (November 11, 1935).

70. Nguyễn Thị Kiêm, "Cô Nguyễn Thị Kiêm nói về vấn đề Nữ lưu và văn học" [Ms. Nguyễn Thị Kiêm Speaks about the World of Women and Literature], *Phụ Nữ Tân Văn* [*New Women's News*] 131 (1932): 32.

71. Translated from Vietnamese by Nguyễn Quốc Vinh, "Love of Men: Xuân Diệu," in *Viet Nam Forum,* ed. Dan Duffy (New Haven, CT: Yale University Council on Southeast Asian Studies, 1997), 16:265.

72. Hữu Nhuận and Vũ Quần Phương, eds., *Tuyển Tập Xuân Diệu* [Selected Works of Xuân Diệu] (Hà Nội: Nhà Xuất Bản Văn Học [Van Hoc Publishing House] 1986), 148; Xuân Diệu, *Toàn Tập Xuân Diệu* [The Complete Works of Xuân Diệu] (Hà Nội: Nhà Xuất Bản Văn Học [Literature Publishing House], 2001).

73. Huy Cận, *Hồi Ký Song Đôi: Tuổi Nhỏ Huy Cận-Xuân Diệu* [Memoirs of Two: The Early Years of Huy Cận and Xuân Diệu] (Hà Nội: Nhà Xuất Bản Hội Nhà Văn [Writers Association Publishing House], 2002), 199.

74. Cận, 209.

75. Cận, 114.

76. Cận, 202.

77. Nguyễn Quốc Vinh, "Deviant Bodies and Dynamics of Displacement of Homoerotic Desire in Vietnamese Literature from and about the French Colonial Period (1858–1954)," 1997, http://www.talawas.org/talaDB/suche.php?res=1056&rb=0503&von=.

78. Hoa Đường, "Trong Chùa Long-Vân Có Gì Lạ?" [What Is Unusual about the Long Van Temple?], *Sài Gòn*, April 23, 1940, 1, 6.

79. "Sau Lưng Phật Tổ" [Behind the Back of the Buddha], *Hà Nội Tân Văn* [New Hà Nội News], May 7, 1940, 3.

80. *Ngày Này* [*These Days*] 208 (May 18, 1940), cover.

81. "Sau Lưng Phật Tổ," 1–2.

82. Tú Mỡ writes: "Pretending to be a woman, that monk there pads his chest/ makes a fraudulent exchange, in order to exploit the nuns" (*Giả làm gái kia sư thầy độn vú/ Để lộn sòng, gà gụ các sư cô*) Although the rhyme is lost in my crude translation, the poem actually parodies a Buddhist chant. T. Mo, "Thơ Trào Phúng: Phá Giới" [Humorous Satirical Poetry: Breaking Commandments], *Ngày Nay* [*These Days*] 209 (May 25, 1940): 9.

83. Như-Hoa, "Nào Sư Muốn Có Gạt Gẫm Ai Đâu" [The Buddhist Priest Muốn Intended to Deceive Nobody], *Sài Gòn,* April 22, 1940, 1.

84. Như-Hoa, "Như-Hoa Muốn Điên Theo Kiểu Đó Quá" [Như-Hoa Wishes to Be Crazy in That Way], *Sài Gòn*, April 26, 1940, 1.

85. Wenqing Kang, "The Language of Male Same-Sex Relations in China," in *Obsession: Male Same-Sex Relations in China, 1900–1950* (Hong Kong: Hong Kong University Press, 2009), 19–40.

Chapter 3

1. As quoted from Martina Thục Nhi Nguyễn, *On Our Own Strength: The Self-Reliant Literary Group and Cosmopolitan Nationalism in Late Colonial Vietnam* (Honolulu: University of Hawai'i Press, 2021), 25.

2. See, for example, the denunciation by the May Fourth intellectuals against an older, more "traditional" cohort of 1910 writers. See Perry Link, *The Uses of Literature: Life in the Socialist Chinese Literary System* (Princeton, NJ: Princeton University Press, 2000), 177–78. See also David G. Marr, *Vietnamese Tradition on Trial, 1925–1945* (Berkeley: University of California, 1981), 342–47; Nguyễn, *On Our Own Strength*, 25.

3. David Marr, "The Question of Women," in *Vietnamese Tradition on Trial* (Berkeley: University of California, 1981), 190–251.

4. For a study on how modern fashion and journalism could serve the basis of a modern Vietnamese nation, see Nguyễn, *On Our Own Strength*. For a study on the literary aesthetic modernity of the Self-Reliant Literary Group, see Ben Tran, *Postmandarin: Masculinity and Aesthetic Modernity in Colonial Vietnam* (New York: Fordham University Press, 2017). For an overview of the modern changes of the period, see Nguyễn Văn Ký, *La société vietnamienne face à la modernité: Le Tonkin de la fin du XIXe siècle à la Seconde Guerre Mondiale* (Paris: L'Harmattan, 1995).

5. The term "classical"—as opposed to "ancient"—is taken from Nguyễn Đinh Hòa's periodization of eighteenth- and nineteenth-century Vietnamese literature. See Nguyễn Đinh Hòa, *Vietnamese Literature: A Brief Survey* (San Diego, CA: San Diego State University, 1994), 1–9.

6. See, e.g., William J. Spurlin, "The Gender and Queer Politics of Translation: New Approaches," *Comparative Literature Studies* 51, no. 2 (2014); Nir Kedem, "What Is Queer Translation?," *symploke* 27, nos. 1–2 (2019).

7. David G. Marr, *Vietnamese Anticolonialism, 1880–1925* (Berkeley: University of California, 1971), 44–76.

8. David Marr, "A Generation of Lasts and Firsts," in *Vietnamese Anticolonialism, 1885–1925* (Berkeley: University of California, 1971), 77–97.

9. Phạm Quỳnh, "Sự Giáo-Dục Đàn Bà Con Gái" [The Education of Women and Girls], *Nam Phong [Southern Wind]* 1, no. 4 (1917): 209.

10. Quỳnh, 208.

11. Quỳnh, 209.

12. Marr, "Question of Women," 203.

13. Marr, 204.

14. Trịnh Thị Minh-hà, *Surname Viet, Given Name Nam*; Marr, "Question of Women," 210.

15. Marr, "Question of Women," 200.

16. Gail Kelly. *Franco-Vietnamese Schools, 1918–1938: Regional Development and Implications for National Integration* (Madison: University of Wisconsin Press, 1982), 14–15.

17. Marr, "Question of Women," 206.

18. Marr, 206.

19. Marr, 204–5.

20. Neil Jamieson, *Understanding Vietnam* (Berkeley: University of California Press, 1995), 146–54.

21. Marr, "Question of Women," 211.

22. Roland Altenburger, *The Sword and the Needle: The Female Knight-Errant (xia) in Traditional Chinese Narrative* Worlds of East Asia 15 (Bern: Peter Lang, 2009), 33.

23. Barbara Watson Andaya, "Rethinking the Historical Place of 'Warrior Women' in Southeast Asia," in *Women Warriors in Southeast Asia*, ed. Vina A. Lanzona and Frederik Rettig (New York: Routledge, 2020), 267–94.

24. *Nữ Lưu Tướng* 將劉女: *Truyện Diễn Ca [Female General Luu: A Story in Plain Verse]*, ed. Phạm Văn Phương (Hà Nội: Mặc Đình Tư Publishers, 1922), 10:10, stanza 2.

25. "Lưu Nữ Tướng [Female General Luu]," in *Tổng Tập Văn Học Việt Nam [General Collection of Vietnamese Literature]*, ed. Lê Văn Quán (Hà Nội: Nhà Xuất Bản Khoa Học Xã Hội [Social Science Publishing House], 1993), 13, stanza 7.

26. "The male transforms clearly into a female" ("Nam nhi phút biến nữ-nhi rõ-ràng"). "Lưu Nữ Tướng," 73, stanza 48.

27. Phan Bội Châu, for instance, recast the story of the two women's fight as a struggle in the name of patriotism. A conventional account of the story would suggest that the reason the older sister went to battle was to avenge her husband killed by the Chinese governor-general. Phan Bội Châu's play, by contrast, recast the fight in the name of love of country within the context of anticolonial struggle against the French. This is the interpretation proffered by Marr. See Marr, *Vietnamese Tradition on Trial*, 200–201.

28. Phan Bội Châu. "A Letter from Abroad Written in Blood" (1907), in *Sources of Vietnamese Tradition*, ed. Jayne S. Werner, George E. Dutton, and John K. Whitmore (New York: Columbia University Press, 2012), 365. On the circulation of the story of Bùi Thị Xuân, see Marr, "Question of Women," 210–11.

29. Phạm Văn Phương, preface to *Nữ Lưu Tướng* 將劉女: *Truyện Diễn Ca [Female Gen-*

eral Luu: A Story in Plain Verse], ed. Phạm Văn Phương (Hà Nội: Mặc Đình Tư Publishers 1922), para. 9.

30. See Feng Lan, "The Female Individual and the Empire: A Historicist Approach to Mulan and Kingston's Women Warrior," *Comparative Literature* 55, no. 3 (2003). See also Lan Dong, "Heroic Lineage: Military Women and Lady Knights-Errant in Premodern China," in *Mulan's Legend and Legacy in China and the United States* (Philadelphia: Temple University Press, 2010), 9–50.

31. Lan, "Female Individual and the Empire," 231.

32. Nguyễn Tử Lăng, *Mộc-lan tòng quân* [*Moc Lan Joins the Army*], trans. Thuyết Phật (Nam Định: Nam Hoa, 1928), 1:7.

33. Lăng, 1:7.

34. Lan, "Female Individual and the Empire," 235.

35. Nguyễn Tử Lăng, "Nhời Nói Sau" [Concluding Remarks], in Lăng, *Mộc-lan tòng quân*, 1:220.

36. These conditions are adapted for the present purposes from Roland Altenburger, "Is it Clothes That Make the Man? Cross-Dressing, Gender and Sex in Pre-Twentieth Century Zhu Yingtai Lore," *Asian Folklore Studies* 64, no. 2 (2005): 165–205.

37. By "pluralism," I borrow Peletz's formulation to mean difference with legitimacy. Difference without legitimacy is not pluralism but potential stigma. See Michael Peletz, *Gender Pluralism: Southeast Asia since Early Modern Times* (London: Routledge, 2009), 7.

38. Nguyễn Tri Phố, "Đoản thiên tiểu thuyết: Hiếu Nữ Nam Trang" [Short Novel: A Filial Female Dressed as a Male, Part 1 of 4]," *Khai hóa nhật báo* 開化日報 [*The Civilizing Daily*] (Hà Nội), 5 September 1923, 2.

39. Feng Menglong, *Stories Old and New: A Ming Dynasty Collection Compiled by Feng Menglong (1574–1646)*, trans. Shuhui Yang and Yunqin Yang (Seattle: University of Washington Press, 2000), 493–501.

40. Menglong, 493.

41. According to Judith Zeitlin, the story of the female character Huang Shancong who dressed as a boy for many years and who managed to raise money to return her father's body to their native place for burial was recorded in the official Ming history in the section "Exemplary Women." See Judith T. Zeitlin, *Historian of the Strange: Pu Songling and the Chinese Classical Tale* (Stanford, CA: Stanford University Press, 1993), 258–59n56.

42. Phố, "Đoản thiên tiểu thuyết," 1.

43. "Phương Hoa," in *Tổng Tập Văn Học Việt Nam* [*General Collection of Vietnamese Literature*], ed. Lê Văn Quán (Hà Nội: Nhà Xuất Bản Khoa Học Xã Hội [Social Science Publishing House], 1993), 330.

44. See Nguyễn Thị Chân-Quỳnh, *"Lối Xưa Xe Ngựa . . ."* [*The Horse Carriage of Former Times*] (Paris: Nhà Xuất Bản An Tiêm [An Tiêm Publishing House], 1995), 149–70.

45. *Nữ Tú Tài* [*Female Baccalaureate Graduate*], ed. and trans. Trần Phong Sắc and Huỳnh Khắc Thuận (Sài Gòn: Marcellin Rey, 1911). According to a secondary source, the story in *quốc ngữ* was also published in 1914. See Nguyễn Văn Minh and Long Điển, *Từ Điển Văn Liệu* [*Dictionary of Literary Material*] (Sài Gòn Nhà Xuất Bản A Châu [A Châu Publishers], 1952), 469. See also *Nữ Tú Tài Truyện, La jeune fille bachelière, en prose rythmée* [*A Story of a Female Baccalaureate Graduate*], trans. Nguyễn Ngọc Xuân (Hải Phòng: Văn

Minh, 1923); *Nữ Tú Tài* 專才秀女 [*Female Baccalaureate Graduate*] (Hà Nội: Kim Khuê, 1927); *Nữ Tú Tài* [*Female Baccalaureate Graduate*] (Hà Nội: Kim Khuê, 1930).

46. "Cải lương: Tối Thứ ba 4 Juin 1929: *Nữ Tú Tài* [Reformed Theatre: Tuesday Evening 4 June: *Female Baccalaureate Graduate*]," *Nông Công Thương Nhật Báo* [*Nông Công Thương Daily*] (Hà Nội), 5 June 1929.

47. Altenburger, "Is It Clothes That Make the Man?," 177.

48. Altenburger, 174.

49. *Nữ Tú Tài* 專才秀女 [*Female Baccalaureate Graduate*], 1.

50. The editors of the *General Collection of Vietnamese Literature* state that *Female Baccalaureate Graduate* is an anonymous *nôm* tale in verse deriving from *Stories Old and New* [*Kim Cổ Kỳ Quan*] but do not specify the name of the original story. A Vietnamese master's thesis focusing on the theme of cross-dressing in *nôm* texts unknowingly treats *Female Baccalaureate Graduate* and the folktale of Liang Shanbo and Zhu Yingtai as distinct stories, perhaps due to the different titles and characters' names. See "Nữ Tú Tài [Female Baccalaureate Graduate]," in *Tổng Tập Văn Học Việt Nam* [*General Collection of Vietnamese Literature*], ed. Lê Văn Quán (Hà Nội: Nhà Xuất Bản Khoa Học Xã Hội [Social Science Literature Publishing House], 1993)], 383–84; Nguyễn Thị Hiền, "Nhân Vật Giả Nam Trong Truyện Nôm [The Characters Who Disguise as Male in Nôm Stories]" (Master's thesis, Trường Đại Học Sư Phạm Hà Nội [Pedagogical University of Hà Nội], 2005), 17–20.

51. Menglong, *Stories Old and New*, 489.

52. Hoa, *Vietnamese Literature*, 94–95.

53. See the brief introduction in "Nữ Tú Tài" [Female Baccalaureate Graduate], in *Tổng Tập Văn Học Việt Nam* [*General Collection of Vietnamese Literature*], ed. Lê Văn Quán (Hà Nội: Nhà Xuất Bản Khoa Học Xã Hội, 1993), 383–84.

54. For more on the "reformed opera," see Khai Thu Nguyễn, "A Personal Sorrow: 'Cải Lương' and the Politics of North and South Vietnam," *Asian Theatre Journal* 29, no. 1 (2012).

55. Altenburger, "Is It Clothes That Make the Man?," 165–205.

56. Keith McMahon, "The Chaste 'Beauty-Scholar' Romance and the Superiority of the Talented Woman," in *Misers, Shrews, and Polygamists: Sexuality and Male-Female Relations in Eighteenth-Century Chinese Fiction* (Durham, NC: Duke University Press, 1995), 99.

57. Daria Berg, "The Happy World of Scholar-Beauty Romances," in *The Columbia History of Chinese Literature*, ed. Victor H. Mair (New York: Columbia University Press, 2001), 666–72. See also McMahon, "Chaste 'Beauty-Scholar' Romance," 99–125.

58. See Emanuel Pastreich, "The Reception of Chinese Literature in Vietnam," in *The Columbia History of Chinese Literature*, ed. Victor H. Mair (New York: Columbia University Press, 2001), 1100–1102.

59. Mark Bender, "Regional Literatures," in *The Columbia History of Chinese Literature*, ed. Victor H. Mair (New York: Columbia University, 2001), 1019–1125.

60. Bender, 1021.

61. Li Guo, "The Legacy of Crossdressing in *Tanci*: On *A Histoire of Heroic Woman and Men*," *Frontiers of Literary Studies in China* 5, no. 4 (2011): 571, https://doi.org/10.1007/s11702-011-0142-x.

62. Siao-chen Hu, "Literary *Tanci*: A Woman's Tradition of Narrative in Verse" (PhD diss., Harvard University, 1994), 31–102.

63. Qingyun Wu, *Female Rule in Chinese and English Literary Utopias* (Syracuse, NY: Syracuse University Press, 1995), 1–17.

64. *Tái Sanh Duyên (sự tích Mạnh Lệ Quân): Giả trai, đậu Trạng, Lê quân cưới vợ [Love Reincarnated (The Story of Manh Le Quan): Disguises as a Man, Passes the Civil Examinations, and Gets Married to a Wife]*, trans. Thanh Phong (Sài Gòn: Tin Đức Thư Xa, 1923), vol. 14.

65. *Tái Sanh Duyên* 再生緣: *Mạnh Lệ Quân toàn truyện [Love Reincarnated: The Complete Story of Manh Le Quan]* (Sài Gòn: Imprimerie Librairie Huỳnh Kim Danh [Huỳnh Kim Danh Publishing House], 1929), vol. 1; *Tái Sanh Duyên* 再生緣: *Mạnh Lệ Quân*, trans. Lê Duy Thiện (Sài Gòn: Xưa Nay, 1930), vol. 1.

66. *Tuồng Hát Cải-Lương: Mạnh Lệ Quân Giả Trai [A Reform Drama: Manh Le Quan Disguises as Male]*, ed. Trương Quang Tiên (Sài Gòn: Imprimerie de l'Union, 1927); Trương Quang Tiến, *Mạnh—Lệ—Quân chăm trường thi gặp chồng: Tuồng hát cải lương [Manh Le Quan Meets Husband at the Exam: A Reform Opera Theatre]* (Sài Gòn: Tín-Đức Thư-Xã, 1928); Trương Quang Tiến, *Tuồng Hát Cải Lương: Mạnh-Lệ-Quân Thoát Hài [Reform Opera: Manh Le Quan Removes Her Shoes]* (Sài Gòn: Tín-Đức Thư-Xã, 1929); Phong Vân, *Mạnh Lệ Quân: thứ nhứt giả trai, thứ hai chẩn mạch, thứ ba thoát hài [Manh Le Quan: To Cross Dress as a Male, to Make a Diagnosis, and to Take Off the Shoes]* (Cholon: Nhà Xuất Bản Phạm Đình Khương, 1933).

67. "Mạnh Lệ Quân thoát hài: Cải lương Nam kỳ [Manh Le Quan Removes Her Shoes: Southern Reform Theatre]," *Hà Thành Ngọ Báo [Hà Thành Midday Newspaper]* (Hà Nội), November 3, 1928, sec. Cuộc Vui Buổi Tối [Evening Entertainment]; "Mạnh Lệ Quân giả trai: Cải Lương Nam Kỳ [Manh Le Quan Cross-Dresses as a Man: Southern Reform Theatre]," *Hà Thành ngọ báo [Hà Thành Midday Newspaper]* (Hà Nội), October 20, 1928.

68. The original: "Cây cỏ bình yên; khuya tĩnh mịch/Bỗng đâu lên khúc Lạc âm thiều / Nhị hồ để bốc niềm cô tịch, / Không khóc, nhưng mà buồn hiu . . . / Điệu ngã sang bài *Mạnh Lệ Quân* / Thu gồm xa vắng tự muôn đời." Xuân Diệu, "Nhị Hồ" [Two Lakes], in *Xuân Diệu Toàn Tập [The Complete Works of Xuân Diệu]* (1938; Hà Nội: Nhà Xuất Bản Văn Học, 2001), 58–59.

69. "Tối thứ bảy: Anh Hùng Náo" [Saturday Evening: The Rowdy Hero], *Hà Thành ngọ báo [Hà Thành Midday Newspaper]* (Hà Nội), November 3, 1928.

70. In her study on the history of foot-binding in China, Dorothy Ko links the practice to the cultural processes of inculcating female identity. See Dorothy Ko, "Becoming a Woman," in *Every Step a Lotus: Shoes for Bound Feet* (Berkeley: University of California Press, 2001). On foot-binding's erotic appeal, see Howard S. Levy, "Wondrousness of the Lotus," in *Chinese Footbinding: The History of a Curious Erotic Custom* (New York: Bell Publishing Co., 1967), 147–56. On the multiple meanings of footbinding, see Dorothy Ko, *Cinderella's Sisters: A Revisionist History of Footbinding* (Berkeley: University of California Press, 2005).

71. For a survey of the interpretations of foot-binding, see Ko, *Cinderella's Sisters*, 1–6.

72. Dorothy Ko, *Every Step a Lotus: Shoes for Bound Feet* (Berkeley: University of California Press, 2001), 15–17.

73. Phú Hà, Tuyết Huy, and Dương Bá Trạc, preface to *Tục Tái Sanh Duyên (Sử Tích*

Mạnh Lệ Quân) [*The Custom of Resurrection (The Story of Manh Le Quan)*] (1924; Hà Nội: Nhà Xuất Bản Văn Hóa Thông Tin, 2000), 6.

74. The original quotation: "Dù trai, dù gái, đã là người thì bốn chữ đó không thể thiếu được."

75. Hà, Huy, and Trạc, preface to *Tục Tái Sanh Duyên*, 6. The original: "Cái đạo cả làm người không có bốn chữ đó thì không phải là người: mà dù có là người cũng không biết là người đã thoái hóa xuống tới giống gì, chứ không còn phải cái hạng người."

76. Another critic's preface, published in 1935, further corroborates this reception of the Mạnh Lệ Quân story. In his preface, Đặng Đình Phương explains that the importance of the story lies in its display of Confucian ethics. He states: "Often when a humble writer merely reads the story of Mạnh Lệ Quân, a thousand sorrows can be resolved. The story contains all of the four proper words, Loyalty, Filial Piety, Altruism, Uprightness [Trung, Hiếu, Tiết, Nghĩa] so when one casually opens the book's covers, one is edifying one's virtue." See Nguyễn Bá Thời, *Mạnh Lệ Quân giả trai* [*Manh Le Quan Feigns Being Male*] (Sài Gòn: Imprimeur Phạm Văn Thình 1935), 1.

77. Tian Min, "Male Dan: The Paradox of Sex, Acting, and Perception in Traditional Chinese Theatre," *Asian Theatre Journal* 17, no. 1 (March 2000): 80.

78. Judith T. Zeitlin, "Heroes among Women," in *Historian of the Strange: Pu Songling and the Chinese Classical Tale* (Stanford, CA: Stanford University Press, 1993), 130.

79. "Đàn bà đời nay: Mạnh Lệ Quân tái thế" [Women Today: The Rebirth of Manh Le Quan], *Phụ Nữ Tân Văn* [*New Women's News*] 1 (May 2, 1929): 23.

80. Studying the "Barker" controversy in English print media, Doan writes that although the scandal took place only three months after the banning of Radclyffe Hall's *The Well of Loneliness*, a novelistic defense of lesbianism, the Barker controversy failed to register any "stable spectatorial effect" (664). If we were to identify a link between female masculinity and homosexual identity, according to Doan, we ought to do so with caution. Laura Doan, "Reading Female Masculinities in the 1920s," *Feminist Studies* 24, no. 3 (Autumn 1998): 663–700.

81. "Nói thêm về chuyện người đàn bà giả trai [More on the Story about the Woman Who Disguised Herself as a Man]," *Phụ Nữ Tân Văn* [*New Women's News*] 6 (June 6, 1929): 26.

82. "Đàn bà đời nay," 23. The original quotation: "Nếu cứ để cho bạn phụ nữ được bình đẳng với đờn ông trong sự học hành và trong giai cấp xã hội, thì ngày xưa chị em mình cũng làm được Trạng nguyên Tế tướng ngày nay cũng làm được Trạng-sư quan toà, chớ có lạ gì."

83. Joan W. Scott, "Fantasy Echo: History and the Construction of Identity," *Critical Inquiry* 27, no. 2 (Winter 2001): 284–304.

84. "Một người con gái Tàu giả trai đi lính, làm tới quan to" [A Chinese Woman Disguises as a Man, Becomes a High-Ranking Official], *Phụ Nữ Tân Văn* [*New Women's News*] 11 (1929): 12.

85. *Trịnh Dục Tú*, ed. Nguyễn Hữu Đạt and Nguyễn Ngọc Hải (Hà Nội: Vĩnh Thành ấn quán [Vĩnh Thành Publishers], 1927), 1:11–12.

86. *Trịnh Dục Tú*, 1:28.

87. *Trịnh Dục Tú*, 1:38.

88. *Trịnh Dục Tú*, 1:9.

89. Trương Hoàn, *Tiểu Thuyết: Nguyễn Tuyết-Hoa: Học sanh Nữ học đường [A Novel: Nguyễn Tuyet Hoa]* (Sài Gòn: Imprimerie Duc-Luu Phuong, 1930), 1:1.

90. Trương Hoàn, preface to *Tiểu Thuyết: Nguyễn Tuyết-Hoa: Học sanh Nữ học đường [A Novel: Nguyễn Tuyet Hoa]* (Sài Gòn: Imprimerie Duc-Luu Phuong, 1930), 1.

Chapter 4

1. See Huệ Tâm Hồ Tài, *Radicalism and the Origins of the Vietnamese Revolution* (Cambridge, MA: Harvard University Press, 1992), 88–113. The figure of the "New Woman" is distinct from that of the "modern girl," although they share some similarities, such as an enthusiasm for mass consumer culture. See Alys Eve Weinbaum et al., "The Modern Girl as Heuristic Device: Collaboration, Connective Comparison, Multidirectional Citation," in *The Modern Girl Around the World: Consumption, Modernity, and Globalization* (Durham, NC: Duke University Press, 2008), 9–10.

2. David G. Marr, *Vietnamese Tradition on Trial, 1925–1945* (Berkeley: University of California, 1981), 191.

3. Shawn McHale, *Print and Power: Confucianism, Communism and Buddhism in the Making of Modern Vietnam* (Honolulu: University of Hawai'i Press, 2004), 173.

4. Studying the publication of the adventures of the cartoon character Ly Toet, George Dutton writes that "Ly Toet's encounters with city life revealed the ambivalence of this new modernity, including its physical dangers and its often-abrupt departures from long-established patterns of daily life." George Dutton, "Ly Toet in the City: Coming to Terms with the Modern in 1930s Vietnam," *Journal of Vietnamese Studies* 2, no. 1 (February 2007): 81.

5. See Dipesh Chakrabarty, "The Time of History and the Times of Gods," in *The Politics of Culture in the Shadow of Capital*, ed. Lisa Lowe and David Lloyd (Durham, NC: Duke University Press, 1997), 35–60; Judith Halberstam, *In a Queer Time and Place: Transgender Bodies, Subcultural Lives* (New York: New York University, 2005); Carla Freccero, *Queer/ Early/Modern* (Durham, NC: Duke University Press, 2006).

6. Nhung Tuyết Tran and Anthony Reid, "The Construction of Vietnamese Historical Identities," in *Viet Nam: Borderless Histories*, ed. Nhung Tuyết Tran and Anthony Reid (Madison: University of Wisconsin Press, 2006), 17.

7. David G. Marr, *Vietnamese Anticolonialism, 1880–1925* (Berkeley: University of California, 1971), 44–156.

8. Hồ Tài, *Radicalism and the Origins of the Vietnamese Revolution*, 34.

9. Mark Bradley, "Becoming Van Minh: Civilizational Discourse and Visions of the Self in Twentieth-Century Vietnam," *Journal of World History* 15, no. 1 (2004): 74.

10. The story of their departure from and eventual return to Vietnam in the early 1930s has already been documented. See, e.g., Scott McConnell, *Leftward Journey: The Education of Vietnamese Students in France, 1919–1939* (New Brunswick, NJ: Transaction Publishers, 1989), 131–70.

11. Hồ Tài, *Radicalism and the Origins of the Vietnamese Revolution*, 146.

12. Pheng Cheah, "Grounds of Comparison," *Diacritics* 29, no. 4 (1999): 12.

13. Neil Jamieson, "Some Things Poetry Can Tell Us about the Process of Social Change in Vietnam," *Southeast Asian Studies* 39, no. 3 (December 2001): 82.

14. For this reason, Judith Henchy describes this period as one of "rapid transition." Judith A. N. Henchy, "Performing Modernity in the Writings of Nguyễn An Ninh and Phan Văn Hùm" (PhD diss., University of Washington, 2005), 208. Shawn McHale calls it a "moral and epistemological chaos" resulting in a "fragmented sense of identity among the men and women members of the élite." Shawn McHale, "Printing and Power: Vietnamese Debates over Women's Place in Society, 1918–1934," in *Essays into Vietnamese Pasts*, ed. K. W. Taylor and John K. Whitmore, Studies on Southeast Asia (Ithaca, NY: Cornell University, 1995), 193.

15. Phan Khôi, "Lịch Sử Tóc Ngắn: Annam Kể Từ 1906" (The History of Short Hair: Annam since 1906)," *Ngày Nay* [*These Days*] 149, Tet ed. (1938): 28–29.

16. Khôi, 29.

17. See Marr, *Vietnamese Tradition on Trial*; Nguyễn Văn Ký, *La société vietnamienne face à la modernité: Le Tonkin de la fin du XIXe siècle à la Seconde Guerre Mondiale* (Paris: L'Harmattan, 1995); Duong Van Mai Elliott, *The Sacred Willow: Four Generations in the Life of a Vietnamese Family* (Oxford: Oxford University Press, 1999); Hồ Tài, *Radicalism and the Origins of the Vietnamese Revolution*.

18. If Laura Doan is right, the necessary link between a fixed gender and (homo)sexual identity in this historical juncture is, at most, tenuous. See Laura Doan, "Reading Female Masculinities in the 1920s," *Feminist Studies* 24, no. 3 (Autumn 1998): 667.

19. Phan Văn Hùm, "Dư Luận và Thời Thượng" [Public Opinion and the Vogue], *Phụ Nữ Tân Văn* [*New Women's News*] 246 (June 14, 1934): 6.

20. Phan Kim Phụng, "Vấn đề hớt tóc của phụ nữ Việt Nam ta" [The Question of Cutting Our Vietnamese Women's Hair], *Tiếng Dân* [*People's Voice*] 168 (April 6, 1929): 3.

21. "Tại sao đàn bà hớt tóc" [Why Women Had to Cut Their Hair], *Phụ Nữ Tân Văn* [*New Women's News*] 26 (October 24, 1929): 22.

22. Kỳ Khôi, "Đàn bà hớt tóc" [Women Trimming Their Hair], *Tiếng Dân* [*People's Voice*] 147 (January 16, 1929): 2.

23. "Độc giả luận đàn: Đàn bà Việt Nam có nên cúp tóc không" [Reader's Discussion: Should Vietnamese Women Clip Their Hair?), *Tiếng Dân* [*People's Voice*] 158 (March 2, 1929): 4.

24. Tam Hữu, "Mái tóc của phụ nữ tương lai" [Women's Future Hairstyle], *Phụ Nữ Tân Văn* [*New Women's News*] 248 (June 28, 1934): 21–22.

25. The original quotation: "Còn thanh niên nước ta thì: dồi mài cạo gọt môi mép, cũng *thoa son đánh phấn như gái*, quần 'charleston,' áo 'Paris mode' chưng diện loẹt loè, rồi thì đoàn năm lủ bảy rủ nhau đi 'thưởng nguyệt ngắm trăng.'" See Thanh Ngôn, "Ý kiến bạn thanh niên: vấn đề đĩ điếm ở xã hội ta" [Ideas from a Young Man: The Issue of Prostitution in Our Society)," *Phụ Nữ Tân Văn* [*New Women's News*] 115 (January 7, 1932): 11.

26. On the dandy's gender crossing, see Susan Fillin-Yeh, "Dandies, Marginality, and Modernism: Georgia O Keefe, Marcel Duchamp, and Other Cross-Dressers," in *Dandies: Fashion and Finesse in Art and Culture*, ed. Susan Fillin-Yeh (New York: New York University Press, 2021), 127–52.

27. Peter Zinoman, ed., *Dumb Luck: A Novel by Vu Trong Phung* (Ann Arbor: University of Michigan Press, 2002), 119.

28. Peter Zinoman, "Vũ Trọng Phụng's *Dumb Luck* and the Nature of Vietnamese Modernism," in *Dumb Luck* (Ann Arbor: University of Michigan Press, 2002), 1–30.

29. Marr, *Vietnamese Tradition on Trial*, 203.

30. The original quotation: "Tôi nói đây chẳng phải bảo chị em bỏ hết cái tánh chất đàn bà, mà làm như đàn ông." Lan Anh, "Tánh e thẹn của phụ nữ" [The Shy Character of Women], *Phụ Nữ Tân Văn* [*New Women's News*] 58 (June 26, 1930): 1.

31. Thạch Lan, "Thơ ở Paris gởi về: Người Đàn Bà Âu-Châu" [Letters from Paris: Women of Europe], *Phụ Nữ Tân Văn* [*New Women's News*] 40 (February 20, 1930): 9–10. The original quotation: "Tôi nghĩ rằng bọn này tự do hơn đàn bà Annam mà rồi không biết cái kết quả sẽ ra thế nào? Ừ, vài mươi năm, một trăm năm nữa, đàn bà ở đây về mặt tự do, sẽ giống như đàn ông cả, nghĩa là họ sẽ chơi và làm việc làm của nam-tử [*sic*], giống hệt nam-tử [*sic*], mà chỉ còn khác một điều: là họ còn kinh-nguyệt, họ phải đẻ và họ yếu đuối hơn! Sự đó không sửa đặng!... [some censored lines] ... *Đàn bà mà đã biến ra đàn ông*... [censored line] ... như thế—vì không làm sao mà đổi cả cái thân thể, cái sánh-lý của họ đặng–thì gia-đình sẽ tiêu, và xã hội cũng sẽ có một cuộc khủng hoảng lớn."

32. See John Dupré, "Gender and the End of Biological Determinism," in *Why Gender?*, ed. Jude Browne (Cambridge: Cambridge University Press, 2021), 57–77; Thomas Laqueur, *Making Sex: Body and Gender from the Greeks to Freud* (Cambridge, MA: Harvard University Press, 1990), 145–88.

33. On the regulation of women's image in contemporary Vietnam, see Lisa Drummond, "The Modern 'Vietnamese Woman': Socialization and Women's Magazine," in *Gender Practices in Contemporary Vietnam*, ed. Lisa Drummond and Helle Ryndstrom (Singapore: Singapore University Press, 2004), 158–78.

34. V.A., "Một vấn đề khoa học: Tại sao lại có đàn bà mọc râu?" [A Question of Science: Why Are There Women Who Grow Beards?], *Phụ Nữ Tân Văn* [*New Women's News*] 84 (May 28, 1931): 23.

35. V.A. The original quotation: "Thế là râu của đàn ông, cũng như kinh của đàn bà, đều thuận theo lý tự nhiên, mà tiết cái huyết dư đi vậy. Theo nghĩa như thế, thì nếu đàn bà huyết hư, mà dứt kinh ở dưới, tức là huyết chạy lên, thành ra mọc râu ở trên, chớ không có gì lạ."

36. See Marr, *Vietnamese Tradition on Trial*, 342–47.

37. H.G.T., "Đã to vú lại rậm râu" [They Have Big Breasts and a Beard!], *Khoa Học Tạp Chí* [*Science Journal*] 25 (July 1, 1932): 23.

38. "Đàn bà có râu" [Bearded Women], *Khoa Học Tạp Chí* [*Science Journal*] 64 (February 15, 1934): 21.

39. Tân Kỹ, "Mấy cái lạ trên thế giới" [Strange and Unusual Phenomena in the World], *Khoa Học Tạp Chí* [*Science Journal*] 87 (February 1, 1935): 5–6.

40. "Đàn bà có râu," 261.

41. V.A., "Đàn Bà quái lạ trên đời: Hai cô dính mình với nhau ma một cô muốn lấy chồng, một cô không muốn; người đàn bà thêu bằng cẳng, phần 1" [Strange women in the world: a Siamese Twin one of whom wishes to get married while the other does not; one who embroiders using her legs, Part 1], *Phụ Nữ Tân Văn* [*New Women's News*] 94 (August 6, 1931): 11; VA, "Đàn Bà quái lạ trên đời: Cô Violetta không tay không chưn, mụ Adrienne mọc râu ghê gớm, phần II" [Strange women in the world: Ms. Violetta has no arms or legs,

Ms. Adrienne grows a frightful beard, Part 2], *Phụ Nữ Tân Văn* [*New Women's News*] 86 (August 20, 1931): 13–14. VA, "Đàn bà quái lạ: trên đời: Người bán nam, bán nữ; cô ngó hình như con beo, người ta gọi là 'femme panthère; một cô gảy đờn bằng cẳng, phần 3" [Strange women in the world: a half man, half woman; a woman who looks like a panther, people call her 'femme panthère; another woman who plucks the guitar using her feet, Part 3], *Phụ Nữ Tân Văn* [*New Women's News*] 99 (September 10, 1931): 16–18.

42. My translation. V.A., "Đàn Bà quái lạ trên đời," pt. 1, 11. The original quotation: "Trên đời này, trong chị em ta, có nhiều người sanh ra tự nhiên là những cái quái-tượng ký hình, không ái có thể tưởng-tượng được. Nào là hai người sinh ra dính lưng với nhau; nào là người không tay, không chưn [*sic*], chỉ [*sic*] trơ trọi có cái mình, thế mà vẫn sống; nào là người mập lớn và cân nặng bằng bốn người thường; nào là người mọc râu ... v.v ... quái quái kỳ kỳ, chẳng biết sao mà nói cho hết" (11).

43. On "crippled" women, some of these documents can be interpreted through a "queer disabilities" lens. See Rosemarie Garland Thomson, *Extraordinary bodies: figuring physical disability in American culture and literature* (New York: Columbia University Press, 1997); Bob Guter and John R. Killacky, eds., *Queer Crips: Disabled Gay Men and Their Stories* (New York: Harrington Park Press, 2004). For a cultural study of the "freak show," see Rosemarie Garland Thomson, ed., *Freakery: Cultural Spectacles of the Extraordinary Body* (New York: New York University, 1996).

44. D.B., "Đàn bà có râu (Women with beards)," *Phụ Nữ Tân Văn (New Women's News)* 185 (January 12, 1933): 29.

45. French in original. V.A., "Đàn Bà quái lạ trên đời: Hai cô dính mình với nhau ma một cô muốn lấy chồng, một cô không muốn; người đàn bà thêu bằng cẳng, phần 1 (Strange women in the world: a Siamese Twin one of whom wishes to get married while the other does not; one who embroiders using her legs, Part 1)," 11.

46. V.A., "Đàn Bà quái lạ," 11.

47. D.B., "Đàn bà có râu" [Women with Beards]," 29.

48. Marr, *Vietnamese Tradition on Trial*, 340.

49. Nguyễn Thị Kiêm, "Cô Nguyễn Thị Kiêm nói về vấn đề Nữ lưu và văn học" [Ms. Nguyễn Thi Kiêm speaks about the world of women and literature]," *Phụ Nữ Tân Văn* [*New Women's News*] 131 (1932): 32.

50. French in original. Kiêm, 32.

51. Thiếu Sơn, "Nữ Sĩ Pháp" [French Women Writers], *Phụ Nữ Tân Văn* [*New Women's News*] 225 (November 23, 1933): 9–10.

52. Kiêm, 34.

53. Kiêm, 34.

54. See Henchy, "Performing Modernity," 85–102.

55. Phan Văn Hùm, "Văn 'Nam Hóa'" ["Masculinization" Literature]," *Phụ Nữ Tân Văn* [*New Women's News*] 245 (June 7, 1934): 11–12.

56. Henchy, "Performing Modernity," 22–23.

57. See Phan Văn Hùm, "Xã hội cần có gia đình không?" [Does Society Need the Family Unit?], *Phụ Nữ Tân Văn* [*New Women's News*] 256 (August 30, 1934): 7–8.

58. Quốc Chi, "Chết hai lần: Trinh thám tiểu thuyết, Số 31" [To die twice: a detective

novel, No. 31], *Khoa Học Tạp Chí* [*Science Journal*] 128 (July 11, 1936): 400. The original quotation: "Người con gái này chính là đứa ăn mày ở bộ câu-lạc ban nay đó. Nó là đàn ông, giả bận đàn bà hoặc nhiều hình khác, chính là viên điều tra."

59. Khái Hưng, "Tiêu Sơn Tráng Sĩ" [The Heroes of Tiêu Sơn], *Phong Hóa* [*Mores*] 147 (January 18, 1935): 6–7.

60. Hưng, 6. The original quotation: "Tuy về dung nhan có kém nhà sư ấy đôi chút, nhưng chàng công tử cũng là một người rất đẹp trai, với cặp mắt phượng long lanh, đôi lông mày bán nguyệt, với hai má trắng hồng và cái mồm cười có duyên. Sự đó chẳng có chi lạ, vì nhà sư và công tử chỉ là hai người thiếu phụ cải nam trang."

61. Vũ Ngọc Phan, "Nhà Văn Hiện Đại" [Modern Writers], in *Vũ Ngọc Phan Tuyển Tập (Selected Works of Vũ Ngọc Phan)*, ed. Nguyễn Thị Hạnh and Nguyễn Hồng Hạnh (Hà Nội: Nhà Xuất Bản Văn Học, 2008), 31.

62. Judith Butler, *Undoing Gender* (New York: Routledge, 2004), 65.

63. French in original. Tung Giang, "Chuyện cổ phương Tây: góc tích đàn bà và đàn ông" [A Western Mythology: On the Origins of Men and Women)," *Phụ Nữ Tân Văn* [*New Women's News*] 81 (December 11, 1930): 13–15.

64. Q.T., "Đàn Bà" [Women], *Phụ Nữ Tân Văn* [*New Women's News*]249 (July 5, 1934): 19–20. The original quotation: "Có một cái thuyết khác . . . nói rằng đàn bà không phải là con mái của đàn ông; xưa kia bạn của đàn bà vốn là cùng giống, cùng nòi, cho nên thân thể nam với nữ không khác nhau nhiều như ngày nay."

65. In turn: Huấn Minh, "Một tiếng đồng hồ với cô vài bút" [An hour with a self-declared "nun"], *Phụ Nữ Tân Văn* [*New Women's News*]198 (May 4, 1933): 21–23; VA, "Đàn bà quái lạ," pt. 3, 16–18; Bích Thuỷ, "Món quà trong lúc nghỉ hè: Dưới biển, trên rừng [A Gift during Summer Break: Under the Sea and in the Jungle]," *Phụ Nữ Tân Văn* [*New Women's News*] 251 (July 26, 1934): 17–19; "Cuộc thí nghiệm kỳ khôi" [A Strange Experiment]," *Khoa Học Tạp Chí* [*Science Journal*] 119 (April 11, 1936): 219; Bản Quán, "Những sự kỳ quán trong vũ trụ xét thấy ở nước Nam" [Strange and Unusual Phenomena in the Country of Nam)," *Khoa Học Tạp Chí* [*Science Journal*] 43 (April 1, 1933): 4–7; "Bán Nam Bán Nữ" [Half Man, Half Woman], *Khoa Học Tạp Chí* [*Science Journal*] 76 (August 15, 1934): 26; Công Ích, "Bán Nam Bán Nữ: Hermaphrodisme, Phần 1" [Half Man, Half Woman: Hermaphroditism, Part 1], *Khoa Học Tạp Chí* [*Science Journal*] 77 (September 1, 1934): 3–4; Công Ích, "Bán Nam Bán Nữ, Phần 2" [Half Man, Half Woman, Part 2]," *Khoa Học Tạp Chí* [*Science Journal*] 77 (September 1, 1934).

66. "Rồi đây khoa học sẽ tạo ra những người bán nam bán nữ" [Science Will Some Day Create Half-Men, Half-Women], *Khoa Học Tạp Chí* [*Science Journal*] 115 (March 1, 1936): 139.

67. "Rồi đây khoa học sẽ tạo ra những người bán nam bán nữ," 139.

68. Chung Anh, "Khoa học triết lý tiểu thuyết: Ngày Mai, số 2" [Philosophical Science Novel: Tomorrow, no. 2], *Khoa Học Tạp Chí* [*Science Journal*] 136 (October 1, 1936): 560. Original quotation: "Thình lình Minh bị một toán người vừa đàn ông, vừa đàn bà . . . chàng vẫn yên trí những người đàn bà kia . . . là những người ái nam, ái nữ."

69. Chung Anh, "Khoa học triết lý tiểu thuyết: Ngày Mai, số 11" [Philosophical Science Novel: Tomorrow, no. 11], *Khoa Học Tạp Chí* [*Science Journal*] 145 (January 12, 1937): 20.

70. Carrol Smith-Rosenberg, "Discourses of Sexuality and Subjectivity: The New

Woman, 1870–1936," in *Hidden from History: Reclaiming the Gay and Lesbian Past*, ed. Martin Duberman, Martha Vicinus, and George Chauncey Jr. (New York: New American Library, 1989), 265.

71. This interpretation of a "sexless" society is slightly different from Marie Louise Roberts' study of a like phenomenon in France where a "civilization without sexes" signified apocalyptic anxieties in the aftermath of World War I. See Mary Louise Roberts, *Civilization without Sexes: Reconstructing Gender in Postwar France, 1917–1927*, ed. Catharine R. Stimpson, Women in Culture and Society (Chicago: University of Chicago, 1994).

72. Anh, "Khoa học triết lý tiểu thuyết," 19.

73. See Anne Fausto-Sterling. "Sex, Glands, Hormones, and Gender Chemistry," in *Sexing the Body: Gender Politics and the Construction of Sexuality* (New York: Basic Books, 2020), 146–69.

74. Vân Anh, "Chuyện Khoa Học nên biết: Thay đầu vật nầy qua vật kia" [A Science Issue Worth Knowing: Changing One Sexual Organ for Another]," *Phụ Nữ Tân Văn* [*New Women's News*] 90 (July 9, 1931): 11.

75. Anh, 10. The original quotation: "Hai cái gà mà độc-giả thấy hình đây, đều là thứ gà trống lớn, cỡ 2 tuổi. Con bên tay trái, mới ngó ai chẳng bảo là gà mái, song kỳ thiệt không phải; lúc trước nó cũng là gà trống như con bên tay mặt vậy, có đều [*sic*] nhà khoa-học làm cách để bọc-trứng vào cho nó, rồi nó biến đổi từ cái mào cho tới lông, mà thành ra gà mái, như ta thấy đó."

76. Emily Martin, "The Egg and Sperm: How Science Has Constructed a Romance Based on Stereotypical Male-Female Roles," in *Feminist Theory and the Body*, ed. Janet Price and Margrit Shildrick (New York: Routledge, 1999).

77. Anh, "Chuyện Khoa Học nên biết," 9, 11.The original quotation: "Ngày nay tuy có nhiều người không tin, chở những nhà bác-học ở Âu-Mỹ có cái mộng-tưởng tới như vậy lận."

78. Heidegger has suggested that this cognitive mode, hegemonic in the modern period, blinds us, fundamentally, to other ways of knowing and understanding. In his words, we become "enframed" (*Gestell*). See Martin Heidegger, *The Question concerning Technology, and Other Essays*, trans. William Lovitt (New York: Harper & Row, 1977).

79. "Một người đàn ông đẻ con" [A Man Who Gives Birth], *Phụ Nữ Tân Văn* [*New Women's News*] 193 (March 30, 1933): 4.

80. Laqueur, *Making Sex*, 145–88.

81. See Barbara Walters's special report on a transgendered man who gives birth. "Pregnant Man Expecting Second Child," *ABC News*, November 13, 2008, https://abcnews.go.com/Health/story?id=6244878&page=1.

82. "Ô! Ai bảo đàn ông không đẻ" [Oh! Who Says Men Cannot Give Birth?], *Phong Hóa* [*Mores*] 146 (April 26, 1935): 8.

83. "Một người đàn ông đẻ con," 4.

84. "Con gái hóa con trai" [A Girl Transforms into a Boy], *Khoa Học Tạp Chí* [*Science Journal*] 81 (November 1, 1934): 25.

85. "Chuyện lạ của khoa học: Rồi đây đàn bà có thể biến thành đàn ông chăng?" [An Unusual Scientific Phenomenon: Will Women Some Day Be Able to Transform into a Man?], *Phụ Nữ Tân Văn* [*New Women's News*] 236 (March 29, 1934): 19.

86. Hữu Sào, "Tại sao đàn ông rậm râu, đàn bà to vú?" [Why Do Men Have Beards and Women Large Breasts?], *Khoa Học Tạp Chí* [*Science Journal*] 93 (May 1, 1935): 2.

87. Hiếu Kỳ, "Tại sao đàn ông có râu, đàn bà tốt tóc" [Why Do Men Have Beards, Women Long Hair?], *Khoa Học Tạp Chí* [*Science Journal*] 108 (December 15, 1935): 3–5.

88. T.V., "Trên đời này có một xứ không cho đàn bà và cho cái bước cẳng đến" [A place where women are forbidden to set foot], *Phụ Nữ Tân Văn* [*New Women's News*] 220 (October 12, 1933): 12–13.

89. H.K., "Có thể biết trước được trứng nào sẽ nở ra gà sống gà mái không? (Is it possible to predict the egg's sex?)," *Khoa Học Tạp Chí* [*Science Journal*] 99 (August 1, 1935): 5; "Đàn bà hóa đàn ông" [A woman transforms into a man], *Khoa Học Tạp Chí* [*Science Journal*] 115 (March 1, 1936): 139.

90. Đồng, "Ảnh hưởng của giáo dục và hoàn cảnh hay là một sự thí nghiệm rất lạ lùng ở Đức" [Societal Influence and Upbringing or a Strange Experiment in Germany], *Phụ Nữ Tân Văn* [*New Women's News*] 236 (March 29, 1934): 24–25.

91. "Nam hóa nữ" [A Man Transforms into a Woman], *Khoa Học Tạp Chí* [*Science Journal*] 147 (January 21, 1937): 57.

92. "Những cái mầu nhiệm của khoa học: người ta có thể đổi giống đực, cái được" [The Miracles of Science: People Can Change Male, Female Genders], *Ngày Nay* [*These Days*] 82 (1937): 887.

Conclusion

1. See "Vietnam Marriage and Family Law 2014," June 26, 2014, https://vietnamlaweng lish.blogspot.com/2014/06/vietnam-marriage-and-family-law-2014.html.

2. For an English version of the law, see "Law on Marriage and the Family (1959)," in *Sources of Vietnamese Tradition*, ed. George E. Dutton, Jayne S. Werner, and John K. Whitmore (New York: Columbia University Press, 2012), 536–542.

BIBLIOGRAPHY

Altenburger, Roland. "Is It Clothes That Make the Man? Cross-Dressing, Gender and Sex in Pre-Twentieth Century Zhu Yingtai Lore." *Asian Folklore Studies* 64, no. 2 (2005): 165–205.

———. *The Sword and the Needle: The Female Knight-Errant (Xia) in Traditional Chinese Narrative.* Worlds of East Asia 15. Bern: Peter Lang, 2009.

Andaya, Barbara Watson. *The Flaming Womb: Repositioning Women in Early Modern Southeast Asia.* Honolulu: University of Hawai'i Press, 2006.

———. "Rethinking the Historical Place of 'Warrior Women' in Southeast Asia." In *Women Warriors in Southeast Asia*, edited by Vina A. Lanzona and Frederik Rettig, 267–94. New York: Routledge, 2020.

Anderson, Benedict. *The Spectre of Comparison: Nationalism, Southeast Asia and the World.* London: Verso, 1998.

Anh, Chung. "Khoa Học Triết Lý Tiểu Thuyết: Ngày Mai, Số 2" (Philosophical Science Novel: Tomorrow, No. 2). *Khoa Học Tạp Chí [Science Journal]* 136 (October 1, 1936): 559–60.

———. "Khoa Học Triết Lý Tiểu Thuyết: Ngày Mai, Số 11" (Philosophical Science Novel: Tomorrow, No. 11). *Khoa Học Tạp Chí [Science Journal]* 145 (January 12, 1937): 19–20.

Anh, Đào Duy. *Hán Việt Từ Điển* [Sino-Vietnamese Dictionary]. Sài Gòn: Trường Thi, 1932.

Anh, Hồng Chung. *Nam Nữ Tu Tri: Guide moral des rapport sexuels [Moral Guide to Sexual Relations].* Hà Nội: Đông Tây, 1932.

Anh, Lan. "Tánh E Thẹn Của Phụ Nữ" [The Shy Character of Women]. *Phụ Nữ Tân Văn [New Women's News]* 58 (June 26, 1930): 1.

Anh, Vân. "Chuyện Khoa Học Nên Biết: Thay Đầu Vật Nầy Qua Vật Kia" [A Science Issue Worth Knowing: Changing One Sexual Organs for Another]. *Phụ Nữ Tân Văn (New Women's News)* 90 (July 9, 1931): 9–11.

Anh Hùng Náo [*The Rowdy Hero*]. Vol. 5. Translated by Vũ Đình Long. Hà Nội: Kim Đức Giang Ấn-Quán, 1924.

Anh Hùng Náo [*The Rowdy Hero*]. Vol. 1. Translated by Vũ Đình Long. Hà Nội: Kim-Đức Giang Ấn-Quán, 1924.

An-Nhân, and Lê-Trúc. *Nam Nữ Bí-Mật Chi Nam* [*Male Female Secrets for Men*]. Hà Nội: Nhật Nam Thư Quán Publishers, 1932.

Au, Sokhieng. *Mixed Medicines: Health and Culture in French Colonial Cambodia*. Chicago: University of Chicago Press, 2011.

"Bán Nam Bán Nữ" [Half Man, Half Woman]. *Khoa Học Tạp Chí* [*Science Journal*] 76 (August 15, 1934): 26.

Bảo, Định Phúc. "Mười Khoản Vệ-Sanh Cốt-Yếu [Ten Cardinal Items on Hygiene]." *Y thoại tùng biên* 醫話叢編 [*Volume Collection of Medical Discourse*] 1 (1931): 32–34.

Barlow, Tani. *The Question of Women in Chinese Feminism*. Durham, NC: Duke University Press, 2004.

Bataille, Georges. *The Accursed Share: An Essay on General Economy*. Vol. 1. Translated by Robert Hurley. New York: Zone Books, 1991.

———. *Eroticism: Death and Sensuality*. 1957. Translated by Mary Dalwood. San Francisco: City Light Books, 1986.

Ben, Paolo. "Global Modernity and Sexual Science: The Case of Male Homosexuality and Female Prostitution, 1850–1950." In *A Global History of Sexual Science, 1880–1960*, edited by Veronika Fuechtner, Douglas E. Haynes, and Ryan M. Jones, 57–91. Oakland: University of California Press, 2018.

Bender, Mark. "Regional Literatures." In *The Columbia History of Chinese Literature*, edited by Victor H. Mair, 1015–31. New York: Columbia University, 2001.

Benstock, Shari. *Women of the Left Bank: Paris, 1900–1940*. Austin: University of Texas Press, 1986.

Berg, Daria. "The Happy World of Scholar-Beauty Romances." In *The Columbia History of Chinese Literature*, edited by Victor H. Mair, 666–69. New York: Columbia University Press, 2001.

Biggs, David. *Footprints of War: Militarized Landscapes in Vietnam*. Seattle: University of Washington Press, 2018.

Bình, Nguyễn Khắc. *Hán Học Nhập Môn Tam Tự Văn*, 漢學入門三字文 [*Three-Character Script for Introductory Sinology*]. Hà Nội: Hợp thành ấn quán, 1928.

Bính, Phan Kế. *Việt-Nam Phong-Tục* [*Vietnamese Customs*]. Sài Gòn: Nhà sách Khai Trí [Khai Trí Publishing House], 1973.

Bình, Tôn Thất. *Đời Sống Cung Đình Triều Nguyễn* [*Life inside the Nguyễn Imperial Court*]. Quảng Trị: Nhà Xuất Bản Thuận Hóa, 1993.

Blackwood, Evelyn, and Mark Johnson. "Queer Asian Subjects: Transgressive Sexualities and Heteronormative Meanings." *Asian Studies Review* 36, no. 4 (2012): 441–51.

Bradley, Mark. "Becoming Văn Minh: Civilizational Discourse and Visions of the Self in Twentieth-Century Vietnam." *Journal of World History* 15, no. 1 (2004): 65-83.

Brocheux, Pierre, and Daniel Hémery. *Indochina: An Ambiguous Colonization, 1858–1954*. Berkeley: University of California Press, 2009.

Bullough, Vern L., and Bonnie Bullough. *Cross Dressing, Sex, and Gender*. Philadelphia: University of Pennsylvania Press, 1993.

Butler, Judith. *Undoing Gender*. New York: Routledge, 2004.

"Cải Lương: Tối Thứ Ba 4 Juin 1929: *Nữ Tú Tài*" [Reformed Theatre: Tuesday Evening 4 June: *Female Baccalaureate Graduate*]. *Nông Công Thương Nhật Báo [Nông Công Thương Daily]* (Hà Nội), June 5, 1929, 3.

Cân, Tôn Văn, and Tứ Quyên. *Thai-Sản Đương Tri* 知當產胎 [*Knowledge on Giving Birth*]. Sài Gòn: Viet&Fils Publishers.

Cang, Quách. *Nam-Nữ Khả-Độc Loại-Dục Vệ-Sinh [The Sexual Education of Males Females]*. Sài Gòn: Imprimerie Chan-Thanh [Chan Thanh Publishers], 1939.

Carter, Philip. "Men about Town: Representations of Foppery and Masculinity in Early Eighteenth-Century Urban Society." In *Gender in Eighteenth-Century England*, edited by Hannah Barker and Elaine Chalus, 31–57. London: Routledge, 2014.

Chaigneau, Michel Đức. *Souvenirs De Hué (Cochinchine) [Memories of Hué (Cochinchine)]*. Paris: L'Imprimerie Impériale, 1867.

Chakrabarty, Dipesh. "The Time of History and the Times of Gods." In *The Politics of Culture in the Shadow of Capital*, edited by Lisa Lowe and David Lloyd, 34–60. Durham, NC: Duke University Press, 1997.

Chân-Quỳnh, Nguyễn Thị. *"Lối Xưa Xe Ngựa . . ." [The Horse Carriage of Former Times]*. Paris: Nhà Xuất Bản An Tiêm [An Tiêm Publishing House], 1995.

Chánh, Hồ Biểu. *Tân Phong Nữ Sĩ [New Styled Women]*. 1937. Sài Gòn: Nhà Xuất Bản Văn Hóa, 2006.

Chauvet, Claire. "Changing Spirit Identities: Rethinking Four Palaces' Spirit Representation in Northern Vietnam." In *Engaging the Spirit World: Popular Beliefs and Practices in Modern Southeast Asia*, edited by Kirsten W. Endres and Andrea Lauser, 85–102. New York: Berghahn Books, 2011.

Cheah, Pheng. "Grounds of Comparison." *Diacritics* 29, no. 4 (1999): 3–18.

Chi, Quốc. "Chết Hai Lần: Trinh Thám Tiểu Thuyết, Số 31" [To Die Twice: A Detective Novel, No. 31]. *Khoa Học Tạp Chí [Science Journal]* 128 (July 11, 1936): 399–400.

Chiang, Howard. *After Eunuchs: Science, Medicine, and the Transformation of Sex in Modern China*. New York: Columbia University Press, 2018.

———. "Castration and the Feminized Male Sex." In *After Eunuchs: Science, Medicine, and the Transformation of Sex in Modern China*, 193–98. New York: Columbia University Press, 2018.

———. "Deciphering Desire." In *After Eunuchs: Science, Medicine, and the Transformation of Sex in Modern China*, 125–77. New York: Columbia University Press, 2018.

———. "Imagining Transgender China." In *Transgender China*, edited by Howard Chiang, 3–19. New York: Palgrave Macmillan, 2012.

Chương, Lộng. "Hầu Thánh: Tiểu Thuyết Phóng Sự" [Serving the Spirits: Novelistic Reportage]. 1942. In *Hầu Thánh [Serving the Spirits]*, 5–175. Hà Nội: Nhà Xuất Bản Thông Tin, 2002.

"Chuyện Lạ Của Khoa Học: Rồi Đây Đàn Bà Có Thể Biến Thành Đàn Ông Chăng? [An Unusual Scientific Phenomenon: Will Women Some Day Be Able to Transform into a Man?]." *Phụ Nữ Tân Văn [New Women's News]* 236 (March 29, 1934): 19.

"Con Gái Hóa Con Trai" [A Girl Transforms into a Boy]. *Khoa Học Tạp Chí [Science Journal]* 81 (Nov 1, 1934): 25.

Corbin, Alain. *Women for Hire: Prostitution and Sexuality in France after 1850.* Translated by Alan Sheridan. Cambridge, MA: Harvard University Press, 1990.

Courouve, Claude. *Vocabulaire de l'homosexualité masculine.* Paris: Payot, 1985.

"Cuộc Thí Nghiệm Kỳ Khôi" [A Strange Experiment]. *Khoa Học Tạp Chí [Science Journal]* 119 (April 11, 1936): 219.

Dân, Chương. "Tình Hình Sanh Hoạt Của Bọn Hoạn Quan Sau Khi Nền Quân Chủ Bị Úp Đổ" [The Circumstances of Palace Eunuchs after the Demise of the Monarch]. *Phụ Nữ Tân Văn [New Women's News]* 91 (July 16, 1931): 9.

"Đàn Bà Có Râu" [Bearded Women]. *Khoa Học Tạp Chí [Science Journal]* 64 (February 15, 1934): 21.

"Đàn Bà Đời Nay: Mạnh Lệ Quân Tái Thế" [Women Today: The Rebirth of Mạnh Lệ Quân]. *Phụ Nữ Tân Văn (New Women's News)* 1 (May 2, 1929): 23.

"Đàn Bà Hóa Đàn Ông" [A Woman Transforms into a Man]. *Khoa Học Tạp Chí [Science Journal]* 115 (March 1, 1936): 139.

Davis, Bradley Camp. "Finding Eunuchs in Imperial Vietnam: Questions and Sources." *South East Asia Research* 30, no. 4 (2023): 426–33.

D.B. "Đàn Bà Có Râu" [Women with Beards]. *Phụ Nữ Tân Văn [New Women's News]* 185 (January 12, 1933): 29.

Dean, Carolyn J. *The Frail Social Body: Pornography, Homosexuality, and Other Fantasies in Interwar France.* Berkeley: University of California Press, 2000.

Devy, Quan Bác Sĩ. *Cho Khỏi Ốm Đau* [To Prevent Illness]. Translated by Đỗ Uông. Hà Nội: Imprimerie Nghiêm-Hàm, 1928.

DeWoskin, Kenneth J. *A Song for One or Two: Music and the Concept of Art in Early China.* Michigan Papers in Chinese Studies. Vol. 42, Ann Arbor: University of Michigan, 1982.

Diệu, Xuân. "Nhị Hồ" [Two Lakes]. 1938. In *Xuân Diệu Toàn Tập [The Complete Works of Xuân Diệu]*, 58–59. Hà Nội: Nhà Xuất Bản Văn Học [Literature Publishing House], 2001.

Định, Vũ Công. "Cái 'Mốt' Mới Của Chị Em Tân-Tiến" [The New Fashion of the New Women]. *Đông Pháp* 報東法 [*Eastern Way Newspaper*], November 16, 1939, 1.

Do, Thien. *Vietnamese Supernaturalism: Views from the Southern Region.* London: Routledge Curzon, 2003.

Doan, Laura. "Reading Female Masculinities in the 1920s." *Feminist Studies* 24, no. 3 (Autumn 1998): 663–700.

"Độc Giả Luận Đàn: Đàn Bà Việt Nam Có Nên Cúp Tóc Không" [Reader's Discussion: Should Vietnamese Women Clip Their Hair?]. *Tiếng Dân [People's Voice]* 158 (March 2, 1929): 4.

Đồng. "Ảnh Hưởng Của Giáo Dục Và Hoàn Cảnh Hay Là Một Sự Thí Nghiệm Rất Lạ Lùng Ở Đức" [Societal Influence and Upbringing or a Strange Experiment in Germany]. *Phụ Nữ Tân Văn [New Women's News]* 236 (March 29, 1934): 24–25.

Dong, Lan. "Heroic Lineage: Military Women and Lady Knights-Errant in Premodern China." In *Mulan's Legend and Legacy in China and the United States*, 9–50. Philadelphia: Temple University Press, 2010.

Dossier relatif aux activités de la prostitution, les faits concernant au filles publiques années,

1916–1931 [*Files on Prostitution Activities, the Facts Concerning the Public Girls, 1916–1931*]. Vietnam National Archives II, Sài Gòn, 1916.

Dror, Olga. *Cult, Culture and Authority: Princess Lieu Hanh in Vietnamese History.* Honolulu: University of Hawai'i Press, 2007.

Drummond, Lisa. "The Modern 'Vietnamese Woman': Socialization and Women's Magazine." In *Gender Practices in Contemporary Vietnam*, edited by Lisa Drummond and Helle Ryndstrom, 158–78. Singapore: Singapore University Press, 2004.

Đức, Hà Minh. Preface to *Tổng Tập Văn Học Việt Nam* [*General Collection of Vietnamese Literature*], edited by Hà Minh Đức, 7–19. Hà Nội: Nhà Xuất Bản Khoa Học Xã Hội [Social Sciences Publishing House], 2000.

Dupré, John. "Gender and the End of Biological Determinism." In *Why Gender?*, edited by Jude Browne, 57–77. Cambridge: Cambridge University Press, 2021.

Durand, Maurice. *Technique et panthéon des médiums viêtnamiens (đồng).* Vol. 45. Paris: École Française d'Extrême-Orient, 1959.

———. "Truyện Quan Âm Thị Kính (觀音氏敬)" [The Story of Kuan Yin]. In *Thế Giới Của Truyện Nôm* [*The Universe of Nom Stories*], edited by Olivier Tessier, 212–22. Ho Chi Minh City: Nhà Xuất Bản Tổng Hợp Thành Phố Hồ Chí Minh [Ho Chi Minh City General Publishing House], 2022.

Dutton, George. "Ly Toet in the City: Coming to Terms with the Modern in 1930s Vietnam." *Journal of Vietnamese Studies* 2, no. 1 (February 2007): 80–108.

———. "'Society' and Struggle in the Early Twentieth Century: The Vietnamese Neologistic Project and French Colonialism." *Modern Asian Studies* 49, no. 6 (November 2015): 1994–2021.

———. *The Tây Sơn Uprising: Society and Rebellion in Eighteenth Century Vietnam.* Honolulu: University of Hawai'i Press, 2006.

Dutton, George E., Jayne S. Werner, and John K. Whitmore, eds. "The Child-Giving Guanyin (Sixteenth-Seventeenth Century)." In *Sources of Vietnamese Tradition*, 180–86. New York: Columbia University Press, 2012.

Edington, Claire E. *Beyond the Asylum: Mental Illness in French Colonial Vietnam.* Ithaca, NY: Cornell University Press, 2019.

Elliott, Duong Van Mai. *The Sacred Willow: Four Generations in the Life of a Vietnamese Family.* Oxford: Oxford University Press, 1999.

Endres, Kirsten W. "Spirited Modernities: Mediumship and Ritual Performativity in Late Socialist Vietnam." In *Modernity and Re-Enchantment: Religion in Post-Revolutionary Vietnam*, edited by Philip Taylor, 194–220. Singapore: Institute of Southeast Asian Studies Publishing, 2007.

Endres, Kirsten W., and Andrea Lauser. "Multivocal Arenas of Modern Enchantment in Southeast Asia." In *Engaging the Spirit World: Popular Beliefs and Practices in Modern Southeast Asia*, edited by Kirsten W. Endres and Andrea Lauser, 2–18. New York: Berghahn Books, 2012.

Fausto-Sterling, Anne. "Sex, Glands, Hormones, and Gender Chemistry." In *Sexing the Body: Gender Politics and the Construction of Sexuality.* New York: Basic Books, 2020.

Fillin-Yeh, Susan. "Dandies, Marginality, and Modernism: Georgia O Keefe, Marcel Duchamp, and Other Cross-Dressers." In *Dandies: Fashion and Finesse in Art and Culture*, edited by Susan Fillin-Yeh, 127–52. New York: New York University Press, 2021.

Firpo, Christina. *Black Market Business: Selling Sex in Northern Vietnam, 1920–1945*. Studies of the Weatherhead East Asian Institute. Ithaca, NY: Cornell University Press, 2020.

———. "Sex and Song: Clandestine Prostitution in Tonkin's Ả Đào Music Houses, 1920s–1940s." *Journal of Vietnamese Studies* 11, no. 2 (2016): 1–36.

Foucault, Michel. *History of Sexuality*. Vol. 1. New York: Vintage, 1978.

———. "Nietzsche, Genealogy and History." Translated by Robert Hurley and Others. In *Aesthetics, Method, and Epistemology*, edited by James D. Faubion, 369–91. Essential Works of Foucault, 1954–1984. New York: New Press, 1998.

Freccero, Carla. *Queer/Early/Modern*. Durham, NC: Duke University Press, 2006.

Fuechtner, Veronika, Douglas E. Haynes, and Ryan M. Jones. "Introduction: Toward a Global History of Sexual Science: Movements, Networks, and Deployments." In *A Global History of Sexual Science, 1880–1960*, 1–22. Oakland: University of California Press, 2018.

Furth, Charlotte. "Androgynous Males and Deficient Females: Biology and Gender Boundaries in Sixteenth- and Seventeenth-Century China." *Late Imperial China* 9, no. 2 (1988): 1–31.

———. *A Flourishing Yin: Gender in China's Medical History*. Berkeley: University of California Press, 1999.

Génibrel, J. F. M. *Dictionnaire Annamite-Française: Comprenant, 1 tous les caractères de la langue annamite vulgaire, avec l'indication de leurs divers sens propres ou figurés, et justifiés par de nombreux exemples, 2 Les caractères chinois nécessaires à l'étude des Tứ Thơ, ou quatre livres classiques chinois, 3 La flore et la faune de l'Indo-Chine*. Sài Gòn: Impr. de la Mission à Tân Định, 1898.

Giang, Kim, trans. "Hào Kiệt Kết Duyên" [Two Heroes Join in Wedlock]." *Khai Hóa Nhật Báo* 開化日報 [*Civilizing Daily*] (Hà Nội), September 20, 1924, 4.

———. "Hào Kiệt Kết Duyên" [Two Heroes Join in Wedlock]. *Khai Hoá Nhật Báo* 開化日報 [*Civilizing Daily*] (Hà Nội), October 4, 1924, 4.

———. "Hào Kiệt Kết Duyên" [Two Heroes Join in Wedlock]. *Khai Hóa Nhật Báo* 開化日報 [*Civilizing Daily*] (Hà Nội), October 6, 1924, 4.

Giang, Tung. "Chuyện Cổ Phương Tây: Góc Tích Đàn Bà Và Đàn Ông" [A Western Mythology: On the Origins of Men and Women]. *Phụ Nữ Tân Văn* [*New Women's News*] 81 (December 11, 1930): 13–15.

Ginio, Ruth. *The French Army and Its African Soldiers: The Years of Decolonization*. Lincoln: University of Nebraska Press, 2017.

Goscha, Christopher. *Vietnam or Indochina? Contesting Conceptions of Space in Vietnamese Nationalism, 1887–1954*. Nordic Institute of Asian Studies 28. Copenhagen: Nordic Institute of Asian Studies, 1995.

———. *Vietnam: A New History*. New York: Basic Books, 2016.

Grand Dictionnaire Ricci de la Langue Chinoise 利氏漢法辭典 [Grand Ricci Dictionary of the Chinese Language]. Vol. VI. Paris-Taipei: Instituts Ricci, 2001.

Gunther, Scott Eric. "Introduction: Republican Values and the Depenalization of Sodomy in France." In *The Elastic Closet: A History of Homosexuality in France, 1942–Present*, 1–24. New York: Palgrave Macmillan, 2009.

Guo, Li. "The Legacy of Crossdressing in *Tanci*: On *A Histoire of Heroic Woman and Men*." *Frontiers of Literary Studies in China* 5, no. 4 (2011): 566–99. https://doi.org/10.1007/s11702-011-0142-x.

Guter, Bob, and John R. Killacky, eds. *Queer Crips: Disabled Gay Men and Their Stories*. New York: Harrington Park Press, 2004.

Hà, Phú, Tuyết Huy, and Dương Bá Trạc. Preface to *Tục Tái Sanh Duyên (Sử Tích Mạnh Lệ Quân)* [*The Custom of Resurrection (The Story of Mạnh Lệ Quân)*]. 1924. Hà Nội: Nhà Xuất Bản Văn Hóa Thông Tin, 2000.

Halberstam, Judith. *Female Masculinity*. Durham, NC: Duke University Press, 1998.

——. *In a Queer Time and Place: Transgender Bodies, Subcultural Lives*. New York: New York University, 2005.

Halperin, David M. *How to Do the History of Homosexuality*. Chicago: University of Chicago Press, 2002.

——. "Sex/Sexuality/Sexual Classification." In *Critical Terms for the Study of Gender*, edited by Catharine R. Stimpson and Gilbert Herdt, 449–86. Chicago: University of Chicago Press, 2014.

Harvey, Elizabeth D. "The Voice of Gender." In *Ventriloquized Voices: Feminist Theory and English Renaissance Texts*, 1–14. London: Routledge, 1992.

"Hát Tại Rạp Cầu-Muối Sài Gòn: Tuồng Hát Tối Thứ Bảy 9 Avril 1927" [Shows at the Cau Muoi Theatre Sài Gòn: Dramas Performed Saturday Evening, April 9, 1927]." *Đông Pháp Thời Báo* [*Đông Pháp Times Newspaper*] (Sài Gòn), April 11, 1927, 3.

Heidegger, Martin. *The Question Concerning Technology, and Other Essays*. Translated by William Lovitt. New York: Harper & Row, 1977.

Hekma, Gert. "'A Female Soul in a Male Body': Sexual Inversion as Gender Inversion in Nineteenth-Century Sexology." In *Third Sexes, Third Gender: Beyond Sexual Dimorphism in Culture and History*, edited by Gilbert Herdt, 213–39. New York: Zone Books, 1994.

Henchy, Judith A. N. "Performing Modernity in the Writings of Nguyễn An Ninh and Phan Văn Hùm." PhD diss., University of Washington, 2005.

Hessney, Richard C. "Beautiful, Talented, and Brave: Seventeenth-Century Chinese Scholar-Beauty Romances." PhD diss., Columbia University, 1978.

H.G.T. "Đã to Vú Lại Rậm Râu" [They Have Big Breasts and a Beard!]. *Khoa Học Tạp Chí* [*Science Journal*] 25 (July 1, 1932): 23.

Hiến, Nguyễn Thị. "Nhân Vật Giả Nam Trong Truyện Nôm" [The Characters Who Disguise as Male in Nôm Stories]. Master's thesis, Trường Đại Học Sư Phạm Hà Nội, 2005.

H.K. "Có Thể Biết Trước Được Trứng Nào Sẽ Nở Ra Gà Sống Gà Mái Không?" [Is It Possible to Predict the Egg's Sex?]. *Khoa Học Tạp Chí* [*Science Journal*] 99 (August 1, 1935): 5.

Hoa, Đường, "Trong Chùa Long-Vân Có Gì Lạ?" [What Is Unusual about the Long Vân Temple?], *Sài Gòn*, April 23, 1940, 1, 6.

Hoà, Nguyễn Đình. *Vietnamese Literature: A Brief Survey*. San Diego, CA: San Diego State University, 1994.

Hoàn, Trương. Preface to *Tiểu Thuyết: Nguyễn Tuyết-Hoa: Học Sanh Nữ Học Đường* [*A Novel: Nguyễn Tuyết-Hoa*]. Sài Gòn: Imprimerie Duc-Luu Phuong, 1930.

————. *Tiểu Thuyết: Nguyễn Tuyết-Hoa: Học Sanh Nữ Học Đường* [*A Novel: Nguyễn Tuyết-Hoa*]. Vol. 1 of 5. Sài Gòn: Imprimerie Duc-Luu Phuong, 1930.

Hội Khai-Trí Tiến Đức Khởi Thảo [The Moral Enlightenment Association]. *Việt Nam Tự-Điển* 越南字典 [*Vietnamese Dictionary*]. Hà Nội: Imprimerie Trung-Bắc Tân-Văn, 1931.

Horton, Paul. "Recognising Shadows: Masculinism, Resistance, and Recognition in Vietnam." *International Journal for Masculinity Studies* 14, no. 1 (2019): 66–80.

Hồ Tài, Huệ Tâm. *Radicalism and the Origins of the Vietnamese Revolution.* Cambridge, MA: Harvard University Press, 1992.

Hu, Siao-chen. "Literary *Tanci*: A Woman's Tradition of Narrative in Verse." PhD diss., Harvard University Press, 1994.

Huang, Martin W. *Negotiating Masculinities in Late Imperial China.* Honolulu: University of Hawai'i Press, 2006.

Hùm, Phan Văn. "Dư Luận Và Thời Thượng" [Public Opinion and the Vogue]." *Phụ Nữ Tân Văn* [*New Women's News*] 246 (June 14, 1934): 6.

————. "Văn 'Nam Hóa' " ["Masculinization" Literature]. *Phụ Nữ Tân Văn* [*New Women's News*] 245 (June 7, 1934): 11–12.

————. "Xã Hội Cần Có Gia Đình Không?" [Does Society Need the Family Unit?]. *Phụ Nữ Tân Văn* [*New Women's News*] 256 (August 30, 1934): 7–8.

Hưng, Khái. "Hồn Bướm Mơ Tiên" [Butterfly Soul Dreaming of an Immortal]. *Phong Hóa* [*Mores*] (Hà Nội), November 4, 1932, 12–13.

————. "Hồn Bướm Mơ Tiên" [Butterfly Soul Dreaming of an Immortal]. *Phong Hóa* [*Mores*] (Hà Nội), January 6, 1933, 2–3.

————. "Tiêu Sơn Tráng Sĩ" [The Heroes of Tiêu Sơn]. *Phong Hóa* [*Mores*] 147 (January 18, 1935): 7–8.

Hương, Văn. "Gái Đời Nay: Lời Một Vị Phu-Nhân Có Nền Nếp Mắng Răn Con Gái Là Bậc Tân Học" [Females These Days: Words of a Dignified Woman Scolding the New Women]. *Phụ Nữ Tân Văn* [*New Women's News*] (September 12, 1929): 10–12.

Hữu, Nhuận, and Vũ Quần Phương, eds. *Tuyển Tập Xuân Diệu* [Selected Works of Xuân Diệu]. Hà Nội: Nhà Xuất Bản Văn Học, 1986.

Hữu, Tam. "Mái Tóc Của Phụ Nữ Tương Lai" [Women's Future Hair Style]. *Phụ Nữ Tân Văn* [*New Women's News*] 248 (June 28, 1934): 21–22.

Hữu-Tiến, Nguyễn. "Nam-Âm Thi-Văn Khảo-Biện" [Survey of Southern Sounds and Poetic Literature]. *Nam Phong* [*Southern Wind*] 3, no. 18 (December 1918): 340–54.

Huy, Cận, *Hồi Ký Song Đôi: Tuổi Nhỏ Huy Cận-Xuân Diệu* [Memoirs of Two: The Early Years of Huy Cận and Xuân Diệu]. Hà Nội: Nhà Xuất Bản Hội Nhà Văn, 2002.

Huyên, Nguyễn Văn. *The Ancient Civilization of Vietnam.* 1945. Hà Nội: Thế Giới Publishers, 1995.

Huỳnh, Sanh Thông. Introduction to *The Tale of Kiều: A Bilingual Edition*, xix–xl. New Haven, CT: Yale University Press, 1983.

Ích, Công. "Bán Nam Bán Nữ, Phần 2" [Half Man, Half Woman, Part 2]. *Khoa Học Tạp Chí* [*Science Journal*] 77 (September 1, 1934): 3–4.

————. "Bán Nam Bán Nữ: Hermaphrodisme, Phần 1" [Half Man, Half Woman: Hermaphroditism, Part 1]. *Khoa Học Tạp Chí* [*Science Journal*] 77 (September 1, 1934): 3–4.

Irigaray, Luce. *Speculum of the Other Woman*. Translated by Gillian C. Gill. Ithaca, NY: Cornell University Press, 1974.

Isobe, Yuko (磯部佑子) and Nguyễn Văn Hoài, trans. "Về Đặc Trưng Truyền Bá Tiểu Thuyết Tài Tử Giai Nhân Trung Quốc Ở Đông Á—Lấy Nhị Độ Mai, Hảo Cầu Truyện Làm Đối Tượng Khảo Sát Chính Yếu" [The Spread of Chinese Scholar-Beauty Romances in East Asia: The Case Study of Er Du Mei and Hao Qiu Zhuan]. *Tạp Chí Khoa Học Văn Hóa và Du lịch* [*Journal of the Science of Culture and Tourism*] 14 (2013).

Jamieson, Neil. "Some Things Poetry Can Tell Us about the Process of Social Change in Vietnam." *Southeast Asian Studies* 39, no. 3 (December 2001), 325–57.

——. *Understanding Vietnam*. Berkeley: University of California Press, 1995.

Johnson, Paul Christopher. "Syncretism and Hybridization." In *The Oxford Handbook of the Study of Religion*, edited by Michael Stausberg and Steven Engler, 754–72. Oxford: Oxford University Press, 2016.

Jordan, Mark D. "Sodomy." In *Gay Histories and Cultures*, edited by George E. Haggerty, John Beynon, and Douglas Eisner, 828–31. New York: Garland Books, 2000.

Kang, Wenqing. "The Language of Male Same-Sex Relations in China." In *Obsession: Male Same-Sex Relations in China, 1900–1950*, 19–40. Hong Kong: Hong Kong University Press, 2009.

Kedem, Nir. "What Is Queer Translation?" *symploke* 27, nos. 1–2 (2019): 157–83.

Kelly, Gail. *Franco-Vietnamese Schools, 1918–1938: Regional Development and Implications for National Integration*. Madison: University of Wisconsin Press, 1982.

Khái, Nguyễn Văn. *Nam Nữ Hôn-Nhân Vệ Sinh* 生衛姻婚女男 [*Male Female Marriage Hygiene*]. Hải Phòng: Văn Minh Publishers, 1924.

Khôi, Kỳ. "Đàn Bà Hớt Tóc" [Women Trimming Their Hair]. *Tiếng Dân* [*People's Voice*] 147 (January 16, 1929): 2.

Khôi, Phan. "Lịch Sử Tóc Ngắn: Annam Kể Từ 1906" [The History of Short Hair: Annam since 1906]. *Ngày Nay* [*These Days*] 149, Tet ed. (1938): 28–29.

Kim, Trần Trọng. *Việt Nam Sử Lược* [*Compendium of Vietnamese History*]. Vol. 2 of 2. 1920. Sài Gòn: Bộ Giáo Dục Trung Tâm Học Liệu Xuất Bản, 1971.

——. *Việt Nam Văn Phạm* [*Vietnamese Grammar*]. Hà Nội: Lê Thăng Xuất Bản, 1940.

Kính, Vũ Văn, and Khổng Đức. *Ngũ Thiên Tự: Trình Bày Việt-Hán-Nôm* [*Five Heavenly Scripts: Presentation of Vietnamese-Chinese-Nôm*]. Ho Chi Minh City: Nhà Xuất Bản Văn Hóa Thông Tin, 1998.

Ko, Dorothy. "Becoming a Woman." In *Every Step a Lotus: Shoes for Bound Feet*, 54–63. Berkeley: University of California Press, 2001.

——. *Cinderella's Sisters: A Revisionist History of Footbinding*. Berkeley: University of California Press, 2005.

——. *Every Step a Lotus: Shoes for Bound Feet*. Berkeley: University of California Press, 2001.

Kỳ, Hiếu. "Tại Sao Đàn Ông Có Râu, Đàn Bà Tốt Tóc" [Why Do Men Have Beards, Women Long Hair?]. *Khoa Học Tạp Chí* [*Science Journal*] 108 (December 15, 1935): 3–5.

Kỹ, Tân. "Mấy Cái Lạ Trên Thế Giới" [Strange and Unusual Phenomena in the World]. *Khoa Học Tạp Chí* [*Science Journal*] 87 (February 1, 1935): 5–6.

Lan, Feng. "The Female Individual and the Empire: A Historicist Approach to Mulan and Kingston's Women Warrior." *Comparative Literature* 55, no. 3 (2003): 229–45.

Lan, Thạch. "Thơ Ở Paris Gởi Về: Người Đàn Bà Âu-Châu" [Letters from Paris: Women of Europe]. *Phụ Nữ Tân Văn* [*New Women's News*] 40 (February 20, 1930): 9–10.

Lăng, Nguyễn Tử. *Mộc-Lan Tòng Quân* [*Moc Lan Joins the Army*]. Translated by Thuyết Phật. Vol. 1. Nam Định: Nam Hoa, 1928.

———. "Nhời Nói Sau" [Concluding Remarks]. Translated by Thuyết Phật. In *Mộc-Lan Tòng Quân* [*Moc Lan Joins the Army*]. Nam Định: Nam Hoa, 1928.

Lang, Trọng. "Hà Nội Lầm Than" [The Wretched of Hà Nội]. 1938. In *Phóng Sự Việt Nam* [*News Reportages of Vietnam*], edited by Phan Trọng Thưởng, Nguyễn Cừ, and Nguyễn Hữu Sơn, 93–243. Hà Nội: Nhà Xuất Bản Văn Học, 2000.

Lang, Trọng. "Đồng Bóng" [Spirit Mediums]. *Phong Hóa* [*Mores*] 166 (December 13, 1935): 10.

———. "Đồng Bóng" [Spirit Mediums]. *Phong Hóa* [*Mores*] 165 (December 6, 1935): 11.

Laqueur, Thomas. "Destiny Is Anatomy." In *Making Sex: Body and Gender from the Greeks to Freud*, 25–62. Cambridge, MA: Harvard University Press, 1990.

———. "Discovery of the Sexes." In *Making Sex: Body and Gender from the Greeks to Freud*, 149–92. Cambridge, MA: Harvard University Press, 1990.

———. *Making Sex: Body and Gender from the Greeks to Freud*. Cambridge, MA: Harvard University Press, 1990.

———. *Solitary Sex: A Cultural History of Masturbation*. New York: Zone Books, 2003.

———. "Why Masturbation Became a Problem." In *Solitary Sex: A Cultural History of Masturbation*, 247–358. New York: Zone Books, 2003.

Le Failler, Philippe, and Olivier Tessier. Preface to *Technique de peuple annamite* [*Mechanics and Crafts of the Annamites*], edited by Philippe Le Failler and Olivier Tessier. Hà Nội: Nhà Xuất Bản Thế Giới, 2009.

"Lê Văn Duyệt." In *Từ Điển Bách Khoa Việt Nam* [*The Encyclopedia of Vietnam*], 672. Hà Nội: Nhà Xuất Bản Từ Điển Bách Khoa, 2002.

Lear, Andrew, and Eva Cantarella. *Images of Ancient Greek Pederasty: Boys Were Their Gods*. New York: Routledge, 2008.

Lee, Haiyan. "The Cult of *Qing*." In *Revolution of the Heart: A Genealogy of Love in China, 1900–1950*, 25–59. Stanford, CA: Stanford University Press, 2007.

Levy, Howard S. "Wondrousness of the Lotus." In *Chinese Footbinding: The History of a Curious Erotic Custom*, 147–56. New York: Bell Publishing Co., 1967.

Liêu, Đ. C., L. K. Kế, et al. *Từ Điển Việt-Anh* [Vietnamese-English Dictionary]. Hồ Chí Minh: Nhà Xuất Bản Hồ Chí Minh, 2000.

Linh, Nhất. Preface to *Tổng Tập Văn Học Việt Nam* [*General Collection of Vietnamese Literature*], edited by Hà Minh Đức. 1933. Hà Nội: Nhà Xuất Bản Khoa Học Xã Hội, 2000.

Link, Perry. *The Uses of Literature: Life in the Socialist Chinese Literary System*. Princeton, NJ: Princeton University Press, 2000.

Long, Vũ Đình. Preface to *Anh Hùng Náo* [*The Rowdy Hero*]. Hà Nội: Kim-Đức-Giang Ấn-Quán, 1924.

Loos, Tamara. "Transnational Histories of Sexualities in Asia." *American Historical Review* 114, no. 5 (2009): 1309–24.

Lương, Tiến. *Nam-Nữ Phòng Trung Bí Mật Tân Y Thuật: Sách Thuốc Chữa Những Bệnh Kín Của Đàn Ông, Đàn Bà, Con Trai Và Con Gái* 男女房中秘密新醫術 [*New Medi-*

cine for the Male and Female Chamber: A Medicine Book to Cure Private Diseases of Men and Women]. Translated by Tô-Linh Thảo. Nam Định: Nhà In Mỹ Thắng, 1933.

"Lưu Nữ Tướng" [Female General Luu]. In *Tổng Tập Văn Học Việt Nam* [*General Collection of Vietnamese Literature*], edited by Lê Văn Quán, 547–74. Hà Nội: Nhà Xuất Bản Khoa Học Xã Hội, 1993.

"Mạnh Lệ Quân Giả Trai: Cải Lương Nam Kỳ" [Mạnh Lệ Quân Cross-Dresses as a Man: Southern Reform Theatre]. *Hà Thành Ngọ Báo* [*Ha Thanh Midday Newspaper*] (Hà Nội), October 20, 1928, 3.

"Mạnh Lệ Quân Thoát Hài: Cải Lương Nam Kỳ" [Mạnh Lệ Quân Removes Her Shoes: Southern Reform Theatre]. *Hà Thành Ngọ Báo* [*Hà Thành Midday Newspaper*] (Hà Nội), November 3, 1928, sec. Cuộc Vui Buổi Tối [Evening Entertainment], 3.

Marr, David. "A Generation of Lasts and Firsts." In *Vietnamese Anticolonialism, 1885–1925*, 77–97. Berkeley: University of California, 1971.

———. "The Question of Women." In *Vietnamese Tradition on Trial*. Berkeley: University of California Press, 1981.

———. *Vietnamese Anticolonialism, 1880–1925*. Berkeley: University of California Press, 1971.

———. *Vietnamese Tradition on Trial, 1925–1945*. Berkeley: University of California Press, 1981.

Martin, Emily. "The Egg and Sperm: How Science Has Constructed a Romance Based on Stereotypical Male-Female Roles." In *Feminist Theory and the Body*, edited by Janet Price and Margrit Shildrick, 179–89. New York: Routledge, 1999.

McConnell, Scott. *Leftward Journey: The Education of Vietnamese Students in France, 1919–1939*. New Brunswick, NJ: Transaction Publishers, 1989.

McHale, Shawn. *Print and Power: Confucianism, Communism and Buddhism in the Making of Modern Vietnam*. Honolulu: University of Hawai'i Press, 2004.

———. "Printing and Power: Vietnamese Debates over Women's Place in Society, 1918–1934." In *Essays into Vietnamese Pasts*, edited by K. W. Taylor and John K. Whitmore, 173–94. Studies on Southeast Asia. Ithaca, NY: Cornell University Press, 1995.

McMahon, Keith. "The Chaste 'Beauty-Scholar' Romance and the Superiority of the Talented Woman." In *Misers, Shrews, and Polygamists: Sexuality and Male-Female Relations in Eighteenth-Century Chinese Fiction*, 99–125. Durham, NC: Duke University Press, 1995.

Menglong, Feng. *Stories Old and New: A Ming Dynasty Collection Compiled by Feng Menglong (1574–1646)*. Translated by Shuhui Yang and Yunqin Yang. Seattle: University of Washington Press, 2000.

Mills, Robert. *Seeing Sodomy in the Middle Ages*. Chicago: University of Chicago Press, 2015.

Min, Tian. "Male Dan: The Paradox of Sex, Acting, and Perception in Traditional Chinese Theatre." *Asian Theatre Journal* 17, no. 1 (March 2000): 78–97.

Minh, Huấn. "Một Tiếng Đồng Hồ Với Cô Vải Bút" [An Hour with a Self-Declared "Nun"]). *Phụ Nữ Tân Văn* [*New Women's News*] 198 (May 4, 1933): 21–23.

Minh, Nguyễn Văn, and Long Điền. *Từ Điển Văn Liệu* [*Dictionary of Literary Material*]. Sài Gòn: Nhà Xuất Bản A Châu, 1952.

Minh-hà, Trịnh Thị, dir. *Surname Viet, Given Name Nam*. 108 minutes. 1989.

Mộng, Nguyễn Can. *Nam Học Hán Văn Khoá Bản*, 南學漢文課本 [*Vietnamese Study of Chinese Characters Textbook*] Hà Nội: Imprimeur Mặc Đình Tư, 1920.

Mộng-Trần, Félix. *Tang-Đại Giả Gái* 桑代野妗 [*Tang-Dai Disguises as Female*]. Sài Gòn: Imprimerie Nguyễn Văn Viết, June 1925.

Monnais, Laurence, C. Michele Thompson, and Ayo Wahlberg. "Southern Medicine for Southern People." Chap. Introduction in *Southern Medicine for Southern People: Vietnamese Medicine in the Making*, edited by Laurence Monnais, C. Michele Thompson and Ayo Wahlberg, 1–20. Newcastle-upon-Tyne, UK: Cambridge Scholars Publishing, 2012.

Monnais-Rousselot, Laurence. "In the Shadow of the Colonial Hospital: Developing Health Care in Indochina, 1860–1939." In *Viet Nam Exposé: French Scholarship on Twentieth-Century Vietnamese Society*, edited by Gisele Bousquet and Pierre Brocheux, 140–86. Ann Arbor: University of Michigan Press, 2002.

"Một người con gái Tàu giả trai đi lính, làm tới quan to" [A Chinese Woman Disguises as a Man, Becomes a High-Ranking Official], *Phụ Nữ Tân Văn* [*New Women's News*] 11 (1929): 12.

"Một Người Đàn Ông Đẻ Con" [A Man Who Gives Birth]. *Phụ Nữ Tân Văn* [*New Women's News*] 193 (March 30, 1933): 4.

Mỹ, Lê Hữu. "Tính Dục Học (Éducation Sexuelle): Thế Nào Là Ái Tình?" [Sexual Education: What Is Love?]. *Y Học Tân Thanh: La nouvelle voix de la médecine* [*New Voice of Medicine*] 5 (December 3, 1938): 57–58.

"Nam Hóa Nữ" [A Man Transforms into a Woman]. *Khoa Học Tạp Chí* [*Science Journal*] 147 (January 21, 1937): 57.

Nga, Vũ Thị and Nguyễn Huy Anh. *Tập Bài Giảng: Lịch Sử Nhà Nước Và Pháp Luật Việt Nam (Từ Nguồn Gốc Đến Giữa Thế Kỷ XX* [*Lectures: History of the Vietnamese State and Law (From the Origins to the Twentieth Century)*]. Hà Nội: Nhà Xuất Bản Chính Trị Quốc Gia, 1996.

Ngày Này [*These Days*] 208 (May 18, 1940), cover.

Ngô, Tất Tố. *Gia-định Tổng trấn Tả-quân Lê Văn-Duyệt* [*The Governor of Gia Định, Lê Văn Duyệt*]. Hà Nội: Nhà In Mai Linh [Mai Linh Publishing House], 1937.

Ngôn, Thanh. "Ý Kiến Bạn Thanh Niên: Vấn Đề Đĩ Điếm Ở Xã Hội Ta" [Ideas from a Young Man: The Issue of Prostitution in Our Society]. *Phụ Nữ Tân Văn* [*New Women's News*] 115 (January 7, 1932): 9–12.

Nguyễn, Khải Thư. "A Personal Sorrow: 'Cải Lương' and the Politics of North and South Vietnam." *Asian Theatre Journal* 29, no. 1 (2012): 255–75.

Nguyễn, Ký Văn. *La société vietnamienne face à la modernité: Le Tonkin de la fin du XIXe siècle à la Seconde Guerre Mondiale*. Paris: L'Harmattan, 1995.

Nguyễn, Martina Thục Nhi. *On Our Own Strength: The Self-Reliant Literary Group and Cosmopolitan Nationalism in Late Colonial Vietnam*. Honolulu: University of Hawaiʻi Press, 2021.

———. "Wearing the Nation." In *On Our Own Strength: The Self-Reliant Literary Group and Cosmopolitan Nationalism in Late Colonial Vietnam*, 79–114. Honolulu: University of Hawaiʻi Press.

Nguyễn, Phúc An. *Tuồng Hát Cải Lương: Khảo & Luận, 10 Năm Bốn Tuồng Đề Yếu (1922–

1931) [Reform Theatre: Research and Writing, 10 Years of Reform Theatre, 1922–1931]. Thành Phố Hồ Chí Minh: Nhà Sách Tổng Hợp Thành Phố Hồ Chí Minh, 2022.

Nguyễn, Quốc Vinh. "Deviant Bodies and Dynamics of Displacement of Homoerotic Desire in Vietnamese Literature from and about the French Colonial Period (1858–1954)." 1997. http://www.talawas.org/talaDB/suche.php?res=1056&rb=0503&von=.

Nguyễn, Quốc Vinh. "Love of Men: Xuân Diệu." In *Viet Nam Forum,* ed. Dan Duffy (New Haven, CT: Yale University Council on Southeast Asian Studies, 1997), 16:265.

Nguyễn, Thế Anh. "The Vietnamization of the Cham Diety Pô Nagar." *Asia Journal* 2, no. 1 (June 1995): 55–67.

Nguyễn, Thị Kiêm, "Cô Nguyễn Thị Kiêm nói về vấn đề Nữ lưu và văn học" [Ms. Nguyễn Thị Kiêm Speaks about the World of Women and Literature], *Phụ Nữ Tân Văn [New Women's News]* 131 (1932): 32.

Nguyễn, Thơ Ngọc, and Phong Thanh Nguyễn. "Philosophical Transmission and Contestation: The Impact of Qing Confucianism in Southern Vietnam." *Asian Studies* 8, no. 24 (2020): 79–112. https://doi.org/10.4312/as.2020.8.2.79-112.

Nguyễn, Thùy Linh. *Childbirth, Maternity, and Medical Pluralism in French Colonial Vietnam, 1880–1945.* Rochester, NY: University of Rochester Press, 2016.

Nguyễn, Trần Mô. *Nam-Hoa Tự-Điển* 南華字典. Hà Nội: Thư Hương Xuất Bản, 1943.

Như-Hoa. "Nào Sư Muôn Có Gạt Gẫm Ai Đâu" [The Buddhist Priest Muon Intended to Deceive Nobody]. *Sài Gòn,* April 22, 1940, 1.

Như-Hoa. "Như-Hoa Muốn Điên Theo Kiểu Đó Quá" [Như-Hoa Wishes to Be Crazy in That Way]. *Sài Gòn,* April 26, 1940, 1.

"Những Cái Mầu Nhiệm Của Khoa Học: Người Ta Có Thể Đổi Giống Đực, Cái Được" [The Miracles of Science: People Can Change Male, Female Genders]. *Ngày Nay [These Days]* 82 (1937): 887.

"Những điều lợi hại của sự nam nữ giao tiếp tự do" [The Harm of Dealings between Men and Women]. *Phụ nữ thời đàm* [Women, Current Events, Commentary] 1 (1931).

Noble, Jean B. *Masculinities without Men? Female Masculinity in Twentieth Century Fictions.* Vancouver: University of British Columbia Press, 2003.

"Nói Thêm Về Chuyện Người Đàn Bà Giả Trai" [More on the Story about the Woman Who Disguised Herself as a Man]. *Phụ Nữ Tân Văn [New Women's News]* 6 (June 6, 1929): 26.

Norton, Barley. "Mediumship, Modernity, and Cultural Identity." In *Songs for the Spirits: Music and Mediums in Modern Vietnam,* 21–53. Urbana: University of Illinois Press, 2009.

———. *Song for the Spirits: Music and Mediums in Modern Vietnam.* Urbana: University of Illinois Press, 2009.

Noseworthy, William B., and Van Son Quang. "A View of Champā Sites in Phú Yên Province, Vietnam: Toward a Longue Durée of Socio-Religious Context." *Religion* 13, no. 7 (2022): 1–15.

Nữ Lưu Tướng 將劉女: *Truyện Diễn Ca [Female General Luu: A Story in Plain Verse].* Edited by Phạm Văn Phương. Vol. 10. Hà Nội: Mặc Đình Tư Publishers, 1922.

Nữ Tú Tài [Female Baccalaureate Graduate]. Hà Nội: Kim Khuê, 1930.

"Nữ Tú Tài" [Female Baccalaureate Graduate]. In *Tổng Tập Văn Học Việt Nam [General Collection of Vietnamese Literature],* edited by Lê Văn Quán, 383–421. Hà Nội: Nhà Xuất Bản Khoa Học Xã Hội, 1993.

Nữ Tú Tài [*Female Baccalaureate Graduate*]. Edited and translated by Trần Phong Sắc and Huỳnh Khắc Thuận. Sài Gòn: Marcellin Rey, 1911.

Nữ Tú Tài Truyện, La jeune fille bachelière, en prose rythmée [*A Story of a Female Baccalaureate Graduate, in Rhythmic Prose*]. Translated by Nguyễn Ngọc Xuân. Hải phòng: Văn Minh, 1923.

Nữ Tú Tài 專才秀女 [*Female Baccalaureate Graduate*]. Hà Nội: Kim Khuê, 1927.

Nye, Robert A. "Sex Difference and Male Homosexuality in French Medical Discourse." *Bulletin of the History of Medicine* 63, no. 1 (1989): 32–51.

"Ô! Ai Bảo Đàn Ông Không Đẻ" [Oh! Who Says Men Cannot Give Birth?]. *Phong Hóa* [*Mores*] 146 (April 26, 1935): 8.

P.G.V. *Dictionnaire Franco-Tonkinois: Illustré (Từ Điển Tiếng Pháp—Tiếng Bắc Kỳ. Có Minh Hoạ)* [*French-Tonkinese Dictionary*]. Hà Nội: F. H. Scheneider, 1898.

Pastreich, Emanuel. "The Reception of Chinese Literature in Vietnam." In *The Columbia History of Chinese Literature*, edited by Victor H. Mair, 1096–1104. New York: Columbia University Press, 2001.

Peletz, Michael. *Gender Pluralism: Southeast Asia since Early Modern Times*. London: Routledge, 2009.

Peniston, William *Pederasts and Others: Urban Culture and Sexual Identity in Nineteenth-Century Paris*. New York: Harrington Press, 2004.

Peycam, Philippe. *The Birth of Vietnamese Political Journalism: Sài Gòn, 1916–1930*. New York: Columbia University Press, 2012.

———. "Exploring the Possibility of a South East Asia-Africa 'Axis of Knowledge.'" *South East Asia Research* 27, no. 1 (2019): 26–30.

Pflugfelder, Gregory M. *Cartographies of Desire: Male-Male Sexuality in Japanese Discourse, 1600–1950*. Berkeley: University of California Press, 1999.

———. "Doctoring Love: Male-Male Sexuality in Medical Discourse from the Edo Period through the Early Twentieth Century." In *Cartographies of Desire: Male-Male Sexuality in Japanese Discourse, 1600–1950*, 135–285. Berkeley: University of California Press, 1999.

Phan, Bội Châu. "A Letter from Abroad Written in Blood." 1907. In *Sources of Vietnamese Tradition*, edited by Jayne S. Werner George E. Dutton, and John K. Whitmore, 353–69. New York: Columbia University Press, 2012.

Phan, Cự Đệ. "Tự Lực Văn Đoàn" [The Self-Reliant Literary Group]. In *Tự Lực Văn Đoàn: Trao Lưu—Tác Giả* [The Self-Reliant Literary Group: Movement and Authors], edited by Hà Minh Đức, 467–92. Huế: Nhà Xuất Bản Giáo Dục, 2007.

Phấn, Lê Văn. *Đông-Tây Y-Học và Nam Nữ Ái Tình (Médecine occidentale et sino-annamite et de l'amour)* [*Western and Sino-Annamite Medicine and Love*]. Vol. 1. Sài Gòn: Imprimerie Trần Trọng Cảnh, 1936.

Phan, Vũ Ngọc. "Nhà Văn Hiện Đại" [Modern Writers]. In *Vũ Ngọc Phan Tuyển Tập* [*Selected Works of Vũ Ngọc Phan*], edited by Nguyễn Thị Hanh and Nguyễn Hong Hanh, 29–50. Hà Nội: Nhà Xuất Bản Văn Học, 2008.

Phan, Vũ Ngọc. "Khái Hưng." 1940. In *Nhà Văn Hiện Đại: Phê Bình Văn Học* [*Contemporary Writers: Literary Criticism*]. Sài Gòn: Nhà Xuất Bản Thăng Long, 1959.

Phát, Lê Văn. *Lê Văn Duyệt*. Sài Gòn: Imprimateur de L'Union Nguyễn Văn Của, 1924.

Philastre, Paul-Louis-Félix. *Le Code Annamite*. Vol. 2 of 2. Paris: Ernest Leroux Éditeur, 1876.

Phinney, Harriet M. "Objects of Affection: Vietnamese Discourses on Love and Emancipation." *positions: east asia cultures critique* 16, no. 2 (Fall 2008): 329–58.

Phô, Nguyên Tri. "Đoàn Thiên Tiểu Thuyết: Hiếu Nữ Nam Trang" [Short Novel: A Filial Female Dressed as a Male, Part 1 of 4]. *Khai hóa nhật báo* 開化日報 [*Civilizing Daily*] (Hà Nội), September 5, 1923, 1–2.

Phụng, Phan Kim. "Vấn Đề Hớt Tóc Của Phụ Nữ Việt Nam Ta" [The Question of Cutting Our Vietnamese Women's Hair]. *Tiếng Dân* [*People's Voice*] 168 (April 6, 1929): 3.

Phụng, Vũ Trọng. "Để Đáp Lời Báo *Ngày Nay* Dâm Hay Là Không Dâm?" [A Response to the Journal *These Days*: Sex or No Sex?]. 1937. In *Tranh Luận Văn Nghệ Thế Kỷ XX* [*Literary and Artistic Debates in the Twentieth Century*], edited by Nguyễn Ngọc Thiện, 1125–33. Hà Nội: Nhà Xuất Bản Lao Động, 2002.

———. *Làm Đĩ: Tiểu Thuyết* [*To Be a Prostitute: A Novel*]. Hà Nội: Nhà Xuất Bản Văn Học, 2005.

———. "Thủ Đoạn" [Stratagems]. In *Chống Nạn Lên Đường* [*The Prevention of Vice on One's Journey*), edited by Lại Nguyên Ân, 27–40. Hà Nội: Nhà Xuất Bản Hội Nhà Văn, 2000.

"Phương Hoa." In *Tổng Tập Văn Học Việt Nam* [*General Collection of Vietnamese Literature*], edited by Lê Văn Quán, 327–80. Hà Nội: Nhà Xuất Bản Khoa Học Xã Hội, 1993.

Phương, Phạm Văn. Preface to *Nữ Lưu Tướng* 將劉女: *Truyện Diễn Ca* [*Female General Luu: A Story in Plain Verse*]. Edited by Phạm Văn Phương. Hà Nội: Mặc Đình Tư Publishers 1922.

Pigneaux, P. J., and J. L. Taberd, *Dictionarium anamitico-latinum, primitus inceptum ab illustrissimo et reverendissimo P. J. Pigneaux. Dein absolutum et editum a J. L. Taberd.* Fredericnagori vulgo Serampore: ex typis J. Marshman, 1838.

Proschan, Frank. "Eunuch Mandarins, Soldats Mamzelles, Effeminate Boys, and Graceless Women: French Colonial Constructions of Vietnamese Genders." *GLQ: A Journal of Lesbian and Gay Studies* 8, no. 4 (2002): 435–67.

Q.T. "Đàn Bà" [Women]. *Phụ Nữ Tân Văn* [*New Women's News*] 249 (July 5, 1934): 19–20.

"Quan Âm Thị Kính." In *Tổng Tập Văn Học Việt Nam* [*General Collection of Vietnamese Literature*], edited by Lê Văn Quán, 425–62. Hà Nội: Nhà Xuất Bản Khoa Học Xã Hội, 1993.

Quán, Bản. "Những Sự Kỳ Quán Trong Vũ Trụ Xét Thấy Ở Nước Nam" [Strange and Unusual Phenomena in the Country of Nam]. *Khoa Học Tạp Chí* [*Science Journal*] 43 (April 1, 1933): 4–7.

Quán, Nguyễn Đạo. *Khai Tâm Hán Văn Giáo Khoa: Năm Thứ Nhất* [*Introduction to Chinese Character Textbook: First Year*]. Hà Nội: Nghiêm Hàm, 1924.

Quỳnh, Phạm. "Sự Giáo-Dục Đàn Bà Con Gái" [The Education of Women and Girls]. *Nam Phong* [*Southern Wind*] 1, no. 4 (1917): 207–17.

———. "Tự Vựng: Quốc Ngữ, Chữ Nho, Chữ Pháp" [Vocabulary: Vietnamese, Chinese, and French]. *Nam Phong* [*Southern Wind*] 3, no. 14 (1918).

———. "Tự Vựng: Quốc Ngữ, Chữ Nho, Chữ Pháp" [Vocabulary: Vietnamese, Chinese, and French]. *Nam Phong* [*Southern Wind*] 1, no. 4 (1917).

Rey, Michael. "Police and Sodomy in Eighteenth-Century Paris: From Sin to Disorder." In *The Pursuit of Sodomy: Male Homosexuality in Renaissance and Enlightenment Europe*, edited by Kent Gerard and Gert Hekma, 129–46. New York: Harrington Press, 1989.

Roberts, Mary Louise. *Civilization without Sexes: Reconstructing Gender in Postwar France, 1917–1927*. Women in Culture and Society, edited by Catharine R. Stimpson. Chicago: University of Chicago Press, 1994.

Rocha, Leon Antonio. "Xing: The Discourse of Sex and Human Nature in Modern China." *Gender and History* 22, no. 3 (2010): 603–28.

"Rồi Đây Khoa Học Sẽ Tạo Ra Những Người Bán Nam Bán Nữ" [Science Will Some Day Create Half-Men, Half-Women]. *Khoa Học Tạp Chí* [*Science Journal*] 115 (March 1, 1936): 139.

Rosario, Vernon A., II. "Pointy Penises, Fashion Crimes, and Hysterical Mollies: The Pederasts' Inversions." In *Homosexuality in Modern France*, edited by Jeffrey Merrick and Bryant T. Ragan Jr., 146–68. Oxford: Oxford University Press, 1996.

Rouzer, Paul. *Articulated Ladies: Gender and the Male Community in Early Chinese Texts in Late Imperial China*. Cambridge, MA: Harvard University Press, 2001.

Salemink, Oscar. "Spirit Worship and Possession in Vietnam and Beyond." In *Routledge Handbook of Religions in Asia*, edited by Brian S. Turner and Oscar Salemink, 231–46. New York: Routledge, 2014.

Sang, Tze-Ian D. "Revisiting Premodern Chinese Female-Female Relations." In *The Emerging Lesbian: Female Same-Sex Desire in Modern China*, 37–65. Chicago: University of Chicago Press, 2003.

Sào, Hữu. "Bà Đồng" [Female Spirit Medium]. *Khoa Học Tạp Chí* [*Science Journal*] 215 (June 1, 1939): 258.

———. "Tại Sao Đàn Ông Rậm Râu, Đàn Bà to Vú?" [Why Do Men Have Beards and Women Large Breasts?]. *Khoa Học Tạp Chí* [*Science Journal*] 93 (May 1, 1935): 2.

Sắt, Nguyễn Chánh, and Tự Bá-Nghiêm. *Hiệp Nghĩa Phong Nguyệt: Đệ Nhị Tài-Tử* 俠義風月第二才子 [*Righteous Heroes of Wind and Moon: The Second Talented Man*]. Vol. 1 of 4. Sài Gòn: Imprimerie Librairie J. Viet et Fils, 1931.

"Sau Lưng Phật Tổ" [Behind the Back of the Buddha]. *Hà Nội Tân Văn* [New Hà Nội News], May 7, 1940, 3.

Schäfer, Dagmar. "Translation History, Knowledge and Nation Building in China." In *The Routledge Handbook of Translation and Culture*, edited by Sue-Ann Harding and Ovidi Carbonell Cortés, 134–53. London: Routledge, 2018.

Schafer, John, and Cao Thi Nhu Quynh. "From Verse Narrative to the Novel: The Development of Prose Fiction in Vietnam." *Journal of Asian Studies* 47, no. 4 (1988): 756–77.

Scott, Joan W. "After History?" In *Schools of Thought: Twenty-Five Years of Interpretive Social Science*, edited by Joan W. Scott and Debra Keates, 85–103. Princeton, NJ: Princeton University Press, 2001.

———. "Fantasy Echo: History and the Construction of Identity." *Critical Inquiry* 27, no. 2 (Winter 2001): 284–304.

Shields, Anna M. *One Who Knows Me: Friendship and Literary Culture in Mid-Tang China*. Cambridge, MA: Harvard University Asia Center, 2015.

Sibalis, Michael David. "The Regulation of Male Homosexuality in Revolutionary and Na-poleanic France, 1789–1815." In *Homosexuality in Modern France*, edited by Jeffrey Merrick and Bryant T. Ragan Jr. New York: Oxford University Press, 1996.

Smith-Rosenberg, Carrol. "Discourses of Sexuality and Subjectivity: The New Woman, 1870–1936." In *Hidden from History: Reclaiming the Gay and Lesbian Past*, edited by Martin Duberman, Martha Vicinus, and George Chauncey Jr. New York: New American Library, 1989.

Sommer, Matthew H. "The Penetrated Male in Late Imperial China: Judicial Constructions and Social Stigma." *Modern China* 23, no. 2 (1997): 140–80.

Sơn, Hoàng Thiếu. "Làm Đĩ: Cuốn Sách Có Trách Nhiệm Và Đầy Nhân Đạo" [*To Be a Prostitute*: A Book with Responsibility and Humanity]. In *Làm Đĩ: Tiểu Thuyết* [*To Be a Prostitute: A Novel*]. Hà Nội: Nhà Xuất Bản Văn Học, 2005.

Sơn, Thiếu. "Nữ Sĩ Pháp" [French Women Writers]. *Phụ Nữ Tân Văn* [*New Women's News*] 225 (November 23, 1933): 9–10.

Spurlin, William J. "The Gender and Queer Politics of Translation: New Approaches." *Comparative Literature Studies* 51, no. 2 (2014): 201–14.

Staves, Susan. "A Few Kind Words for the Fop." *Studies in English Literature, 1500–1900* 22, no. 3 (1982): 413–28.

Stewart, Charles. "Creolization, Hybridity, Syncretism, Mixture." *Portuguese Studies* 27, no. 1 (2011): 48–55.

Stryker, Susan. "(De)Subjugated Knowledges: An Introduction to Transgender Studies." In *The Transgender Studies Reader*, edited by Susan Stryker and Stephen Whittle, 1–17. New York: Routledge, 2006.

Surkis, Judith. *Sexing the Citizen: Morality and Masculinity in France, 1870–1920*. Ithaca, NY: Cornell University Press, 2006.

Tạ, Văn Tài. *The Vietnamese Tradition of Human Rights*. Berkeley: Institute of East Asian Studies, University of California, 1989.

Tái Sanh Duyên (Sự Tích Mạnh Lệ Quân): Giả Trai, Đậu Trạng, Lê Quân Cưới Vợ [*Love Reincarnated (The Story of Mạnh Lệ Quân): Disguises as a Man, Passes the Civil Examinations, and Gets Married to a Wife*]. Translated by Thanh Phong. Vol. 14. Sài Gòn: Tín Đức Thư Xã, 1923.

Tái Sanh Duyên 再生緣: *Mạnh Lệ Quân*. Translated by Lê Duy Thiện. Vol. 1 of 15. Sài Gòn: Xưa Nay, 1930.

Tái Sanh Duyên 再生緣: *Mạnh Lệ Quân Toàn Truyện* [*Love Reincarnated: The Complete Story of Mạnh Lệ Quân*]. Vol. 1. Sài Gòn: Imprimerie Librairie Huỳnh Kim Danh, 1929.

"Tại Sao Đàn Bà Hớt Tóc" [Why Women Had to Cut Their Hair]. *Phụ Nữ Tân Văn* [*New Women's News*] 26 (October 24, 1929): 22.

Tana, Li. *Nguyễn Cochinchina: Southern Vietnam in the Seventeenth and Eighteenth Centuries*. Ithaca, NY: Cornell Southeast Asia Program Publications, 1998.

Taylor, Gary. "Contest of Reproductions: The Rise of the Penis, the Fall of the Scrotum." In *Castration: An Abbreviated History of Western Manhood*, 85–110. London: Routledge, 2000.

Taylor, Keith. "The Early Kingdoms." In *Cambridge History of Southeast Asia*, edited by Nicholas Tarling, 137–82. Vol. 1. Cambridge: Cambridge University Press, 1999.

———. *A History of the Vietnamese.* Cambridge: Cambridge University Press, 2013.

Taylor, Philip. *Goddess on the Rise: Pilgrimage and Popular Religion in Vietnam.* Honolulu: University of Hawai'i Press, 2004.

Thạch, Lam. 1936. "Sự Nghiệp của Ông Vũ Đình Long (The Career of Mr. Vũ Đình Long)." *Phong Hóa (Mores)* 184 (April 24, 1936): 8.

Thanh, Hoài, and Hoài Chân. "Một Thời-Đại Trong Thi Ca" [A Period of Poetry]." 1942. In *Thi Nhân Việt-Nam [Vietnamese Poets]*, 9–55. Sài Gòn: Nhà Xuất Bản Hoa Tiến, 1968.

Thế, Phụng. "Bài Phản Đối của ông Thế Phụng" [A Rebuttal by Mr. Thế Phụng], *Phụ Nữ Tân Văn [New Women's News]* 6 (1929): 13.

Thinh, Ngo Duc. "The Mother Goddess Religion: Its History, Pantheon, and Practices." In *Possessed by the Spirits: Mediumship in Contemporary Vietnamese Communities,* edited by Karen Fjelstad and Hien Thi Nguyễn, 19–30. Ithaca, NY: Cornell Southeast Asia Program Publications, 2006.

Thịnh, Ngô Đức. *Lên Đồng: Hành Trình Của Thần Linh Và Thân Phận [Len Dong: Journeys of Spirits and Fates].* Ho Chi Minh City: Nhà Xuất Bản Trẻ, 2007.

Thời, Nguyễn Bá. *Mạnh Lệ Quân Giả Trai [Mạnh Lệ Quân Feigns Being Male].* Sài Gòn: Imprimeur Phạm Văn Thình, 1935.

Thompson, C. Michele. "Indochina." In *The Cambridge History of Science: Modern Science in National, Transnational, and Global Context,* edited by Hugh Richard Slotten, Ronald L. Numbers, and David N. Livingstone, 593–608. Cambridge: Cambridge University Press, 2020.

Thomson, Rosemarie Garland. *Extraordinary Bodies: Figuring Physical Disability in American Culture and Literature.* New York: Columbia University Press, 1997.

———, ed. *Freakery: Cultural Spectacles of the Extraordinary Body.* New York: New York University, 1996.

Thủy, Bích. "Món Quà Trong Lúc Nghỉ Hè: Dưới Biển, Trên Rừng" [A Gift During Summer Break: Under the Sea and in the Jungle]. *Phụ Nữ Tân Văn [New Women's News]* 251 (July 26, 1934): 17–19.

Tiến, Trương Quang. *Mạnh—Lệ—Quân Chấm Trường Thi Gặp Chồng: Tuồng Hát Cải Lương [Mạnh Lệ Quân Meets Husband at the Exam: A Reform Opera Theatre].* Sài Gòn: Tín-Đức Thư-Xã Publishers, 1928.

Tiến, Trương Quang. *Tuồng Hát Cải Lương: Mạnh-Lệ-Quân Thoát Hài [Reform Opera: Mạnh Lệ Quân Removes Her Shoes].* Sài Gòn: Tín-Đức Thư-Xã Publisher, 1929.

"Tìm Tri Kỷ Trong Mục Sợi Tơ Hồng" [Finding a Soulmate in the Red Silk Column]. *Báo Loa [The Loudspeaker]* 91 (November 11, 1935): 14.

"Tối Thứ Ba 3 Décembre 1929: Anh Hùng Náo" [Wednesday Night December 3, 1929: The Rowdy Hero]. *Hà Thành ngọ báo [Hà Thành Midday Newspaper]* (Hà Nội), December 3, 1929, 3.

"Tối Thứ Bảy: Anh Hùng Náo" [Saturday Evening: The Rowdy Hero]. *Hà Thành ngọ báo [Ha Thanh Midday Newspaper]* (Hà Nội), November 3, 1928, 3.

Tracol-Huỳnh, Isabelle. "Between Stigmatisation and Regulation: Prostitution in Colonial Northern Vietnam." *Culture, Health & Sexuality* 12 (2010): S73–S87.

———. "Prostitutes, Brothels and the Red Light District: The Management of Prostitution in the City of Hà Nội from the 1870s to the 1950s." In *Translation, History and the Arts: New Horizons in Asian Interdisciplinary Humanities Research*, edited by Ji Meng and Atsuko Ukai, 176–93. Newcastle, UK: Cambridge Scholars Publishing, 2013.

Trần, Ben. *Postmandarin: Masculinity and Aesthetic Modernity in Colonial Vietnam*. New York: Fordham University Press, 2017.

———. "Queer Internationalism and Modern Vietnamese Aesthetics." In *Post-Mandarin: Masculinity and Aesthetic Modernity in Colonial Vietnam*, 105–18. New York: Fordham University Press, 2017.

Trần, Liên Thị "Henriette Bui: The Narrative of Vietnam's First Woman Doctor." In *Vietnam Exposé: French Scholarship on Twentieth-Century Vietnamese Society*, edited by Gisele Bousquet and Pierre Brocheux, 251–78. Ann Arbor: University of Michigan, 2005.

Trần, Nhung Tuyết, and Anthony Reid. "The Construction of Vietnamese Historical Identities." In *Viet Nam: Borderless Histories*, edited by Nhung Tuyết Trân and Anthony Reid, 3–22. Madison: University of Wisconsin Press, 2006.

Trần, Richard Quang-Anh. "An Epistemology of Gender: Historical Notes on the Homosexual Body in Contemporary Vietnam, 1986–2005." *Journal of Vietnamese Studies* 9, no. 2 (2014): 45.

———. "Sex in the City: The Descent from Human to Animal in Two Vietnamese Classics of Urban Reportage." *International Quarterly of Asian Studies* 50, nos. 3–4 (2020): 171–92.

Trần, Văn Quế, *Côn Lôn Quần Đảo Trước Ngày 9-3-1945* [The Poulo Condore Archipelago before March 9, 1945]. Sài Gòn: Thanh Hương Tùng Thơ, 1961.

Trịnh Dục Tú. Edited by Nguyễn Hữu Đạt and Nguyễn Ngọc Hải. Vol. 1 of 3. Hà Nội: Vĩnh Thành ấn quán, 1927.

Trumbach, Randolf. "The Birth of the Queen: Sodomy and the Emergence of Gender Equality in Modern Culture, 1660–1750." In *Hidden from History: Reclaiming the Gay and Lesbian Past*, edited by Martin Duberman, Martha Vicinus, and George Chauncey Jr., 129–40. New York: Meridian, 1989.

———. "Gender and the Homosexual Role in Modern Western Culture: The 18th and 19th Centuries Compared." In *Homosexuality, Which Homosexuality?*, edited by Dennis Altman, Carol Vance, Martha Vicinus, and Jeffrey Weeks, 149–70. Amsterdam: An Dekker; London: Schorer, GMP, 1989.

Trương-Vĩnh-Ký, P. J. B. *Petit dictionnaire Français-Annamite*. Sài Gòn: Imp. de la Mission, à Tân-Định, 1884.

Từ Điển Tiếng Việt [Vietnamese Dictionary]. Hà Nội: Nhà Xuất Bản Văn Hóa Thông Tin, 2005.

Tục Anh Hùng Náo 續英雄鬧 [The Rowdy Hero Continued]. Translated by Vũ Đình Long. Vol. 4. Hà Nội: Thực Nghiệp 1925.

Tục Anh Hùng Náo 續英雄鬧 [The Rowdy Hero Continued]. Translated by Vũ Đình Long. Vol. 3. Hà Nội: Thực Nghiệp, 1925.

Tùng, Thanh, ed. *Nguyễn Vỹ, Văn Học Từ Điển: Tiểu Sử Tác Giả* [Literary Dictionary: Biographies of Writers]. Sài Gòn: Nhà Xuất Bản Khai-Trí, 1973.

Tùng-Linh [PuSongling], Bồ. "Duyên Chàng Lại Cái" [Fate of Female Contaminated Male]. Translated by Huyền-Mặc Đạo-Nhơn. In *Liêu-Trai Chí Dị (異誌齋聊) [Strange Tales from Liao Zhai]*, 80–91. Sài Gòn: Nhà in Đức-Lưu-Phương, 1933.

Tuồng Hát Cải-Lương: Mạnh Lệ Quân Giả Trai [A Reform Drama: Mạnh Lệ Quân Disguises as Male]. Edited by Trương Quang Tiên. Sài Gòn: Imprimerie de l'Union, 1927.

T.V. "Trên Đời Này Có Một Xứ Không Cho Đàn Bà Và Cho Cái Bước Cẳng Đến" [A Place Where Women Are Forbidden to Set Foot]. *Phụ Nữ Tân Văn [New Women's News]* 220 (October 12, 1933): 12–13.

V.A. "Đàn Bà Quái Lạ Trên Đời: Hai Cô Dính Mình Với Nhau Ma Một Cô Muốn Lấy Chồng, Một Cô Không Muốn; Người Đàn Bà Thêu Bằng Cẳng, Phần 1" [Strange Women in the World: A Siamese Twin One of Whom Wishes to Get Married While the Other Does Not; One Who Embroiders Using Her Legs, Part 1]. *Phụ Nữ Tân Văn [New Women's News]* 94 (August 6, 1931): 11.

V.A. "Đàn Bà Quái Lạ Trên Đời: Cô Violetta Không Tay Không Chưn, Mụ Adrienne Mọc Râu Ghê Gớm, Phần Ii" [Strange Women in the World: Ms. Violetta Has No Arms or Legs, Ms. Adrienne Grows a Frightful Beard, Part 2]. *Phụ Nữ Tân Văn [New Women's News]* 86 (August 20, 1931): 13–14.

———. "Đàn Bà Quái Lạ: Trên Đời: Người Bán Nam, Bán Nữ; Cô Ngó Hình Như Con Beo, Người Ta Gọi Là 'Femme Panthère; Một Cô Gảy Đờn Bằng Cẳng, Phần 3" [Strange Women in the World: A Half Man, Half Woman; a Woman Who Looks Like a Panther, People Call Her 'Femme Panthère; Another Woman Who Plucks the Guitar Using Her Feet, Part 3]. *Phụ Nữ Tân Văn [New Women's News]* 99 (September 10, 1931): 16–18.

———. "Một Vấn Đề Khoa Học: Tại Sao Lại Có Đàn Bà Mọc Râu?" [A Question of Science: Why Are There Women Who Grow Beards?]." *Phụ Nữ Tân Văn [New Women's News]* 84 (May 28, 1931): 23.

Vân, Phong. *Mạnh Lệ Quân: Thứ Nhứt Giả Trai, Thứ Hai Chẩn Mạch, Thứ Ba Thoát Hài [Mạnh Lệ Quân: To Cross Dress as a Male, to Make a Diagnosis, and to Take Off the Shoes]* Cholon: Nhà Xuất Bản Phạm Đình Khương [Pham Dinh Khuong Publisher], 1933.

Vandermeersch, Patrick. "Sodomites, Gays and Biblical Scholars: A Gathering Organized by Peter Damian?" In *Sodom's Sin: Genesis 18–19 and Its Interpretation*, edited by Eibert Tigchelaar, 149–71. Boston: Brill 2004.

"Vietnam Marriage and Family Law 2014." Vietnam Law in English. June 26, 2014. https://vietnamlawenglish.blogspot.com/2014/06/vietnam-marriage-and-family-law-2014.html.

Việt Nam Tự Điển/Hội Khai-Trí-Tiến-Đức Khởi [Vietnamese Dictionary]. Hà Nội: Trung-Bắc Tân-Văn, 1931.

Vĩnh, Nguyễn Văn. "Hương Sơn Hành Trình" [A Journey to Hương Sơn Temple]. 1914. In *Hầu Thánh [Serving the Spirits]*, 242–64. Hà Nội: Nhà Xuất Bản Văn Hóa Thông Tin, 2002.

Warner, Ding Xiang. *A Wild Deer amid Soaring Phoenixes*. Honolulu: University of Hawaiʻi Press 2003.

Weinbaum, Alys Eve, Lynn M. Thomas, Priti Ramamurthy, Uta G. Poiger, Madeleine Y. Dong, and Tani E. Barlow. "The Modern Girl as Heuristic Device: Collaboration, Connective Comparison, Multidirectional Citation." In *The Modern Girl around the World:*

Consumption, Modernity, and Globalization. Durham, NC: Duke University Press, 2008.

Weiss, Andrea. *Paris Was a Woman: Portraits from the Left Bank.* San Francisco: Harper San Francisco, 1995.

Weng, Jeffrey. "What Is Mandarin? The Social Project of Language Standardization in Early Republican China." *Journal of Asian Studies* 77, no. 3 (August 2018): 611–33.

Wheeler, Charles. "Interests, Institutions, and Identity: Strategic Adaptation and the Ethno-Evolution of Minh Hương (Central Vietnam), 16th–19th Centuries." *Itinerario* 39, no. 1 (2015): 141–66.

Woodside, Alexander. "Early Ming Expansionism, 1406–1427." *Papers on China* 1 (1963): 1–37.

———. *Vietnam and the Chinese Model: A Comparative Study of the Nguyễn and Ching Civil Government in the First Half of the Nineteenth Century.* Cambridge, MA: Harvard University Press, 1971.

Wu, Qingyun. *Female Rule in Chinese and English Literary Utopias.* Syracuse, NY: Syracuse University Press, 1995.

Xuân, Diệu. *Toàn Tập Xuân Diệu* [The Complete Works of Xuân Diệu]. Hà Nội: Nhà Xuất Bản Văn Học, 2001.

Yü, Chün-fang *Kuan-Yin: The Chinese Transformation of Avalokiteśvara.* New York: Columbia University Press, 2001.

Yue, Audrey. "Queer Singapore: A Critical Introduction." Introduction to *Queer Singapore: Illiberal Citizenship and Mediated Cultures*, edited by Audrey Yue and June Zubillaga-Pow, 1–25. Hong Kong: Hong Kong University Press, 2012.

Zamperini, Paola. *Lost Bodies: Prostitution and Masculinity in Chinese Fiction.* Women and Gender in China Studies. Leiden: Brill, 2010.

Zeitlin, Judith T. "Heroes among Women." In *Historian of the Strange: Pu Songling and the Chinese Classical Tale*, 116–31. Stanford, CA: Stanford University Press, 1993.

———. *Historian of the Strange: Pu Songling and the Chinese Classical Tale.* Stanford, CA: Stanford University Press, 1993.

Zhou, Zuyan. *Androgyny in Late Ming and Early Qing Literature.* Honolulu: University of Hawai'i Press, 2003.

Zinoman, Peter, ed. *Dumb Luck: A Novel by Vu Trong Phung.* Ann Arbor: University of Michigan Press, 2002.

———. "The Question of Communism." In *Vietnamese Colonial Republican: The Political Vision of Vũ Trọng Phụng*, 85–130. Berkeley: University of California Press, 2014.

———. "The Crisis of Vietnamese Sexuality." In *Vietnamese Colonial Republican: The Political Vision of Vũ Trọng Phụng*, 131–55. Berkeley: University of California Press, 2014.

———. "Vũ Trọng Phụng's *Dumb Luck* and the Nature of Vietnamese Modernism." In *Dumb Luck*, 1–30. Ann Arbor: University of Michigan Press, 2002.

INDEX

Page numbers in italics denote figures, and endnotes are indicated by "n" followed by the endnote number.

The authorized representative in the EU for product safety and compliance is:
Mare Nostrum Group B.V.
Mauritskade 21D
1091 GC Amsterdam
The Netherlands
Email address: gpsr@mare-nostrum.co.uk

KVK chamber of commerce number: 96249943

The authorized representative in the EU for product safety and compliance is:
Mare Nostrum Group
B.V Doelen 72
4831 GR Breda
The Netherlands

www.ingramcontent.com/pod-product-compliance
Lightning Source LLC
Chambersburg PA
CBHW030818270326
41928CB00007B/787